D0788746

ASPECTS OF GREEK AND ROMAN LIFE

General Editor: H. H. Scullard

* * *

CRAFTSMEN IN GREEK AND ROMAN SOCIETY

Alison Burford

CRAFTSMEN
IN GREEK AND
ROMAN SOCIETY

Alison Burford

CORNELL UNIVERSITY PRESS

ITHACA, NEW YORK

First published 1972

This edition is not for sale in the
United Kingdom and British
Commonwealth.

International Standard Book Number 0-8014-0717-6

Library of Congress Catalog Card Number 71-37630

PRINTED IN GREAT BRITAIN

CONTENTS

LIST OF ILLUSTRATIONS 6

PREFACE 9

I INTRODUCTION 11

II GREEK AND ROMAN SOCIETY 28

III ARTISTS AND CRAFTSMEN AT WORK 68

IV CRAFTSMEN AND THEIR PATRONS 124

V OUT OF WORKING HOURS 153

VI CONCEPTS OF THE NATURE OF CRAFTSMANSHIP 184

NOTES 219

SOURCES OF ILLUSTRATIONS 251

MUSEUM LOCATIONS 251

INDEX 252

24180

LIST OF ILLUSTRATIONS

PLATES

1   Dedication base of Euthykartides
2   *Kouros* figure
3   Cobbler making shoes to measure
4   Cobbler at work
5   Relief of a Gaulish shoemaker
6   Grave relief of Xanthippos, a shoemaker
7   Shoemaker and rope–maker in their workshop
8   Grave stele of P. Beitenos Hermes, a couch-maker
9   Grave stele of P. Longidienus Camillus, a shipwright
10   Argus working on the prow of the *Argo*
11   Boeotian sawyer
12   Wall-painting of festival in honour of Perdix
13   Digging clay for potting
14   Potter at work
15, 16   Firing a kiln
17   Work in a pottery
18   Potter burnishing an unglazed skyphos
19   The Potter's Stele
20   Terracotta figurine by Diphilos of Myrina
21   Cast from an Arretine ware mould
22, 23   Terracotta lamps from similar moulds
24   Terracotta lamp with Athena Promachos
25   Glass cup signed by Ennion
26   Glass beaker by Neikaios
27   Entrance to silver mine, Laureion
28   Washing table near silver mines, Laureion
29   Two smiths smelting ore
30   Blacksmith's shop
31   An armourer at work
32   Plaque from Pheidias' workshop, Olympia
33   Grave stele of a Romano-British blacksmith

34 Dedicatory relief to Vulcan
35 A smith on holiday
36 Grave relief of L. Cornelius Atimetus, a smith
37 Silver cup signed by Cheirisophos
38 Athena modelling a horse in clay
39, 40 The Berlin Foundry Cup
41 Relief showing a gold-leaf worker
42 Silver wreath of myrtle
43 Gold necklace with *aureus* pendant
44, 45 Impressions of engraved gems by Dexamenos of Chios
46 Grave relief of Demetrius and Philonicus
47 Plaque with mint-tools
48 Relief of a coin-striker at work
49, 50 Archaic Athenian tetradrachm
51, 52 Syracusan tetradrachm
53 Gold *aureus* of Augustus
54 Roman engineering, a treadmill hoist
55 Modern lifting device on Athenian acropolis
56 Grave relief of C. Vedennius Moderatus, a military architect
57 A Greek automatic calculator
58 The Hephaisteion, from the west
59 Athena directing the building of the acropolis
60 Foundation course, temple of Apollo, Delphi
61 The Erechtheion, from the east
62 Detail of *tholos* interior, Epidauros
63 Pentelic marble column drum
64 The Pantheon, exterior
65 The Pantheon, interior of the dome
66 The arch of Titus
67 Trajan's forum and column
68 House of Diana, Ostia
69 House-builders at work
70 Roman legionaries as road-builders
71 Mason's graffito, Thasos
72 Acropolis wall, Thasos
73 The theatre at Aspendos
74 Pont du Gard aqueduct
75 Unfinished colossal statue, Naxos
76 Graffiti on a statue base from Persepolis

77   Sculptor carving a herm
78   The Strangford shield
79   Reconstruction of the statue of Athena Parthenos
80   Winged Victory by Paionios
81   Death of Laocoon and his sons
82   Commodus as Hercules
83   Bust of a Roman lady
84   Grave stele of Megistokles, a sculptor
85   Grave stele of M. Se. . . Amabilis, a sculptor
86   The garden of Livia
87   Mosaic signed by Gnosis
88   Mosaic signed by Dioskourides

FIGURES

I   *Winged Victories crowning vase-painters, p. 71*
II   *Map of the Athenian agora and surroundings, p. 81*
III   *Map of the Athenian agora and workshop district, p. 83*
IV   *Bronze-worker's shop, p. 169*
V   *Hephaistos making the armour of Achilles, p. 195*

PREFACE

WHILE WRITING THIS BOOK I have received generous help of many kinds and from many people. I am most grateful to the Trustees, the Director and the Senior Fellows of the Center for Hellenic Studies, where I held a Junior Fellowship in 1965–6, and to the University of Nebraska for research leave during 1970. Additionally I should like to thank in particular Professor M. I. Finley for constructive criticism at various stages of composition; Miss J. M. C. Toynbee, Professor D. Strong and Mr G. de Ste Croix for helpful discussion; Professor Sterling Dow for comment on the penultimate draft; Professor H. H. Scullard for his editorial encouragement and advice; Mr Peter Clayton at Thames and Hudson for resolving so many of the problems which the illustration of the subject has presented; and Dr Guy L. Cooper for invaluable secretarial assistance.

I should point out that the spelling of Greek proper names in this book has been kept as close as possible to the Greek form, except where common usage has rendered this impracticable. No apology is made for the inevitable inconsistencies to which this gives rise.

Asheville,   A.B.
North Carolina

CHAPTER I

INTRODUCTION

'EUTHYKARTIDES THE NAXIAN MADE AND DEDICATED ME'[1]

AT SOME POINT IN HIS CAREER the sculptor Euthykartides felt called upon to fashion a monument in local stone, and to dedicate it, on his own behalf, to Delian Apollo (*Pl.* 1). He incurred considerable trouble and expense in quarrying, working and transporting across a dozen miles of the temperamental Aegean Sea two sizable blocks, statue and base, of heavy, fragile marble. What manner of man was he, that he should have displayed the cultural ambition usually expected at all periods of the rich and, at this period (the seventh century BC) especially, of the aristocracy, and have put his signature to this statue he had made at a time when literacy itself was still comparatively rare, and craftsmen's personal records virtually unknown in the ancient world, Mediterranean or Near Eastern?

If Euthykartides was unusual, he was not unique. Other craftsmen were already beginning to speak in their own name, and thereafter the consciousness (however limited in concept) of their creative powers came to be expressed more and more frequently throughout antiquity. But apart from the fact that Euthykartides was able to advertise his own individuality, so to speak, there are other things we need to know in order to begin to understand not only Euthykartides' situation, but the position of craftsmen generally in the society in which they worked and lived. Euthykartides' name, domicile, and to some degree his skill, are made clear by the inscription and the remnants of the monument; but these facts provide little basis for assessing his economic status, his standing in Naxian society, his relationship with his customers, the compulsions which had led him to take up sculpture, his dependence on other skilled workers, or the attention he is likely to have given to affairs outside the stonemason's workshop. Various comments in ancient literature on sculptors and other skilled workers in general make it clear that for some sections of society, at least, Euthykartides was one of the *banausoi*, the manual workers, the men who exploited a skill for their living, the artisans; men to whom the nature of their employment denied all possibility of moral or political virtue; men with reference to whom it could be said that 'banausic activities are held in complete disdain in the Greek cities . . . they spoil the bodies of the workmen and the overseers, because the nature of the work compels them to sit indoors, and in some cases to spend the day by the fire. Softening of the body leads to softening of the mind.'[2] Lucian of Samosata, writing in the imperial age of Rome, was moved to speak of the sculptor's life thus:

> If you become a stone-cutter you will be nothing more than a workman, doing hard physical labour. . . . You will be obscure, earning a small wage, a man of low esteem, classed as worthless by public opinion, neither courted by friends, feared by enemies, nor envied by your fellow-citizens, but just a common workman, a craftsman, a face in a crowd, one who makes his living with his hands.[3]

The truth of these assertions requires considerable qualification. For the moment, however, they serve to point out the existence of a group which was thought of as distinguished from the rest of society by the nature of its members' occupations. They also indicate the paradox in certain aspects of ancient thinking about the respective merits of the *banausoi* and the things they made, which was most sharply put by Plutarch in his life of Pericles: 'It does not necessarily follow that if a work is delightful because of its gracefulness, the man who made it is worthy of our serious regard. . . . No one, no gifted young man, upon seeing the Zeus of Pheidias at Olympia or the Hera of Polykleitos at Argos ever actually wanted to be Pheidias or Polykleitos.'[4]

No matter how useful or how beautiful the object, how essential to the physical or spiritual needs of the individual or community for whom it was made—be it hunting-knife, defence tower, or gold and ivory cult statue—the maker was in no way admirable.

That opinions such as these, held though they were by many of the greatest philosophers and men of letters in antiquity, reveal only part of the story is immediately clear from the existence of records like Euthykartides' dedicatory inscription, of the later seventh century BC; or the gravestone which commemorated the painter Loukios Sossios' admission to the city council of Cyrene, in recognition of his achievements in his art, at some point in the second century AD; the decree of civic honours granted at Olbia to the architect Epikrates, who came from Byzantium to build up the city's defences in the third century BC; or the grave reliefs with accompanying inscriptions of sculptors, masons, cobblers and smiths in Roman Gaul (e.g. *Pl. 5*).[5] Men who could so handsomely fulfil cult obligations, gain such high public honours, or consider themselves worthy of comemmoration in pictorial relief were not just 'common workmen, faces in a crowd'.

In discussing the craftsmen of antiquity, we need first to make clear who is included under the heading *craftsman*, and secondly to emphasize that for us, if not in their own time, the majority of ancient craftsmen are anonymous and even less than 'faces in a crowd'. The question then arises whether the craftsmen of whom record survives are typical, the mere tip of an iceberg of self-expressing and socially accountable skilled workers whose memorials have perished, or whether they represent the exceptional minority.

The term 'craftsman' is here used of every skilled worker whose labours contributed to the manufacture of objects in durable materials, and who depended on the exercise of his craft for a living.[6] Defined thus, the miner, the bronze nail-maker, the goldsmith, the jeweller, the quarrymason, the sculptor, the architect, the tanner, the cobbler, the harness-maker, the lumberman, the shipwright, the joiner and inlayer, the potter, the figurine-maker, the vase-painter, the mosaic-layer, the catapult-builder and the glass-blower are all equally deserving of consideration. None was any more or less a professional and a craftsman than any other. Something which gives complete validity to the grouping together of what are at first sight such dissimilar kinds of skilled worker is the fact that the modern distinction between the arts and the crafts, between the artist and the craftsman, was unknown in antiquity, the most obvious indication of this conceptual difference being given by the language. In Greek, *technē* and, in Latin, *ars* were used indiscriminately of painting and cobbling alike, just as the *technitēs*, *cheirotechnēs* or *dēmiourgos*, the *faber* or *artifex*, could be either a sculptor or a miner, a quarry-man or an architect.

This does not mean that no one in fact appreciated the character of the artistry which produced a piece of fine painted pottery, as opposed, let us say, to the technical skill by which elemental silver was refined from its ore, or made any distinction between the aesthetic qualities expressed in a Doric temple and the purely utilitarian nature of a well-built, weather-proof pigsty.[7] It is simply that both temple architect and pigsty builder were seen to draw on precisely the same source for the success of their work—and that was craftsmanship. The line and form of statues and warships alike were achieved by the application of exact and well-learnt craft rules; whatever additional quality the individual worker might bring to bear, it was experience in the ways of the craft that counted for most.

The layman's admiration for craftsmanship was frequently expressed in the ancient literature. The Homeric poems include many descriptions of marvellous handiwork, not only that of the smith-god Hephaistos or the 'much-devising' hero, Odysseus, but of a more realistic kind; the poet shows that excellence of craftmanship had a strong fascination for his audience:

The first prize was a mixing bowl of chased silver, holding six pints; it was the loveliest thing in the world, a masterpiece of Sidonian workmanship, which had been shipped across the misty seas by Phoenician traders.[8]

The concern of later ages for the quality of craftsmanship is reflected in the comment of the Hellenistic historian Diodorus, speaking of sculptors in the Classical period: 'It was not possible for even these men to be so successful in their work that they could put on display a finished product of their skill which was completely flawless.'⁹

The craftsman provided the specialized skill, the technical know-how necessary to civilized life. Without him, the layman could only produce at best a poor imitation of the required object's proper form; for the most part he would be unable to make anything that worked as it should—a pot which stood steady on its base, or a cult statue which conveyed the full dignity and power of the deity whom it represented; even to begin the process of preparing suitable materials for the job would in many cases be beyond him. Once society had moved on from the stage of hunting or food-gathering, once the community had evolved a lasting pattern of relationships and a regular economic give and take, there began to develop a place for the specialist craftsman who supplemented the production of the household or the cross-section of the community hitherto responsible (in the case of pottery manufacture, for example, the women of the community), and then gradually replaced it.¹⁰

At no period of antiquity could there be any doubt that craftsmen had a great economic importance; their distribution was a matter of almost constant concern.¹¹ They provided not only the essentials—lasting shelter, durable clothing, shoes that wore well, effective weapons and tools, walls which withstood attack—but also the trappings of the community's cultural life. With craftsmanship it was possible to have houses, shrines, drinking vessels, armour, street complexes, fortifications, and aqueducts which both functioned perfectly adequately and were things of beauty as well (Pls. 69, 74). A lack of craftsmanship, the absence from the community of the men capable of working according to the highest standards, meant not merely an incidental lack of beautiful objects and luxuries, but an overall cultural poverty, a depression of the quality of life, as anyone moving from the city of Athens to the villages of Arcadia or the hinterland of Macedonia, or from Rome to Tomi on the Black Sea would have been fully aware.[12]

Every community had its craftsmen, every village its blacksmith, cobbler, carpenter-cum-builder, or at least its jack-of-all-trades. The bigger the settlement, naturally, the larger the craftsman population was likely to be, and the more diverse, with greater opportunities for the more exotic crafts to find patronage. In all but the most squalid hamlets, then, craftsmen had a role to play, irrespective of whether they were, legally speaking, citizens, slaves or free resident aliens. It is in this sense that they can be surveyed as a cohesive entity within ancient society.

TIME AND PLACE—THE ANCIENT WORLD

For the purposes of this discussion, the ancient world comprises Greece and Rome from the earliest historical period—that is, from *c.* 700 BC onwards—down to the later Roman Empire of the fourth and fifth centuries AD. Within this time span some further definition is needed: the Greek period means roughly the sixth, fifth, and fourth centuries BC; the Hellenistic period applies to the Greek world from Alexander's time to the end of the Roman Republic and the reign of Augustus; the Roman Republic, to the city of Rome and Italy between the sixth century BC and the time of Augustus; and the Roman Empire, to the period from Augustus onwards. The later Roman Empire may be thought of as extending from the time of Septimius Severus, *c.* AD 200, to about the fifth century AD. Within these eleven hundred years or so the balance of power in the ancient world shifted and altered in character considerably; great changes took place in the ways of thought reflected in and shaped by differing political institutions, as in the design and function of the objects the craftsmen were called upon to make. At the same time, there was some fundamental continuity of thought, attitude and life-style, so that it is feasible to bring together evidence for a general description of the ancient craftsman's situation in spite of the extent of the period of history from which it is culled.

Sometimes it is necessary to refer to the Greek world as opposed to the Roman. Geographically speaking, the Greek world consisted of Greece proper (the mainland, the Aegean islands and the west coast of Asia Minor), the cities in Sicily and south Italy, the Greek communities on the Black Sea and the Mediterranean coasts of Spain and France; it also extended north and north-east to the tribal and nomadic communities of Thrace and the Scythians in south Russia, eastwards into Mesopotamia and Persia, to Afghanistan and north-west India (as a result of Alexander's exploits), and southwards into Syria, Egypt and Libya. In talking of the Greek world in the time of the Roman Empire, however, one means the eastern half of the empire, simply, which always remained predominantly Greek in language, institutions and culture. The Roman world may be seen to consist of Rome itself, Italy and the western and northern provinces of the empire, including Africa, Spain, Gaul, Germany, Britain and the Danube provinces, where the Latin language and Roman institutions prevailed. But these distinctions are not always meaningful, for among the reasons why the ancient world can be seen as one historical cultural unit are first, the Romans' long if gentle subjection to Greek influences, transmitted indirectly by the Etruscans to the north and directly by the Greek cities in southern Italy itself from the sixth century B C onwards, and secondly the Romans' entry into the Greek world in 200 B C, which marked the beginning of the shift of power from the Hellenistic monarchies to the Republic of Rome in central Italy. The Romans then gradually inherited much of the Greeks' sphere of influence. They not only absorbed Greek culture from centres in Greece itself and employed Greek craftsmen in increasing numbers, but extended Greek stylistic and technical influences, along with other benefits of Roman imperialism, to the provinces in the north and west.[13]

Obviously, the ancient world encompassed many political changes. The Greek city-states experienced the entire range of constitutional forms from aristocracy to tyranny, from radical democracy to narrow oligarchy—all these types of government existed alongside each other at various times within the Greek world—and from independence of, if not supremacy over, other states to subjection under a neighbour or, from the late fourth century onwards, to one or another of the Hellenistic monarchies, and then to Rome. The Roman state, on the other hand, underwent slow transformation from a republic, controlled by the preoccupations of its aristocracy and the relationships of that group to the rest of a numerically small and geographically circumscribed society in central Italy, to the leadership of an Italian confederacy which became at the same time ruler of a world empire. While retaining something of its original republican character, it came to resemble in certain respects the absolute monarchies of the ancient east.

There were marked differences in the composition of the Greek and Roman communities. Though fundamentally the same rigid distinctions are to be found in both, the most important being that between citizen and non-citizen, social distinctions at Rome were far more intricate, and at the same time social mobility was much greater. These two characteristics are perhaps responsible for another marked difference in the social climate: the great formality which prevailed at Rome was in sharp contrast to the simplicity and directness of relationships in the Greek city, where groupings tended to depend far more on the actualities of the present situation than on longstanding ties of family or clientship as at Rome. The following epitaphs, both of craftsmen, indicate the difference in tone between the two societies. In the late fifth century BC a wood-cutter of Attica chose to be remembered thus:

> Mannes, son of Orymaios, who was the best of the Phrygians in the spacious lands of Attica, lies in this fine tomb. And by Zeus I never saw a better woodman than myself. He died in the war.[14]

Contrast this concisely *personal* statement with the onerously honorific epitaph of a Roman carpenter:

> (Memorial) to Tiberius Flavius Hilarion, freedman of Tiberius, *decurion* of the *collegium* of carpenters in the 15th *lustrum*, inspector of the ballot-box for the elections in the 16th *lustrum*, quinquennial officer of the *collegium* of woodworkers in the 17th

lustrum, honoured in the 18th, twice censor for appointing officials in the 19th and 20th, and judge among the chosen twelve from his rank (?) in the 22nd. This monument was put up by Claudia Prisca to the best of husbands.[15]

The traditional connection between patron and client, which influenced relationships in Roman society so strongly, may very well have affected the relations between patrons of the workshops and the craftsmen; an entire habit of thought existed ready-made for the Roman who commissioned a special piece of work, as it did not in the Greek world. Thus the emperor extended his patronage from his own household and dependants to the whole state; his personal servants became part of the central machinery of government. Nothing resembling this situation could ever arise in the Greek world.

On the other hand, much the same economic and social problems prevailed in both societies. In particular an institution common to them both, and one which they shared with other less 'enlightened' societies, was slavery. Slave labour was basic to the economy; the relationship between free men and slaves remained a prominent feature of the social intercourse of the ancient world, and not a few craftsmen were themselves slaves at the start of their working lives, if not for all of them.

Alongside this so to speak negative characteristic we have to take into account a development of a far more positive nature, which to some extent counterbalanced the depressing fact of the existence of slavery. Political and social thinking in the ancient world went a considerable way beyond the concepts of the ancient Near East; in the eighth and seventh centuries it was already diverging quite sharply from that of contemporary Oriental societies—Assyria, Babylon, Egypt, to which the later empire of the Achaemenid Persians succeeded. The city-state was something quite new, and inextricably involved in it was the development of a way of thinking in its turn peculiarly relevant to the status of the craftsmen: the individual began to be important in his own right.

The existence of a certain respect for the individual in earlier societies cannot be altogether denied, but the significant difference is that it receives scarcely any acknowledgment in the sources and was surely a mode of thought generally discouraged. What mattered most was the preservation of the social order, to which the individual was entirely subordinated; only the ruler, the Pharaoh, the Great King, King of Kings, could express his personality, and that only in the formal terms prescribed by the character of Oriental monarchy.

The Greek sources show an entirely different temper. Hesiod, the peasant-farmer poet who wrote in the early seventh century, railed against the miseries of farming and the injustice of the government of his day.[16] Both he and the lyric poet Archilochos, the aristocratic rebel who flaunted his scorn of the conventions, positively boasting, for instance, that he had abandoned his shield on the battlefield in order to be able to run away more swiftly, demonstrate that entirely new opportunities for saying what one thought had now come into being.[17] Among other indications is the fact that, from the seventh century onwards, men were concerned to commemorate the names of the dead by inscribing them on that most durable material, stone.[18] And this was the very period when the sculptor Euthykartides was pleased to make himself known to posterity. In the societies of the Near East, craftsmen remained anonymous.

The differences in concept come over clearly in a comparison of the record which Darius, Great King of Persia, published of the palace built at Susa *c.* 500 B C, with the Athenian building accounts for the Erechtheion, near completion in 408/7 B C. The Persian document says:

This is the palace which I built at Susa. From afar its ornamentation was brought; the earth was dug deep down until I reached rock-bottom. . . . The cedar was brought from Lebanon, the Assyrians brought it to Babylon, and from Babylon the Ionians [Greeks] and Carians brought it to Susa. . . . The stone pillars were brought from Elam; the craftsmen who dressed the stone were Ionians and Lydians. . . . At Susa here a great work was ordered; it turned out very splendid. May Ahura Mazda protect me and Hystaspes who is my father, and my land.[19]

The Athenian inscription includes such items as these:

> Salaries. To the architect Archilochos of Agryle, 36 dr. To the under-secretary Pyrgion, 30 dr. . . . To the encaustic painter Dionysodoros living in Melite, for treating the kymation on the inner epistyle, at 5 ob. per foot, 113 feet, we gave out in addition to what he had before, his guarantor being Herakleides of Oe, 44 dr. 1 ob. . . . For fluting a column, . . . Ameiniades living in Koile, 18 dr., Lysamas, 18 dr., Somenes (slave) of Ameiniades, 18 dr., Timokrates, 18 dr.[20]

Again in strong contrast to the situation obtaining in the Near East, employees of the Roman emperors were quite often allowed the right to put their names to the works they had achieved, even to the extent of eclipsing their patron, as did the architect of Hadrian's temple at Cyzicus:

> From the foundations, with money from the whole of Asia, and with the help of many hands, the noble [god-like or heroic] Aristainetos raised me up.[21]

As for the work in which craftsmen of the ancient world were engaged, there were, to be sure, great stylistic changes, differences in design dictated by differences in function which in turn depended on dissimilar ritual and variant belief; an example is the case of temples, which in the Greek world were regarded primarily as shelter or as a frame for the cult statue of the god, whereas in the Roman world the temple was more properly a framework for ritual procedure, sacrifice, and so on, and far less emphasis was placed on the statue of the god. There were also some regional differences, such as those resulting from the development of the individual portrait at Rome as opposed to the idealizing type characteristic of Greece. But craft traditions as a whole, the methods of production and many of the designs and motifs themselves suffered no sudden or dramatic alteration. Rather it is their capacity for endurance that is striking. Many variant interpretations of the traditional forms were made, but they remained within the limits of the inherited canons; they did not break out into new dimensions. Regional differences were never so great that no connection can be traced from one to another, and the techniques of manufacture altered very little. There were changes in the manner in which materials were exploited; the Romans, for example, used coloured marble more extensively—and of course private houses were built and embellished on a far grander scale—than had been customary in the Greek period; but, more important, they also explored the potentialities of brick and cement. Mechanical invention, on the other hand, always remained slight; when it did occur, it had only limited application, for the devices employed in catapults and other siege engines were never transferred to the workshops, and steam power remained merely a motivator of toys. In civil engineering the Romans did go beyond the achievements of the Greeks, as their drainage works and aqueducts alone show (Pl. 74). Nevertheless the Greeks too could overcome formidable technical problems on occasion; in the sixth century BC Eupalinos of Megara had engineered a tunnel through a thousand yards of solid rock in order to bring water within the city walls of Samos. So, technologically speaking, the preoccupations of the craftsmen remained fundamentally unshaken.

THE EVIDENCE AND ITS LIMITATIONS

Certain aspects of the craftsman's lot are sufficiently well documented to warrant the making of fairly broad assumptions which seem to hold good for ancient craftsmen in general—though it is often enough quite clear that what may have been relevant to their situation in the Greek period was no longer so in the Roman, and vice versa. Nevertheless it must be admitted that the evidence is for the most part fragmentary in all senses, and that therefore the only picture we can achieve is incomplete at best.

For one thing, statistics are hard to come by, and unreliable even when they are available.[22] It is impossible to do more than hazard a guess at the proportion of craftsmen to the rest of the population in any given community, or of the relative strength of the various crafts within any one city. The slave population of Athens can only be gauged very approximately, and even then we have no idea what proportion of the craftsmen were slaves and how many were citizens and metics. Similarly, although in this case census figures survive, it is equally impossible to estimate the proportion of one group to another in Rome, particularly within the working class. A proper appreciation of the craftsman's standard of living could only come from knowing what the wages and prices of a wide range of occupations and commodities were over a statistically significant period of time. The evidence does not provide an adequate basis for more than the most general inferences; neither the building accounts for Greek public works, nor the objects themselves, neither references in the ancient literature nor documents like Diocletian's price edict provide enough data for the precise comparison of costs at any period.[23]

For another thing it is impossible to speak with any assurance of the social context in which craftsmen existed anywhere but at Athens and Rome, with fragmentary evidence from other places. How did the Greek stonemasons who went from Synnada in Asia Minor to work at Leptis Magna and other places in Roman Africa fit into the community?[24] What sort of existence did they lead at home in Asia Minor? Only the most general assumptions can be made from what we know of city life in the Roman empire as a whole.

Some crafts are far better documented than others; just as some kinds of artefacts have survived in far better condition and greater numbers than others. This is particularly true of the crafts of monumental building and sculpture, so that inevitably illustrations in the following discussion are drawn more frequently from what we would call the fine arts than from the more mundane crafts. But where possible evidence for the latter is brought forward too, in accordance with the proposition that professionally speaking the master of a blacksmith's shop was seen as, and felt himself to be, a man of no less consequence than the chief sculptor of a monumental mason's shop; that the painter's least experienced colour-mixer was in no way superior to the tanner's apprentice; and that it was in no sense inevitable that the silversmith should enjoy a higher standard of life than the cobbler.

The archaeological material illustrates the range of the crafts-men's skills and the high standards they could achieve. It has drawbacks, however, of which one is the temptation to over-interpret. For example, the finely worked Ionic columns on the east façade of the Erechtheion by themselves give no indication of the relationships within the work-group which produced them, of the individual member's earnings, place of residence, or legal position in Athenian society; it is only when we consider the inscribed building accounts and the colonnade together that we realize that work of such great excellence was done by six small gangs working independently on each of the six columns—citizens, metics and slaves alongside one another, with absolutely no distinction apparent in the quality of their craftsmanship or the wages they received.[25] Conversely, while neither inscribed accounts nor literary references survive to amplify in any way the evidence for the workings of the craft which is supplied by the makers' marks on Arretine pottery (Pl. 21) of the late Republic and early Roman Empire, these on their own reveal much of the organization of the craft, and of the status of owners and assistants in the various workshops in Italy and Gaul.[26]

But if there is something to be said about the potters and painters of fine pottery in Athens of the sixth and fifth centuries BC, little or nothing can be done along the same lines for the (presumably more numerous) makers of the far commoner coarse wares, cooking pots, storage jars and so on, because these pieces were never signed nor did the potters responsible make themselves known in any other way—such as by dedications and epitaphs.[27] If the products of the silversmith and imperial freed-man Cheirisophos (Pl. 37) have survived, those of countless bronzesmiths and ironworkers have altogether perished, and with them the memory of their makers.

As for written records, the inscribed accounts of public works in some of the Greek cities and international sanctuaries contain details of how such work was organized, the conditions under which craftsmen were employed, the prices and sometimes the wages which were paid. Inscriptions of this kind have survived in greatest number at Athens, mainly from the later fifth and fourth centuries BC, and in the Delian sanctuary from the late fourth to the second century; others are also known from fourth-century Delphi and Epidauros, and isolated examples have survived elsewhere.[28] But although they provide very specific data on some aspects of the craftsman's lot, they are too specialized in subject-matter to relate usefully to manual workers in general. Public works, whether temple construction or fortification building, were by no means everyday occurrences, and further-more they were subject to adjustment by the state or sanctuary administration; so that there is, therefore, no certainty that day-wages paid to the builders of the Parthenon in fifth-century Athens bore more than a tenuous relationship to the earnings of a craftsman in the workshops of fifth-century Thebes. And if it is possible to see how craftsmen may have fared on public works in Greece, there is no basis for comparison with the situation in the Roman world, since virtually no Roman building records have so far come to light.[29]

The ancient literature shows only a passing concern for all but the technical and stylistic aspects of the craftsmen's way of life. Comments on the economy are rarely more than incidental to the main theme, which is as often as not political history, or political and personal morality. Remarks made by Plato or Aristotle, Cicero or Seneca, revealing as they may be of the moralists' and philosophers' attitudes towards the crafts and the manual workers, do not necessarily tell the whole story.[30] Their bias is clear; the question is, to what extent other sections of society subscribed to it. That by no means all Greeks considered work degrading in itself becomes clear as one examines the craftsmen's own statements; but more significant of the division in Greek thinking on this matter is the point of view put across by Xenophon, himself one of the aristocrats who despised *banausoi*, in his anecdote about Euthemeros. It was not work to which Euthemeros objected, but being under the control of an employer; independence, not clean hands, was the desired state.[31] Although not stated so clearly in the Roman sources, the same difference can be seen between the Roman moralists' attitude to manual work and the view of the man in the street, or the man on the job. Nevertheless, the prejudice against manual work did not always remain a mere intellectual quirk, but occasionally had a real effect on political thinking in some Greek cities and at Rome, to the extent that association with the crafts could debar a man from participation in government. If it is clear that we are dealing here with an aristocratic or upper-class sentiment, we must surely allow that throughout antiquity the aristocracy to a very large extent set the tone of public opinion. The answer then is neither to accept the opinions of Plato and other aristocratic philosophers as the only true view of the situation, nor to dismiss them as the idiosyncrasies of entirely unusual thinkers, but to steer a course somewhere in between. For little as we may like it these thinkers are in some sort spokesmen for their time.

Writers on great craftsmen and their works, exemplified by the elder Pliny in his *Natural History*, reflect the rich man's concern to know the right things and to be able to obtain the best *objets d'art*. Attention is concentrated on the differentiation of one sculptor's style from another's, or the way in which famous painters achieved their effects; incidentally included in this information are many anecdotes more or less revealing of the craftsman's circumstances, but here one has to beware of rhetorical exaggeration, the literary cult of personality, and a love of the squalidly picturesque on the part of the dilettante.[32] Works seriously devoted to the techniques of various crafts were written in some number, but only their memory survives, apart from Vitruvius' study *On Architecture* and some rather more theoretical accounts of mechanical inventions.

Vitruvius' treatise is the product not of a theoretician but of a professional architect, revealing the full range of his concerns, both technical and intellectual. His is the fullest, but by no means the only articulate expression of the craftsman's commitment to his work. The inadequacies of the public records and the literary sources are to a large extent compensated for by the personal documents of the skilled workers themselves—the signatures, sometimes accompanied by some amplification on the signer's situation in life, or his feelings about craftsmanship; the dedications and the epitaphs, which also frequently included data of this kind; and records of public honours granted to individual crafts-men, and of the activities of the various craft associations.

The point has already been made that only a very small propor-tion of the craftsmen in the ancient world is known to us even by name, let alone in any more detail, and that in using material of this kind one must attempt to decide to what extent it is typical of craftsmen in general. In this study I have chosen to take the opinions expressed by the few on the nature of their craftsmanship as being representative of the views of the majority of craftsmen, some of whom might perhaps have left us such testimony of their existence had they not been illiterate, others of whom could not afford to do so, and still others simply never thought of it. What it is impossible to do, of course, is to assume that because some craftsmen were sufficiently affluent and well-placed in society to achieve high honours and considerable per-sonal wealth, skilled workers in general lived in similar style. But it seems legitimate to argue that they all shared to some extent a positive attitude towards their profession, which gave them all a certain confidence and independence of mind in the face of whatever pressures the rest of society saw fit to bring to bear upon them.

CHAPTER II

GREEK AND ROMAN SOCIETY

THE CRAFTSMAN WAS NOT BORN a craftsman, but a citizen, the son of a slave, a metic, or a total foreigner. Like any other member of the community he was subject to all the prejudices and psychological pressures which society brings to bear on the individual—anxieties as to whether or not he belongs to any particular group within the community and, if not, whether perhaps he ought to belong to one; the nature of his rights and duties; public issues and common dangers; his role in the community, the recognition for which he can hope, and the positions to which he might aspire. In order to appreciate the varying conditions of life enjoyed by craftsmen, therefore, we should perhaps consider briefly the background of the society in which they lived and worked.

CONCEPTS OF CITIZENSHIP

There were two closely connected preoccupations fundamental to the thinking of most free men about their political and economic status. The first related to the question of whether or not one was a citizen, and if not, to which section of society one did belong; the other, to whether or not one owned any land, and if not, who did. These concerns remained close. At first—in the period of shifts towards the city-state during and after the Dark Age and in many states for a long time after—qualification for citizenship depended partly on owning land within the bounds of the national territory. Citizenship was moreover the only key to membership of the most privileged group in the community. The city provided the most meaningful social context available to the individual, one which provided wider horizons and hence more fascination, with greater opportunities for a man to exert his personality, than the immediate family or kinship group. The very fact that this citizenship was limited gave a sense of distinction and exclusiveness to its members.

Manual workers, craftsmen, unskilled labourers and peasants were denied full citizen rights in some communities, even well on into the historical period, because they were *banausoi*. And even where it was no longer reflected in law, the prejudice against manual workers remained widespread; nowhere was it aired more frequently than in democratic Athens. What lay at the root of this antipathy? Perhaps as good an explanation as any is Xenophon's statement that

> banausic occupations leave no spare time for friendship or for the affairs of the city: the practitioners of such occupations are . . . bad friends and bad defenders of the city. . . . If during an invasion the farmers and the craftsmen were separated out, and each group was asked whether it would vote for the defence of the country or for withdrawal to the fortresses, the farmers would vote for fighting, whereas the craftsmen would elect to sit still and risk nothing. . . . The farmers therefore make the best and most loyal citizens.[33]

The craftsman had no connection with the land, neither owning any himself nor tilling anyone else's as a peasant. Land had always retained its superiority over all other forms of wealth, a superiority based not on moral considerations—these came second—but on the plain unvarnished fact that only by the production of food could Man ensure his survival; a starving man in the desert has no use for gold. The peculiar importance attached to the land is seen at Athens, for example, in that only citizens could actually own it; and so strong was this idea that even in the late fifth century, despite Athens' industry being bigger and busier than most, it is reckoned that perhaps four-fifths of the citizens owned at least a vegetable patch, if not more.[34] The social and political ideal of the good citizen remained for many—for Hesiod in the seventh century BC as for Aristotle in the fourth, for the elder Cato in the second century as for Cicero in the first—the self-sufficient farmer.

Farming was the chief preoccupation of the vast majority of the population throughout antiquity. Cicero remarked that 'of all the productive occupations there is none better, more fertile, sweeter, or more worthy of a free man' than farming—by which, of course, he meant farming one's own land.[35] Land formed the foundation of most of the large fortunes known to us; even when a man had made his money by other means he would put it into land if he could, a habit common among successful trades-men in other periods too.[36] Nevertheless this was not an article of faith which was strictly adhered to in practice, even by the aristocracy; many Athenian aristocrats, as well as commoners, owned both land and workshops. The ambiguity of the situation did not disturb anyone, however, as the accounts of the clash between Nikias and Kleon show. Both were elected, in the period after Pericles' death, to the board of ten generals; both were therefore rich, influential, and popular. The big difference between them was that, while Nikias was one of the *kaloi k'agathoi*, a 'gentleman' of dignity and prudence, Kleon was a commoner, brash, rash and self-seeking; his awfulness (in the eyes of some) was crowned by his association with a tannery—his manners and his wealth alike came from the workshop, as contemporary comedy was pleased to declare.[37] It is natural to assume that Nikias' wealth, by contrast, lay entirely in land, but in fact he owned one thousand mine slaves who were let out very profitably by his Thracian slave overseer.[38] The same contradictions underlie Roman thinking on land and commerce; according to the elder Cato, the ancient virtues of the Roman farmer were what had made Rome great and would keep her so, but he himself used slave labour very economically, and through his slave agent conducted various trading ventures.[39] Cicero, too, for all his scorn of the manual worker and his enthusiasm for farming as a way of life, could just bring himself to let out property to shop-keepers.[40]

Technically speaking, full citizenship laid on the citizen rights and duties which only the self-supporting man could encompass. In the formative period of the city-state the landless man had little or no alternative means of getting a living. As a member of the family, he could generally depend on handouts from one or another of his kin; he retained his birthright to a place in the kinship structure; but he was a liability, if anything, because he had nothing to offer and nothing to risk if and when common action was called for—neither arms or followers in time of crisis, nor weight of authority in debate. Throughout the long period of the city-state's formation, the landless man was not taken seriously, whether citizen-born or not. So, for Xenophon and many like him, despite the fact that the political organization and economy of Athens had long since given such men a full role to play, the landless craftsman had none of the right things to offer, and might even refuse to give the state what support he was able to provide, since he was cut off from the things that mattered.

Citizenship embodied the right to live as a free man within the bounds of the community, and to own property; it also allowed a man the possibility of helping to determine the city's policy by exercising his vote in the Assembly. The citizen could look to his city for protection in time of war; for food in time of famine—discussion of the corn supply came up regularly on the Athenian Assembly's agenda, and the corn dole was a matter of great political moment in the later Roman Republic and under the Empire; for justice in case of injury, damage to property or attack on his personal freedom, whatever the rank or political influence of the perpetrator; and for divine guidance and sanction of the community's activities, through the cults of the city. In return, the city demanded the rendering of certain services; the citizen must contribute money, labour or supplies, according to his means and as the city required, for fortifications, ships, temple building and other public undertakings; he must help to ensure the safety of his fellow-citizens, as well as his own, by fighting alongside them in the city's defence. In many cities this last requirement remained, with land owning and citizen birth, a fundamental qualification for citizenship; it was always retained for citizens at Sparta, but was modified at Athens under the radical democracy, where by the mid-fifth century there had arisen a strong connection between the political rights of the lowest class and its usefulness in serving in the fleet; at Rome military service, though enforceable, seems not to have been expected of all citizens after the fourth century BC.

The early development of the city-state followed much the same pattern in the Greek world and at Rome. The three basic elements, annual magistrates (replacing the original monarchy), council of elders and assembly of citizens, were common to both, and much the same problems arose as the city-states became more competent to deal with the community's affairs, and their members more aware of the power exploitable by one group or another.[41] For greater men must always have tended to exert their power over lesser men; thus in the eighth and seventh centuries BC, when the Greek city-states were evolving the first principles of government, it was aristocratic power which counted, power based on the possession of land and maintained by the members of a few families, or in some places a single clan. Aristocratic influence lasted long; and even when the aristocratic monopoly of office was broken by the rise of men made rich by trade and industry the antithesis of influential and weak, rich and poor, always endured. The rich took to themselves, if they did not hold it already, the aristocratic belief that political power and political virtue were exclusive to a select group of families. Adherents to this belief did not go unchallenged, however, and long and bitter quarrels developed in many cities. Yet it is significant that when the many rose against the few, their leaders were often, as at Athens, men who themselves came from the upper class; this demonstrates the profound and enduring influence of the concept of aristocracy, and its resistance to all efforts to destroy it.

In states where democracy did not prevail, the holding of political power was restricted; citizenship by itself did not qualify a man for office. In early Rome, for instance, only patricians could hold office; then from the mid-fourth century onwards a few wealthy plebeian families joined this privileged circle, so that despite the apparent success of this challenge to the old aristocratic monopoly, real power in the state was still held by a small group, which relied upon intermarriage and the descent of power within the group to maintain its hold. Only very occasionally did men from other families reach the highest office, by means of army and magisterial appointments and the backing of a noble patron. Under the Empire offices were still restricted to the upper classes, the senatorial and equestrian, but by then new men had more opportunity to rise. In the later Empire, however, from the third century onwards, the two top classes became virtually closed and the appointment of officials to places in the imperial bureaucracy came to depend on finer and finer distinctions of rank and precedent within these upper classes. The ordinary citizen had not the slightest chance of gaining a post, except by advancement in the army.

At no period could anyone doubt the distinctions between the three main groups recognized in Greek and Roman society of citizens, free non-citizens and slaves, or mistake the slight differences in status existing within each group. The craftsmen, whatever their personal feelings in the matter, belonged at all periods to one or another of several clearly defined social orders. What flexibility was there in the system? To what extent were they able to participate in public affairs, supposing they wished to do so? A problem of particular relevance to their position concerns the change that wealth could effect in status; for it is clear that, once the early principle of qualification for political rights by birth had been modified, a man had the chance to escape from the status he had inherited (or had had forced upon him, as in the case of slaves and freedmen). Thus in Athens, after Solon's reforms in 594, a very wealthy commoner could hold office with the highest-born; and by the time of Pericles, men of quite modest means could hold most offices. At Rome, a slave became a citizen on gaining his freedom, and a freedman's grandson might, if his forbears had done well in business and married judiciously, become an equestrian and so eligible for office; the Emperor Augustus' great-grandfather was said to have been a freedman rope-maker, and Pertinax, the son of a freedman, became emperor (briefly) in AD 193.[42]

Even where political and social prejudices against manual work remained very strong, even in those states whose constitutions denied active citizen rights to the *banausoi*, barriers not only to communication but to actual social contact between them and the citizens must always have been breaking down. Despite the apparent rigidity of the antipathy to *banausoi* in the literature, opinions on eligibility for citizenship varied; and constitutions can be seen to have varied accordingly. Aristotle said, 'No man can practise virtue who is living the life of a mechanic', and went on to say that 'in the oligarchies no labourer can ever be a citizen'.[43] This we know was true of Sparta; but Aristotle only quotes the instance of Thebes, where the law said that no one could hold office for ten years after he had given up business.[44]

That such restrictions were less the rule than the exception is suggested by Plutarch's report of a military gathering of the Spartans and their allies called by King Agesilaus in 396; when he asked for artisans of various kinds to stand up, most of the allies rose, while all the Spartans of course remained seated.[45] The story may be apocryphal, yet reflect something of the truth; Herodotus reports that

the Egyptians . . . and indeed almost all foreigners reckon craftsmen and their descendants as lower in the social scale than people who have no connection with manual work . . . (and) the Greeks have adopted this attitude, especially the Spartans; the feeling against handicraft is least strong in Corinth,

which city happens to have been Sparta's most powerful ally in the Peloponnese, down to the fourth century when Agesilaus called the gathering.[46] The Ephesians we know granted citizenship to two Athenian potters in the fourth century.[47]

The citizen's immediate horizon was bounded not by the city walls but by his family and kinship group. Citizenship embodied the recognition of citizen marriage, and conferred legitimacy on the offspring. The city provided legal protection of the family's business—property, inheritance, restitution of dowries on the breakdown of marriages, and so on. The citizen's private life was as important as his role in public, and the state's acknowledgment of the fact allowed dignity and stability to the family. There could be no separation of family interests from the city's concerns; there was no competition between the city and the family for a man's loyalty. The individual's religious beliefs were catered for partly by the cult associations based on family and clan, and by local cults subscribed to by neighbours who were not necessarily related. These cults were either linked to the state cults, or at any rate in no conflict with them.

A man with no settled home, who moved about at will from one place to another, might gain in personal freedom by not having to pay taxes (apart from incidentals like harbour dues and sales taxes), by not being obliged to serve in the army, and by not sharing in the collective misfortune of a defeated or dearth-stricken city. He might in many places find that, though rootless, he could claim some hearing before the law, and even share in cult observances. Nevertheless he could not be certain of obtaining justice; nor could he benefit (except incidentally and merely as a bystander) from the good fortune of the city, and all that this might mean to the full citizen.[48]

But the vast majority of non-citizens in the Greek world had a recognized place in the cities. Metics, free resident aliens of a certain standing, are known to have existed in at least seventy Greek cities, where they probably enjoyed much the same privileges and duties as at Athens.[49] The Athenian metics were outsiders, some Greek, some barbarian, who had either come freely to Attica to take advantage of the opportunities it offered for trade and industry, or had been brought in as slaves and then given their freedom, choosing to stay where they knew they could make a living rather than returning to the clan or tribe which had as likely as not sold them into slavery in the first place. Metics were long-term residents, not itinerants flitting from place to place. They had no active political rights, but were guaranteed some protection under Athenian law, and bore some responsibility to their adopted place of residence; they paid the metic tax, contributed along with the citizens to special war taxes, served in the army and the fleet, and took part in the national festival of the Panathenaia. But though they were free to do business, make contracts and lend money, they were not allowed to own land.

Legally speaking the division between citizens and metics was sharp; but individual metics could, by rendering services to the state, gain certain rights which distinguished them from their fellow metics but still left them non-citizens; one such privilege was *isoteleia*, the right to pay taxes on the same rating as citizens (i.e. at a lower rate than other metics), another was *epigamia*, recognition of the children of a marriage between a metic and an Athenian as of citizen birth, and another, *enktesis*, the right to own land. Privileges of this kind were only granted occasionally; what is remarkable is, first, the fact that metics supported the Athenians so loyally, especially at the time of the city's defeat and the democrats' struggle with the oligarchs in 404/3, and secondly, that though the Athenian attitude to metics was favourable on many counts, the Athenians never integrated them completely.[50]

The status of the resident alien before the law was much more explicit than that of the citizen of another state. But the Greeks moved a little way towards the concept of international law, in that each city might if it felt so moved appoint, as an honour and privilege, someone in another city to be *proxenos*; if for example the Athenians appointed a *proxenos* in Sicyon, then he must stand as protector and advocate for any Athenian citizen who required assistance in Sicyon. Even so, it appears that special provisions had to be made in individual building contracts for the settlement of disputes between state officials and workers who came in from elsewhere; no generally accepted principle of inter-state arbitration could be called on, nor, except in isolated instances, was there any question of dual citizenship being established.

ROMAN POINTS OF VIEW

In the Roman world, of course, international law became a reality in that Roman citizenship eventually lost all local connection and indeed all political significance, transformed as it was after AD 212 into world citizenship. In the later Roman Empire a single code of law was recognized throughout a wider area than ever before in the ancient world. Yet originally Rome had been, and remained for several centuries, a city-state in which the same concern prevailed as in the Greek cities for preserving the privileges of citizenship, with very similar attitudes towards non-citizens. Landowning and military service were as important in the early period as citizen birth, and they remained essential for all who aimed at holding high office; but though the peasant farmer who would fight for his land and his country continued to predominate in the citizen body, the landless and those too poor to provide their own arms also had a place among the citizens. The Romans differed markedly from the Greeks in their approach to the question of admitting new men to the citizen body; though they steadfastly refused to give the franchise to their Italian allies until forced to do so (in the early first century BC), in general they granted their citizenship much more generously, and they had always permitted the slave of a Roman citizen to become a citizen himself immediately on gaining his freedom, a thing totally inconceivable to the Greeks.[51] Roman thought on this matter in particular was influenced by two relationships peculiar to Roman society, which together made for a wider spectrum of statuses within the citizen body (the distinction between the lowest echelons of citizens and both non-citizens and slaves was far less at Rome than anywhere in the Greek world).

One of these elements was the *patria potestas*, the father's authority over every aspect of his children's private lives, extending to all sons and unmarried daughters, and to the son's sons and other male descendants until his death.[52] Only the *pater familias* had the right to own property, for anything acquired by members of the family went to him (and in strict law continued to do so until the time of Constantine); no child could marry without his permission, and the sons' wives passed into his authority too. One of the chief concerns underlying this aspect of the law was to ensure the right control of property; and adoption, another constantly recurring feature of Roman family life, was the means by which a childless man could ensure that his property went to an heir.

The other peculiarly Roman element affecting relationships within the citizen body was patronage.[53] In early Rome the patrons were the aristocrats, the heads of the great houses, and their clients the followers, their supporters at election time, men who attended daily on their patrons in return for past, and in the hope of future, financial assistance or legal protection. They included the patron's freed slaves and their families, immigrants perhaps who needed a protector, poor relations, needy tenants, or badly off neighbours. And at all periods the effect must have been to strengthen the loyalties of lesser men to greater—the tie between patron and client was hereditary—and to discourage radical change.

This patron-client relationship was of particular significance for artists and craftsmen, since many of them were ex-slaves. The freedman's position at Rome demonstrates all the ambiguities and legal tortuosities of the Roman concept of citizenship; for, though a freedman was a Roman citizen according to the law, he remained, as a client to his patron, under heavy obligation to his former master, and in addition had set upon him many of the limitations that a freeborn son suffered under the *patria potestas*. According to the *Digest*, 'the person of the patron or the father should always be honoured and held sacred by the freedman or son.' A condition of some manumissions, of particular relevance to the craftsman, was that the freedman was expected to perform *operae*, that is, to do so many days' work in the patron's household or workshop, a duty which could descend to the patron's heirs, though the freedman's obligation ended with his death; *operae* could be hired out to a third person, presumably with no regard for the freedman's wishes, unless he happened to have a sympathetic patron. This duty might be commuted to a cash payment, but even so the freedman suffered a limitation on his earning powers.[54]

The freedman was a Roman citizen. Nevertheless he was distinct from free-born citizens, the *ingenui*, and known as a *libertinus*, slave-born; only his sons, as long as they were born after his manumission, could count as *ingenui*. Freedmen's names very often, because they were Greek or Asiatic, betrayed their status, and so their sons were generally given Latin names, as a necessary aid to integration. If, however, the children had been born before their father's manumission, they remained slaves, a harsh condition not alleviated until Hadrian's time; nor was a marriage contracted before manumission recognized afterwards as a citizen marriage—it remained a slave union, *contubernium*.

At all periods, except when imperial patronage (especially that of Claudius and Nero) elevated certain individuals to high administrative office, the freedman's hope of gaining an influential position was slight in the extreme; he could not rise by military achievements, since the freedman could not serve in the legions. A law of Tiberius' reign forbade the freedman to become a member of the local senate in the provincial cities, and by the time of Nero legislation had rendered it possible only for a freedman's grandson to stand on equal terms with the free-born.

Wealth made a difference. Under the early Empire it became possible for more new men to find their way into the two upper classes, the senatorial and the equestrian, from which officials were appointed; one of the means to entry was a large fortune. But a strong prejudice against banausic occupations, with the inevitable political overtones, always persisted. Even if the Romans had never held that manual workers and traders should be excluded from the citizen body, some traces of deep antipathy did exist, for instance in the tradition that if a bird of ill omen perched on the Capitol, the *pontifex maximus* should order artisans and slaves to withdraw, and then read out the customary formula of supplication which the citizens repeated after him.[55]

Any association between senate or magistrates and trade and industry was felt to be objectionable, and the feeling was formally expressed in a law of 218 BC which severely limited senatorial participation in overseas trade.[56] The detestation in which contact between members of the Roman government and trade was held appears in Livy's description of one of the consuls of 216 BC, C. Terentius Varro: 'He was of humble, indeed mean origin; his father is said to have been a butcher who retailed his own meat, and employed his son in the servile office of his trade.'[57] Similarly, Augustus' great-grandfather, the freedman rope-maker, was suddenly remembered by Mark Antony in one of his attacks on Augustus as they struggled for power. The same prejudices are to be found in the literature of the imperial period, and in the legislation of the emperors too:

> if a freedman, having promised to perform *operae*, then rises to a station in which it would be unsuitable for him to perform them for his patron, he may forego them.[58]

The same prejudices prevailed from one century to the next, even though the nature of Roman citizenship itself was translated into something totally different from the Greeks' view of the subject. The Greeks only gradually moved beyond the concept of a limited community, as far as possible independent, whose citizen body might number anything between 5,000 and 20,000, one of over 35,000 being exceptional; this was the kind of community which came into being during the ninth, eighth and seventh centuries, and which continued to be founded in Egypt, Asia Minor, Mesopotamia, Persia and Bactria as a result of Alexander's conquests. Rome remained for generations a city-state very similar in scale and preoccupations, but then evolved into the capital city of an empire surrounding the Mediterranean and stretching beyond; from a state which maintained a number of 'special relationships' with neighbouring communities in Italy into the centre of a vast administrative network by grace of which, as early as the late Republic, Roman citizenship was being extended to communities far distant from the city. As the number of citizens increased, Roman citizenship lost more and more of its original political significance, retaining only its legal and private privileges when after AD 212, by decree of the Emperor Caracalla, it was extended to virtually all inhabitants of the empire.[59]

The wide extension of Roman citizenship did not mean that the local citizenships already existing were automatically can-celled. Far from it; local city administrations continued, under the eye of the Roman provincial governor, to have not only the power but the duty to manage their own affairs. Many Roman citizens throughout the provinces therefore enjoyed dual citizenship.[60] And with the decline in the political value of Roman citizenship itself, as the empire became far too large to attract the individual's active loyalty, local affairs could provide a substitute for policy-making and empire-building for those excluded from the central imperial administration. In cities in the provinces office depended on rank determined by wealth just as much as in the imperial structure. The power of the people, originally vested in the right to elect magistrates, gradually dwindled until all they could do to influence policy was to shout loudly, in approval or dissent, on the occasion of imperial proclamations, or to riot in the theatre or at the games put on by local magistrates if the price of bread had risen too high or the services demanded by the central government, such as providing horses and carts for the imperial post, were too burdensome.

Executive power lay in the hands of the upper class; the local city's senate of decurions managed affairs, but imperial permission had to be sought for every constitutional adjustment or major public expense, whether for essential waterworks, theatres, or statues of the emperor himself. Qualification for office and for membership of the senate had become hereditary by the third century AD; freedmen were excluded from office by law, but if they were wealthy enough they could enter the minor priesthood of the Augustales, which administered the imperial cult. The dislike of banausic occupations rears its head in the story of Thalassius, who was refused entry to the senate of Constantinople in the fourth century because he owned a knife factory and was suspected of having worked in it himself.[61] On the other hand, Caecilianus, a linen-weaver in the small city of Aptungi in Africa, became a *duovir*, one of the two chief magistrates, even though he seems to have shared both meals and labour with his craftsmen.[62] It must be that the general ban on manual workers had to be relaxed in smaller communities. At Tarsus in the second century AD citizenship itself still depended on a property qualification of 500 dr., an amount some linen-weavers were too poor to raise.[63]

SLAVES

Roman citizenship encompassed a far wider range of social positions than ever existed in the Greek cities. The reverse seems to be true of the institution of slavery. In the Roman world the slave's status, though complicated by the legalistic formulations inherent in Roman social thinking, always remained straightforward in the sense that there were no halfway measures —a slave was unfree, and that was that. Greek citizenship covered a far smaller range of differences between more and less privileged citizens, and the difference between citizens and non-citizens was clear, while that between free men and unfree was even more distinct; within the category of unfree, however, were many shades of unfreedom, ranging from chattel slavery, according to which the slave was a beast differing from other domestic animals only in the number of his feet, a piece of property which happened to be human but which was entirely at its owner's disposal, through helots, *pelatai* and others tied to the land but slightly better off than chattel slaves, to that of the man who was technically free but who was bound for a period of time to work for another, either to pay off a debt or even as part of the conditions on which he had been manumitted.[64]

Nevertheless, despite certain obvious institutional differences, the condition of the slave throughout antiquity was in practice determined on one hand by the fact of his being enslaved, and on the other by the kind of work he did, the temper of his owner and the rapport he was able to establish with him; neither Roman law nor Greek legal particularizations could by themselves dictate the kind of life a slave might lead. Individual circumstances could vary enormously; the life of the chattel slave in fifth-century Athens might be grim if he was a mine slave let out to a succession of mine lessees, but rewarding, both spiritually and materially, if he was a stonemason working on equal terms with free masons; yet the legal status of both was the same, just as was that of the farm slaves in the Italian *ergastula* of the second and first centuries BC and Cicero's slave architect Cyrus.[65] The slave was a thing, a possession. But this had its positive side, in that as property he was valuable, and so the owner was inhibited to some extent from punishing him too hard or starving him completely; for a dead slave was a dead loss.

There always lingered a slight uneasiness about the rights and wrongs of slavery. Aristotle declared that slavery was natural, that slaves were slavish by nature, while others, including the Roman jurists, said that it was a convention only. But whatever the theorists' doubts, the reality of slavery remained unchallenged throughout antiquity; no one ever thought seriously of abolishing it, neither Stoic philosophers, Church fathers nor the slaves themselves, whose only thought was to regain their own freedom. Enslavement meant that the owner of a slave could put the slave's labour to whatever purposes he saw fit; and, though the importance of slavery in ancient society was primarily economic, this fact alone had immediate and far-reaching social significance. Adequate estimation of numbers is impossible; yet, where it can be calculated, the proportion of slave to free gives some indication of slavery's impact on society. At Athens in the later fifth century the slave population was perhaps 60,000–80,000, and the proportion of slave to free 1:2 or 3. At Sparta, an extreme example, the proportion of helots to all free men was perhaps 3:1, and of helots to born citizens, 7:1. The proportion of slave to free in most other cities will have been smaller.[66]

The distribution of slaves was determined by their place in the economy. The largest individual holdings of slaves known at Athens are the 1,000 mine slaves of Nikias in the later fifth century.[67] This was exceptional, however; otherwise, the largest unit of slaves known is the shield workshop of the metic Polemarchos, employing 120, while Demosthenes' father owned 52 or 53 slaves in his knife and ivory-bed factory; Timarchos owned 9 or 10 cobblers and a sewing woman.[68] Most slave-owners will have had one or two, or half a dozen slaves at the most.

The sharpness of distinction between slave and free in the Greek world was complementary to their strength of feeling for the value of citizenship and the contrast made between citizens and outsiders. By the Classical period the enslavement of Greeks by other Greeks, as well as of fellow-citizens, was considered a bad thing; Philip II of Macedon, for example, was fiercely criticized after his enslavement of the population of Olynthos.[69] At Athens we can see how the development of the city as a positive entity was matched by an increased regard for the citizen, and by a growing distinction between those whom it was suitable to enslave and those whom it was not. In the early sixth century Solon abolished debt bondage (which went out at Rome too in the fourth century), so that a citizen debtor could no longer fall completely into the possession of his creditor by pledging his own person, thus rendering his citizenship valueless; for citizenship was too precious to be so abused. As the city offered more and more positive advantages to its citizens, so the most extreme form of slavery, chattel slavery of the kind known in Classical Athens, emerged; and chattel slaves came almost entirely from outside the Greek world. The halfway status of helot, *pelates*, *penestes* and the like prevailed in areas where the city's development was less sophisticated, or static as in Sparta, Thessaly or Crete—at Sparta, for instance, the citizen body was small and the indigenous non-citizen population (including the *perioikoi*) large. Perhaps partly because these people were not complete outsiders but had ties of cult if not kinship with the land in which they lived, they could not so readily be considered as mere human beasts of burden after the manner of chattel slaves. Since it was in the more advanced communities, where chattel slavery prevailed, that most slave craftsmen eked out their existence, our discussion is best confined to what we know of chattel slavery, mainly from the Athenian evidence.

Chattel slaves, mostly from non-Greek-speaking areas,[70] fell into slavery in one or another of several ways: either they were captured in war and then passed to slave-dealers and so into the Greek world, or they were kidnapped by pirates and brigands, constant menaces in the Mediterranean world, and put on the market thereafter. No doubt some kings were not at all averse to selling unwanted subjects into slavery, nor was it unheard of to sell children to the slave-dealers.[71] At Athens there appears to have been a constant recurrence of the same nationalities during the fifth and fourth centuries, which implies fairly steady contact between certain sources of supply and the Athenian slave market. Another means of supply was breeding. The status of slavery was heritable, and there were always house-born slaves; but we do not know the proportion of bought to bred slaves at any period.

The nationalities represented among the slaves at Athens included Thracians, Scythians, Bithynians, Phrygians, Paphlagonians, Colchidians, Carians, Lydians, Cappadocians, Syrians, Egyptians, an occasional Ethiopian, some Persians and other Middle Easterners captured by the Greeks in the Persian invasions of Greece, or in campaigns in Cyprus or Egypt, and even Illyrians and Macedonians, semi-Greeks if not exactly literate. A Messenian appears among household slaves in a late fifth-century sales list; although it was surely rare for Greeks to fall into slavery at Athens in this period, self-sale was never entirely out of the question.[72] A man who was destitute or who simply wished to vanish might choose slavery as a refuge, servitude being preferable to free beggary, prison or death.

Most slaves in Attica were privately owned, but some belonged to the state—the Scythian archers who composed the police force, for example. Others were attached to the temples; fourth-century accounts from Eleusis list hats, tunics, shoe repairs and food 'for the public slaves'.[73]

It was said that the three preoccupations governing a slave's existence were work, punishment and food.[74] The slave could not keep anything of his own without his master's consent; he had no power to take his owner to court, and so no protection whatsoever against ill-treatment; if he was a witness at a trial he could be tortured with his owner's consent; unlike the free man, he was not protected from corporal punishment. However, only the owner was lawfully permitted to beat a slave; and if the master saw fit, a slave might work apart from the household, in a separate workshop, virtually independent except that he had to pay over a regular portion of his earnings—the rest he kept for himself. With savings of this kind, the *apophora*, the slave might pay his own manumission price and so gain freedom. The owner's consent was required, but it was probably difficult to refuse when the slave had the fee in his hand, so to speak.

The slave had no civic rights, and (unlike the Spartan helots) did not serve with the army. But slaves did on occasion help to man the Athenian fleet; in 406, at a time of great crisis, some were recruited and, after the battle of Arginusae, set free with a grant of limited citizen rights. As for private rights, these were in principle non-existent; but for the slaves who lived and worked apart from their owners, life must have been, within limits, very much what they could make of it. Others doubtless led wretched lives, made miserable both by the kind of work they did and the brutishness of their masters, or their overseers. But for the industrial and house slaves in and around the city, was life necessarily so bad? The bleak summary of the slave's preoccupations quoted above is not altogether borne out by what we know of the possibilities open to slaves with wits and skill, or by the fact that several of the public slaves employed in the sanctuary at Eleusis were initiated in the Mysteries.[75]

The mid-fifth-century pamphleteer known as the Old Oligarch said, rather sourly, that

> the slaves and metics, indeed they live in Athens the most unrestrained life; to beat them is not permitted there, and a slave will not even stand out of your way in the street. The reason is . . . that if the free citizen were allowed to beat the slave or the metic the freedman, he might hit an Athenian citizen by mistake. For the people there are no better dressed than the slaves and metics.[76]

Plato remarked too that 'the climax of popular liberty is attained in such a city (a democracy) when the purchased slaves, male and female, are no less free than the owners who paid for them.'[77]

Both writers, one suspects, exaggerated the degree of liberty enjoyed by slaves, for both were embittered critics of Athenian democracy. Nevertheless they should not be dismissed out of hand. The large number, twenty thousand, which is said to have fled during the Peloponnesian War is no clear indication that slaves in Attica were badly off,[78] for freedom is as a rule the slave's foremost desire, whatever his conditions; certainly the murder of masters by their slaves seems to have been rare, in contrast to the situation in Roman society.

Most of the slaves in Attica were non-Greek by origin, and many must have been non-Greek-speaking. How did they fit in? The question of racial prejudice in antiquity is touched on below, so that it is enough here to point out that, while the house-born slaves can have experienced no language difficulty, even an Asiatic working in the silver mines was moved to have an epitaph in Greek hexameters, with Homeric allusions thrown in, and many others set up simpler dedicatory and funerary inscriptions, again in Greek.[79] The range of occupations which slaves followed suggests that there was virtually no sphere of Athenian activity in which they could not play some part, however menial; they worked in the households as nurses, cooks, cleaners, on the land as bailiffs, labourers, herdsmen, in the workshops at every kind and level of skilled work, as state secretaries, temple servants, public and private entertainers, confidants and private secretaries.

Their status after manumission is not clear; ultimately they became metics (and a very few gained citizenship thereafter), but to begin with they were perhaps in a lower category of 'freedmen'.[80] Occasionally the state manumitted slaves *en masse*, as in 406 BC. But manumission was principally the concern of private owners, since most slaves were privately owned; the slave might be manumitted by will, or as at Delphi by means of a fictitious sale to the god Apollo, who was then assumed to let the slave go free. By law the ex-slave need have no further links with his former master; in some cases, however, the freedman was bound by the terms of the manumission agreement itself to work for his former owner for a certain length of time, perhaps even for the rest of his life. Documents from second-century Delphi show that a weaver who had been manumitted was pledged to train an apprentice to take his place before he could leave his master's service for good; another freedman was bound to support one of his manumittors in old age.[81] So the question arises, in what sense was the freedman in such cases free? Conversely, can one not say, as Aristotle did, that any free man who contracted to work for another thus put himself under a degree of servitude? This is a point of view which profoundly influenced ancient attitudes to work, and it takes the argument from the realm of law to that of economic status. Legally the distinction between slave and free may have been crystal clear; in practice, the two states overlapped. There is no knowing how far services after manumission were expected of Athenian craftsmen. One can imagine that a slave-owner might often have found it inconvenient to let a man go free the moment he had saved up his manumission price or had morally qualified for freedom by some good deed, so that Athenian manumissions may also have entailed further duties in the former owner's workshop. The Greeks' interest in holding on to the freedman in this way stemmed directly from the concern which lay at the roots of slavery, the concern *to control labour outright*, and nothing more nor less than that.[82]

Much the same interests prompted the preservation of the Roman freedman's obligations to his former owner. Their origins, however, lay in an entirely different context, that of the *patria potestas*, which, as we have seen, had nothing to do with slavery as such. The evidence for the circumstances of Roman slaves is abundant, for since slaves were valuable pieces of property they were the subject of frequent adjustments to the law and figured large in the legal opinions of the jurists. Slave status was complicated in detail, but more clear-cut in concept than among the Greeks in that there existed no halfway statuses, and no one of whom it could be said, as was possible in the Greek world, 'Yes, he is free—partly free—in a way.' It was thus impossible to make a clear distinction between chattel slavery, which was seen by the Greeks as a status to be inflicted on outsiders, and less extreme forms.

The Romans' attitude to slavery, besides being in many respects less complex than the Greeks', was if possible even more hard-headed. A single quotation from the *Digest* puts the matter in its true perspective:

The slave who does anything to remove himself from mankind is regarded as vicious; as for example if he makes a noose or

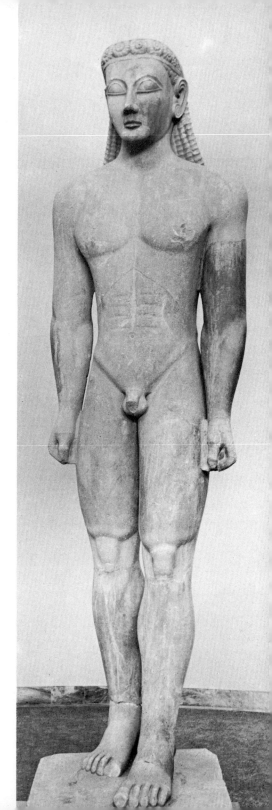

1, 2 Euthykartides' dedication to
Delian Apollo. It is a triangular
marble base with a Gorgon's head
at two of the corners and a ram's
head at the third. The base would
originally have supported a *kouros*
of the type shown here.

3 An Athenian vase-painting showing a cobbler at work in his shop. He is cutting a pair of shoes to measure for the small boy standing before him on the bench.

4 The cobbler at work in early fifth-century Athens

5-7 *Above*, two grave stelai; *left*, that of a Romano-Gaulish shoemaker at work at his last; *right*, that of Xanthippos, a shoemaker in Athens, *c*.420 BC. *Below*, a Roman relief of a shoemaker and a rope-maker at work in their workshop

8-10 The carpenter's trade.
Above left, the grave stele of
P. Beitenos Hermes, a couch-
maker; *right*, the grave stele
of P. Longidienus Camillus, a
shipwright, inscribed 'Publius
Longidienus hastens to get on
with his work'. *Left*, a
terracotta plaque showing
Argus working on the prow
of the *Argo*

11, 12 The small terracotta figurine, *above*, of the fifth century BC, shows a Boeotian sawyer at work. *Right*, a wall-painting from Pompeii illustrates a festival in honour of Perdix, the inventor of the carpenter's saw. He was killed out of jealousy by his brother, Daidalos, and a model of the event was carried in procession, possibly by carpenters.

13-16 Various stages in the manufacture of pottery. *Above*, a Corinthian terracotta plaque of the seventh-sixth centuries BC shows the clay being dug out. *Left*, a potter works a kylix on his wheel, and, *below*, two more plaques show kilns being fired.

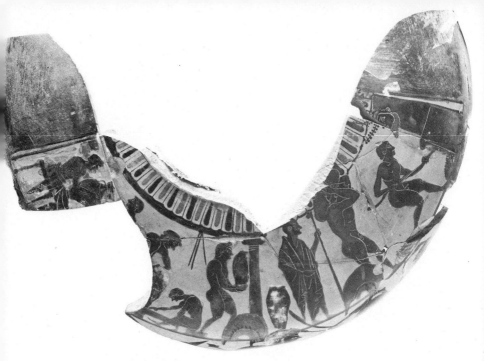

17, 18 Potters at work. *Above*, all aspects of work in a pottery are shown, from painting to firing – notice the apotropaic mask hanging on the kiln. *Below*, *left*, a potter burnishes an unglazed skyphos.

19 The Potter's Stele, *right*, dedicated (probably) by the potter Pamphaios and made by the sculptor Endoios in the late sixth century BC

20, 21 Terracotta products. *Left*, a figurine made in the workshop of Diphilos of Myrina and signed on the base, second century BC. *Above*, a cast from an Arretine ware mould, signed 'M. Peren.', showing Alexander the Great hunting a lion, late first century BC

22-24 Roman terracotta lamps. They illustrate how some were made from worn moulds and subsequently touched up. Others, such as the design on the right, inspired by the statue of Athena Promachos of Pheidias, were individually modelled.

drinks medicine as a poison, or throws himself from a height, hoping to achieve death. For one who will do this to himself will have no scruple about what he does to others.[83]

The impact of slavery on Roman society can be judged to some extent from the proportion of slave to free, where and when the evidence allows. In the early period slaves were comparatively few; but from 200 BC onwards, as Rome became more and more involved in conquests to west and east, vast numbers of slaves were available to the Italian economy. In 167 alone, the Roman general Aemilius Paullus sold 150,000 Epirotes into slavery, many of whom must have come to Italy, and it is calculated that between 200 and 167 something like 250,000 slaves entered Roman and Italian households and estates.[84] By 28 BC the total population of Italy is reckoned to have been about twelve million, of whom perhaps one-third were slaves;[85] however, the proportion of slaves to free in Italy as a whole will have been somewhat lower. The number of slaves acquired by war obviously decreased after the first century AD, as wars of conquest became less frequent, and subject peoples were left to till the fields in the new provinces rather than being put on the slave market. But the proportion of slaves itself need not have diminished accordingly, for breeding would have helped to maintain numbers; the house-born slave figured large in most occupations, apart from mining and quarrying. The slave trade, carried on between the frontier provinces and the tribes beyond, and within the empire by brigands and pirates whom the Romans never succeeded in suppressing entirely, would also have maintained the supply. Slavery for long remained a vital feature of the economy. In the later Empire a change in status did come about, however, connected with the decline in the value of citizenship; the difference between the free poor, by then mostly tied to hereditary occupations or tenancies, and the slaves decreased almost to vanishing point.

There must always have been a few Italians among the slave population. But after 200 BC the main sources of slaves were the theatres of Rome's wars: Greece, Asia Minor, Thrace and beyond, the Near East, Africa, and the German, Gallic and

Spanish territories to the north and north-west of the empire. Revolts in the provinces might result in the enslavement of the rebels too; the pro-Roman writer Josephus says that 97,000 Jews were enslaved by Vespasian after the war of AD 66–8, and many may have suffered the same fate after the revolt in Hadrian's time.[86]

Some slaves belonged to the state, but the majority were in private ownership. Many rich men owned hundreds of slaves each, often as a matter of prestige, to serve as retainers rather than to do anything productive. Augustus felt it necessary to limit the number of slaves an owner might manumit by will, probably to protect the heirs from undue loss of property, and it is interesting to see that the limits quoted in the law run from a modest five out of ten slaves owned altogether, to one hundred out of a total of five hundred, and that this was the upper limit, however many more slaves the owner might have.[87] Crassus, who was renowned for his wealth and avarice, made money by buying slaves who were carpenters and masons, and when he had more than five hundred of them speculating on properties damaged or destroyed by fire, which he used his slave gang to rebuild.[88] But though some men owned slaves on a huge scale, the majority, as in Greece, will only have owned one or two, or half a dozen at the most. Nevertheless, the slave population of Rome alone was considerably larger than that of the entire Greek world.

Legally, the slave was completely at his master's disposal. The position did not alter very much throughout Roman antiquity, although from the first century AD onwards it was slightly modified by occasional laws framed with humanitarian principles somewhere in view, as Stoicism and then Christianity began to make some impression on the social thinking of influential Romans. Even so, they left much to be desired.[89] Until Augustus' time, slaves could be tortured when giving evidence in any kind of trial; Augustus restricted the use of torture to really serious trials, for treason and the like. The master could kill his own slave with impunity, until slave-killing was officially equated with murder in the second century AD; the killing of someone else's slave had always been taken seriously, of course, since this constituted damage to property. A jurist of the second century states with obvious pride that 'nowadays neither Roman citizens nor any other member of the Roman empire may use excessive or groundless cruelty against their slaves'.[90]

Slaves employed in business and in the workshops could (depending on their ability and on the attitude of their owners) achieve semi-independence by means of the *peculium*, the proportion of their earnings which could be kept for personal use. This system had advantages for both sides. A degree of free enterprise encouraged the hard-working slave to work better—he produced a regular profit for the owner, and could retain what he earned over and above that to build up his own business. The owner could then stop worrying about the expense of maintaining him, and might hope to gain considerably if the slave died, because his property would revert to the owner. This system also meant that the slave could do business quite independently, using his *peculium* to back a deal; if the deal fell through, the owner was involved in no loss. Roman slaves and freedmen played a far larger part in the business life of the Roman world than their Athenian counterparts.

The private lives of slaves, even those who were allowed a *peculium*, were circumscribed by law. Legal marriage was impossible, but urban slaves could usually enjoy a stable family life, the great difference between theirs and the free man's situation being that their partners were not recognized as wives nor their union sanctioned by anything but the master's goodwill; the children came under not their parents' but the master's authority.

Ultimately, the condition which most closely determined the kind of life a slave might lead was the relationship he had with his master. For some slaves, especially in agriculture, the nature of their work meant that the connection was very remote, if not non-existent, and that they were left to the care of slave and freedman bailiffs and overseers who cared for little beyond getting work out of them. In the household and the workshop, the master's opportunities for sadism of every kind were vast; on the other hand, the conjunction of a temperate master and an intelligent and patient slave could mean that in all senses the slave led a most profitable life, even to the extent of having houses, workshops and slaves of his own.[91]

NATIONAL PREJUDICES

In the ancient world, foreigners, outsiders in the sense that they were not natives of the city in which they found themselves, came to represent a sizable proportion of many communities. Among the Greeks distrust of strangers—*xenoi*, Greeks from other cities—had given way to acceptance on limited terms, so that, for example, the itinerant craftsman could expect some degree of recognition before the law. Thus at Rome during the Republic treaties made with other communities in Italy defined very clearly the rights which Latins and Italians could enjoy when they came to the city. After this came the changes in the economy which brought about the use of chattel slaves and which introduced increasing numbers of complete aliens, whose speech and culture were quite strange to their Greek and Roman owners. In the case of a highly trained finely skilled slave or freedman worker, racial origins, skin colour and accent counted for little, professionally speaking, in comparison with his ability. But the man of alien origins—the non-Greek speaker in Greece, and in Italy anyone from overseas—whatever his skill or the degree of social and cultural integration he had achieved, always ran the risk of intolerance from those who chose to insist upon their prerogatives as being free-born. On what, precisely, were Greek and Roman prejudices against other nationalities based?

Undoubtedly the Greeks had a strong sense of national unity, and considered themselves superior to other peoples, subscribing to a nationalism based to some extent on race. But, like the Romans, they distinguished themselves most markedly by their culture and especially by the language they spoke. Thus in the Roman period, the Emperor Claudius, though far more enthusiastic than most of his contemporaries about extending citizenship to the provincials, yet refused it to those who did not know Latin or Greek.[92] The Athenians assured the Spartans in 479 BC that of course they would not yield to Persian pressure, because Greeks were 'of the same stock, the same speech, and shared common shrines of the gods, common rituals, and similar customs'.[93] The Greeks could understand each other; the barbarians only babbled. As was to be expected of so fluent a people, living lives so much more interesting than those of their neighbours—subjects of the Persian king in the east, uncouth tribes to the north and un-inspiring Italian and native Sicilian communities in the west—they scorned non-Greeks.

Aristotle's remarks on the slavishness of barbarians—'The poets say that "it is fitting that barbarians should submit to the Greeks", as if a barbarian and a slave were one and the same by nature'—reflects a large body of opinion or prejudice, to be sure.[94] Euripides expresses the view that all but the rulers were slaves among the eastern nations, and Aristophanes makes fun of Persian diplomatic and court procedure.[95] But this is by no means the whole story. The Greeks could also take a keen interest in other cultures, sophisticated and primitive alike; Herodotus shows this in his history, which is as much an anthropological survey of the world known in his time, ranging from the burial practices of the Scythians to the customs of the Iranian nobility and to Egyptian temple lore. Aeschylus' tragedy, *The Persians*, portraying the effect of their defeat at Salamis and produced a mere eight years after the event, contains no hint of mockery; it is, rather, a respectful portrayal of the Persian king and court at a moment of dreadful disaster, with clear indications that Aeschylus took pains to get the detail right.[96] Some Spartans detested all things Persian, while others became the firm friends of Persian princes. Certainly, Alexander's Macedonian troops were upset when he promoted Persians and other Orientals to serve alongside them in the army, but this was surely less a racist reaction than the natural jealousy of a loyal corps.

Something can be deduced of the Greeks' attitude to non-Greeks from the latter's reactions to living in Greece. Mannes, son of Orymaios, is commemorated as a Phrygian, in Greek; pride is expressed in his skill as a woodman, and in the fact that he died in the war.[97] In southern Attica there was a large number of

Phrygians, Paphlagonians and other Asiatics among the miners; their origins are apparent in their names, and sometimes in the names of the deities to whom they made dedications, but again all these records were inscribed in Greek. These people were culturally integrated, but their origins were not forgotten. They were neither so fully submerged in the present that their past faded from them, nor so depressed by their new life that they could not bear to leave any memorial at all, nor discouraged by the temper of the society they lived in from advertising their ethnic origin; and this they did not in their own tongue, but in Greek.[98]

There were no episodes in Attica comparable to the slave wars in Sicily towards the end of the second century BC, one of the attendant characteristics of which was Syrian nationalism.[99] And though there were jokes enough in Attic comedy about barbarians and alien habits, can anyone, even Kleon himself or the Paphlagonian community in Attica, have been deeply upset by Aristophanes' insulting portrayal of Kleon as a Paphlagonian slave defeated by a sausage seller? Did deep racial prejudice lurk in the twisting of the apotropaic phrase 'Be off, you Keres [demons of death]' to 'Be off, you Carians'?[100]

Lack of culture and obvious dissimilarities in physique as well as customs, these were the things which the Greeks and, even more, the Romans abominated in other peoples. Sardinians, Thracians and Germans were terrible creatures, fit only for the foulest work. The Lusitanians in Spain were the most bestial of humans, according to Strabo, because they lived on acorn meal, drank beer instead of wine, and slept on the ground, to mention just a few of their loathsome habits.[101] Besides lacking culture, Germans, Britons and Gauls tended to be disgustingly tall, and frightened the smaller Roman soldier, though of course he was more than a match for them in the end; their tallness is emphasized not only by the literary historians, but also by Caesar, who actually faced them in the field. The Gauls wore trousers, a point of oddness thought worthy of labouring even by so eminent a man as Cicero; he called Piso, whose family had slight connections with a Roman settlement in Gaul, a 'disgrace to your trousered kinsmen', and referred to Gallic witnesses in another case as 'giants in trousers'.[102] But with regard to distinction of dress it is perhaps relevant to recall the contrasting enthusiasm of some Athenian aristocrats for Scythian trousers.[103]

It was also possible in the Roman view to have too much culture. Although the Romans always acknowledged their own cultural debt to the Greeks, there were those who feared and detested Greek philosophy, culture, and even the Greek language. The elder Cato continually criticized those who succumbed to the temptations of Greek luxuries and Greek ways of thought. Greek philosophers were expelled from Rome later in the second century, and on various occasions in the first century AD were declared *personae non gratae*.[104] Greeks and Orientals were taken into the great Roman households as teachers, confidential secretaries or artists, to supply the aptitudes which their masters lacked; the reverse side of this cultural dependence appears in the epithet *Graeculus*, which was more or less synonymous with deceit, trickery, being clever at one's master's expense, venality, and everything else which was underhand. The Greek writer Lucian, in a study of a Greek tutor's sufferings in the household of his Roman patron, says that any charge made against the tutor is believed simply because he is Greek and therefore a man of easy virtue, ready for any villainy.[105] The quantity of evidence for legislation against the ill-treatment of slaves suggests that this kind of contempt, together with the carelessness of the over-rich, was often expressed in physical terms.

What was the attitude of the aliens to Rome? The barbarians, the Germans, Gauls, Spaniards, Sardinians, Thracians, have left no record, though the activities of the Thracian gladiator Spartacus speak for themselves. The Greeks' opinion of Rome, high in the second century BC, as the writings of Polybius demonstrate, was lowered not only by such events as the sack of Corinth in 146 or of Athens in 86, but by the increasing wealth and vulgarity of the Roman rich.[106] Rome was a modern Babylon, and the Romans were obsessed with property. This was of course chiefly the opinion of the intellectuals. The pressure exerted on ordinary slaves and freedmen by the Romans' racial or cultural prejudices seems to have been much greater than at Athens in that the aliens' own records, their dedications and epitaphs, show far greater signs of wishing to be assimilated; the high proportion of Latin to Greek or Oriental names for the sons of freedmen is but one example of this ambition.[107] And though ethnic names can sometimes be detected in the name of the slave or freedman himself, it is rare for a man to declare with open pride that he came from Syria or Egypt or Phrygia, in the same way that Mannes or Atotas had felt free to do in Attica. It would seem that aliens in Rome did suffer not only because of their status but because of their origins.

On the whole intolerance found expression only in social and private life, and could, with luck and a little cleverness, be avoided. There was no active colour bar, no consistent religious persecution of any cult or sect, and very little national discrimination in politics. By the second century AD, most provinces in the empire were represented in the Roman senate (apart from north Gaul, Britain, and the German provinces), and an African provincial became emperor in AD 193. Racial prejudice was prevented from breaking out into active hostility by a fundamental lack of anxiety about the presence and power of aliens in the community. No single ethnic group was felt to pose a threat, political or otherwise, by the mere fact of its presence—and certainly the Syrian slave revolts in Sicily seem to have taken the Roman authorities by surprise. The barbarians, despite their ferocity and height, had all been defeated by the Roman armies in the end; and there was no sense of economic competition between free poor and slave labourers. The upper classes in Rome, the great slave-owners (many of whom, under the Empire, were themselves *nouveaux riches*), might sneer at Greeklings and trousered Gauls, and shudder in fear of their own slaves, approving still in the late first century AD the law which laid down that if a master had been murdered, however brutal he was, *all* his slaves should be executed for the crime.[108] But nothing equivalent to the 'poor-white' attitude to minority groups and imported labour emerges from the evidence, and the inference is that virtually none existed.

SKILLED LABOUR AND THE ECONOMY

The economy of ancient society was simple, and its organization, to modern ways of thinking, inadequate. In some respects, the ancient attitude to economic problems was mainly one of resignation, as to bad weather; but sometimes a plaintive note creeps in, there is some expression of the realization that *if only* something could be done about it, the situation might improve. A recurrent theme in Aristotle's economic thought might be rather loosely summed up thus: 'if only we could return to the self-sufficiency of the household, and not have to depend on traders, money-making craftsmen, imports and the like.'[109] Related to this economic wishful thinking is the subject, frequently raised during the fifth century, of Athens' vulnerability as a land power: 'if only Athens were an island, able to rely entirely on sea power to maintain necessary imports, and to conduct her affairs free from interruption by her present neighbours on land.'[110] The Peloponnesians' lack of resources and of means of challenging Athenian supremacy at sea is expressed, at the beginning of the Peloponnesian War, in similar 'if-only' terms in the speech which Thucydides attributes to the Spartan King Archidamos.[111] Xenophon's *Ways and Means*, written when the Athenian economy was less healthy than it had been, expresses the sentiment, 'if only the city's resources were properly exploited, and (especially) if only the silver mines were made to produce at maximum capacity'. For if more silver were produced and put into circulation, this alone would restore the city's prosperity.

Failures of supply might be met by going to alternative sources, but very often they simply had to be endured. Corn shortages might be alleviated by incidental gifts of grain, like the one sent by the ruler of Egypt to the Athenians in 445 BC or the grants made by Alexander to various states in 326, but very often no relief was possible—famine in inland areas could not be ended simply by transporting corn from elsewhere, for land transport always remained a cumbersome and exorbitantly expensive procedure.[112] Although some steps were taken to improve the management of farms, and no doubt to cut down waste in the workshops, ancient methods of keeping accounts indicate that the chief concern was to check dishonesty, not to be able to see at once from the record of expenses how one might economize by running things more efficiently. Neither Greeks nor Romans knew the double-entry method of accounting, and even to check the accuracy of Greek accounts (let alone see any proper balance of receipt against expenditure) means reading through long and entirely narrative records, with big and small expenses, totals and incidentals all following one upon another.[113]

One of the most important limiting factors in the ancient economy, and one which was partly responsible for the institution of slavery, was the distribution of skilled labour. The skilled craftsman was an economic necessity in all but the most primitive communities; yet such was the balance of demand against availability that skilled workers were very often not there when you wanted them.[114] The only means of overcoming the lack was to try to tempt them from elsewhere or, if they were likely to have continuous employment, to buy slaves. Mechanization, either to supplement manpower or to produce goods more cheaply, was, despite Aristotle's brief fantasy of mechanical weavers replacing slaves, Homer's account of the automatic tripods made by Hephaistos, or the intricate mechanisms devised by Hellenistic engineers (Pl. 57), never a meaningful alternative to skilled manpower.[115] If labour was unavailable, then one did without the fancy shoes, the chased silver, the inlaid footstool, or the new temple for the sanctuary. No ancient government's economic policy ever actively concerned itself with anything beyond ensuring food supplies; once mines had been opened, the state would assume control insofar as it let out concessions and imposed a tax on the product, and it was pleased to exact harbour dues from traders entering its ports, yet the state had no hand in establishing either mines or harbours. Thus, while it was some-times a matter of policy to try to attract skilled workers from elsewhere to settle, the main reason for their being willing to come would be, not the invitation, but the city's economic prosperity as a whole and the opportunities she could offer. During the fifth century, Athens' sea power and her imperial concerns meant that the city exercised sway over the whole of the Aegean, so that the Piraeus became the great *entrepôt* and Athens the labour exchange of the Greek world, to which discontented craftsmen naturally gravitated. But after the Peloponnesian War, when the city had lost its power and prosperity, the state could do nothing to hold skilled workers if more attractive conditions were offered elsewhere.

The Roman state was no more concerned to protect or promote industry by any positive policy. It was not imperial edicts which prompted the expansion of crafts and trade in the north-western provinces, where the market for Italian-made goods was gradually taken over by local producers; for although the distribution of trades and personnel certainly became a matter of active concern to the government in the later Empire, when more and more occupations were made hereditary, until the third century AD industry, like trade, was left entirely to private enterprise.[116]

It is often suggested that free and slave labour competed for the employment available, and that the use of slaves who could, it is assumed, live more cheaply, depressed the wages of the free workers. But surely in general slave labour supplemented free, or was used to make up a work-force which would otherwise be short-handed or completely non-existent. Since no wages, free or slave, were ever particularly high (except in one or two quite unusual instances), there is no reason to suppose that the quite modest rates of pay apparent in the Athenian evidence of the late fifth century were lower even than they might have been because slaves also were employed.[117]

Contrary to what is often stated as concrete fact, slave labour was not necessarily cheaper than free; a slave required constant maintenance (even if it was no more than enough to keep body and soul together), whereas a free man could only expect to be paid for the job he had done, after which he was responsible for his own keep.[118] The accounts for work on the Erechtheion show that slave and free received exactly the same pay for the same kind of work; and on other temple building sites, at Delphi, Delos and Epidauros, architects who were surely neither slaves themselves nor suffering competition from slaves in their profession (whether or not there were some slave architects is an entirely different point), received salaries on the same or even a slightly lower scale.[119]

At Rome in the second and first centuries B C, free labour on the land was widely displaced by slave, but this change came about in the first instance because many free farmers had lost their farms to bigger landowners after having spent years away from home serving in the army and the new landowners required labour to supplement or replace their free workers. Thereafter, slaves could be kept constantly on the land, whether or not the Roman army was at war. As for Greek and Oriental slaves who came into service as personal servants, business agents, craftsmen and so on in increasing numbers during the second century B C, they were not replacing free Roman and Italian counterparts; they were a new phenomenon, part of a new way of life in which more complicated demands came to be answered by more sophisticated products.

What then was the economic tempo in antiquity? Slow, at all periods. The scale of production did alter in some crafts—the production of fine painted pottery shifted almost entirely from Corinth to Athens during the sixth century B C, and developed into a somewhat larger operation; and the Arretine potteries in Italy of the late first century B C were gradually replaced by numerous offshoots in Gaul and the Rhineland. But the number of workshops involved in such changeovers and expansions was pretty small, compared with the size of the population as a whole in any given area, and whatever the amount of pottery produced, its appearance on the market will have had but a limited impact— no shares rose or fell, no banks failed or prospered as a result. More workshops might be opened, thus producing more goods overall, but by the same methods as before. Ready-made goods certainly became a feature of many city workshops, but even in the most ordinary crafts making things to order remained a very common practice. In any case, even though there was some ready-made stuff, it can rarely have piled up in large quantities; far from attempting to induce the public to buy more, the suppliers often seem to have been unable to satisfy the existing demand. Bishop Synesius of Cyrene refers to a maker of fine cloaks who regularly brought a stock to Alexandria from Athens, and always sold out very quickly; he did not, however, presumably because he could not, expand his business and so satisfy more customers on his occasional visits to Alexandria.[120]

Methods of production altered comparatively little. Craftsmen might become more specialized as and when they could be sure of finding a demand for their specialization; the city craftsman was therefore better off than the jack-of-all-trades, who as Xenophon remarked had to work at all sorts of jobs 'in the villages and small towns'.[121] It would, however, be a mistake to press the argument that specialization increased between the Homeric and the Classical period in Greece, or the early and the late Republic at Rome. The quality of workmanship in an eighth-century Geometric-style vase and a red-figure amphora from fifth-century Athens was of much the same high level, as were the best examples of moulded Arretine ware in the first century BC. Neither the methods of production nor the degree of specialization exercised by the potters and painters changed very much.

As household production declined in many crafts (even in the making of textiles, which, though it remained very much a domestic skill, was extensively supplemented by professionals), the number of workshops increased. This increase complemented the growing sophistication of life in the city-state. Even so, one has to remember that the total number of people concerned in the crafts made up only a part of that small proportion of the population which was not engaged in agriculture. But how many were they? The shortcomings of the evidence in this regard especially have already been pointed out. But even though almost the only basis for calculation is provided by Athens, and although data for the useful crafts—metalwork, masonry, carpentry, shoemaking and so on—is not available, it is worth taking a look at the figures which do emerge.

Considerable quantities of coarse pottery have survived, cooking and ordinary house ware, but so far this material has not produced anything like the kind of information yielded up by fine painted pottery, so that it is impossible to say how many workshops or how many individuals were employed in its production at any given period. Fine painted pottery, on the other hand, has been so exactly identified as to enable us to say that during the fifth century not more than about 125 people need have been involved in its manufacture at any one time— this is somewhat surprising, especially in the light of the emphasis laid on fine painted pottery by many archaeologists and ancient historians.[122]

Temple building accounts give some indication of the numbers concerned in this highly specialized, but at the same time very diversified, work. In 408-7, the Erechtheion accounts show that over one hundred men were engaged on the final stages of decorating and finishing—44 masons, 9 sculptors, 7 woodcarvers, 22 carpenters, sawyers and joiners, a lathe worker, 3 painters and a gilder, 9 labourers and other unspecifiable workers.[123] At this time Athens was fighting for survival in the Peloponnesian War; it may be that the only available resources of highly skilled labour were concentrated on the Erechtheion, that there were no more in the city. Of course these workers should not be thought of exclusively as temple builders, for when the temple was finished they reverted of necessity to more ordinary tasks— house building, gravestone cutting, perhaps even shipbuilding.

The accounts for the Parthenon, thirty years earlier, provide a slight hint of the number of sculptors who were employed on the pediment sculptures. Payment of salaries for the year to workers 'on the pediments' seems to allow for a group of between twenty and twenty-five; stylistic analysis of all the temple sculptures suggests that perhaps seventy men worked on both pediments and the frieze reliefs.[124] Although many of these sculptors were probably itinerants attracted to Athens by the general prosperity and the employment offered, so that they do not tell us anything about the number of Athenians permanently employed in the sculptor's craft, they may have constituted the major part of the top sculptors in the Greek world as a whole, since it was at Athens that there was most activity in their field at this time. That is to say, there were perhaps not more than seventy or eighty really competent sculptors of the calibre indicated by the Parthenon sculptors, then, before, or after, anywhere or at any time in the Greek world.

Temple building elsewhere depended far more heavily on imported labour. The accounts for the Epidaurians' temple of Asklepios of about 370 BC show that masons, sculptors and fine carpenters came in from Argos, Corinth, Athens, Paros, Arcadia and even the neighbouring city of Troizen, whose economy was probably slighter even than the Epidaurians', who themselves could provide little more than plain smiths, simple builders and odd-job men; if we estimate that perhaps two hundred people were required to build the temple, this still tells us nothing about the numbers of craftsmen in either Epidauros or the surrounding cities.[125] Of Argos we can say that although there was a very flourishing group of sculptors and masons there in the fifth and early fourth centuries they nevertheless required the help of Athenian masons in 418 to build their long walls down to the sea at high speed; just as the Athenians in 479 could only build their defences rapidly enough with the help of every able man, woman, and child in Athens, and during the 390s were helped by carpenters and masons sent in from Megara and Thebes to rebuild the walls destroyed by Sparta in 404. For unusual projects such as public works, no city, not even Athens, had a sufficiently large skilled labour force to do the job by itself.[126] It was certainly not the case that any of the cities of the Roman empire, in the African provinces, for example, or in Asia Minor, managed to carry out their magnificent building programmes unaided; the monumental fortifications and civic amenities of Perge, Selge, Telmessos, Termessos and Aspendos, along the south coast of Asia Minor, must all have been built principally by itinerant crews of skilled workers, with the local craftsmen contributing what expertise they could.

As for the size of other crafts, the Athenian silver mines are said to have employed at least twenty thousand slaves at the height of their productivity, in the fifth century.[127] Whether or not this figure is correct, it seems unlikely that it can ever have been higher; but whatever the actual total at any given time, the impression is that the mining area of Attica was fairly heavily populated, and that there was quite a community, or strings of communities scattered over it. The number of miners elsewhere can only be guessed at in even more general terms.

Another craft vital to those cities which maintained fleets, outstandingly Athens, was that of shipbuilding. Large numbers of men, architects and the shipwrights working under them, must have been employed at Athens, Corinth, Syracuse, Corcyra and in the larger of the Aegean island states, by the Hellenistic kings of Macedon, Pergamon, Syria and Egypt, and by the Roman state from the mid-third century BC onwards. Yet such is the state of evidence that all we can say is that at Athens between about 360 and 320 BC at least fifty-seven master-shipwrights were at work; which means that perhaps thirty will have been active at any one time.[128] Individual shipbuilders are known elsewhere at other periods, but numbers in the industry altogether are unobtainable —nor can we say, for example, how many men it took to build a trireme.

The labour force in the Roman period is no more open to calculation. We know that in imperial Rome there were at some point at least three hundred sandal makers;[129] that the Emperor Claudius' engineering and water works employed thirty thousand men for eleven years;[130] and that at all periods the Roman army itself constituted much of the skilled manpower required for the great public works all over the empire—witness the number of inscriptions recording the work of military detachments on wall, tower, bath and guardhouse along Hadrian's Wall alone.[131] From Agrippa's time onward, if not even earlier, the legions were well equipped to provide for their own needs in the way of perishables like boots, pots, undershirts, harness, armour, as Vegetius, a writer of the fourth or fifth century AD, also makes clear:

The legion has carpenters, masons, wagon makers, smiths, painters, and other artisans on hand for the construction of the barracks and the winter quarters, for making or repairing damaged machines, wooden towers, and other equipment for . . . siege and defence; . . . they also have workshops for shields, cuirasses and bows, arrows, missiles, nets and all types of weapons. . . . They are especially concerned that whatever seems necessary for the army should never be lacking in camp. . . . The officer in charge is the prefect of the workmen.[132]

But the size of the so-called state factories of the later Roman Empire, the number of ordinary craftsmen resident in Ostia or Pompeii, to name one of the biggest ports and one of the most comfortable residential cities in Italy, or the labour forces which produced the mass of tiles and bricks used for buildings in Rome (Pl. 68), all these are truly unknown quantities.

Given the scale of the economy even in the larger cities of the ancient world, it is clear that the craftsmen who worked in expensive materials and unusual techniques—not, of course, the shoemakers, blacksmiths, weavers, house builders, harness makers and so on—had to face the problem at one time or another of finding adequate employment for their special skills. Local demand for all but the most utilitarian articles could fall off for a variety of reasons; at the same time, such was the delicacy of balance of under-employment against demand, especially in the finest crafts, that an immediate shortage could be remedied by moving elsewhere to a more active market. Eventually the place from which the sculptor, bronze-caster or fine stonemason had moved would begin to feel the lack of his services, so that there was a constant shift. Illustration of the effects of skilled mobility may be seen in the Epidaurians' experience: during the last third of the fifth century they saw their god Asklepios gain an international reputation, but they were unable to build up his sanctuary in a manner befitting a Panhellenic god of healing for about fifty years.[133] The absence of temple building has usually been attributed to lack of money or the prevalence of war, but neither of these factors constitutes the whole answer to the problem. In the first instance, it was the shortage of skilled workers which was the main stumbling block. The Epidaurians could not find a sufficient concentration of architects, sculptors, masons and other skilled workers because in the late fifth and early fourth centuries they were scattered far and wide or out of circulation.

Athens, the great labour market and a major employer during the fifth century, had come more or less to the end of her vast building programmes, and, more important, had suffered a tremendous economic setback with her defeat in 405. Craftsmen hitherto based in Athens tended to seek employment far afield; and as for Epidauros, neither Corinth nor Argos harboured sufficient skilled labour to do the work alone—both cities may in any case also have suffered somewhat from the repercussions of war.

The movement of skilled labour was not confined to the Greek and Roman world but went on between the Mediterranean and the Near East. On many occasions, craftsmen found themselves employed by Persia, whether willingly or not is unclear—probably the Ionian Greeks working for Darius in *c.* 500 BC had been compelled to go.[134] Greek smiths produced marvellous works of art for Scythian patrons, working in the Greek cities of south Russia or perhaps even within Scythian territory.[135] In the Roman period craftsmen went to or were taken by the Parthians.[136] The desert principality of Palmyra, which took to monumental building from Tiberius' time onwards, though culturally closer to the Near East, turned to the builders and sculptors of the Roman imperial world in order to obtain the most splendid city architecture available.[137]

Within the Mediterranean world, in the Greek period Dionysius of Syracuse was obliged to advertise for armaments workers from the rest of Greece when he was preparing to resist the Carthaginians at the end of the fifth century.[138] Sculptors moved from city to city and from sanctuary to sanctuary: Myron of Eleutherai worked at Athens, Olympia, in the islands of Aegina and Samos, at Ephesos, Orchomenos, and Akragas in Sicily; Skopas and Satyros of Paros were among the sculptors engaged on the Mausoleon at Halikarnassos, after completion of which Satyros took up a commission at Delphi, and Skopas went to direct work on the temple of Athena Alea at Tegea, taking at least one assistant across with him; Spintharos of Corinth was the architect of the fourth-century temple of Apollo at Delphi; in the second century, Epikrates was especially brought from Byzantium to Olbia, to fortify that city.[139] The potters Bakchios and Kittos found employment and political honours at Ephesos in the later fourth century, when the pottery craft at Athens was no longer as prosperous as it had been.[140] Workers from islands all over the Aegean, and from the mainland too, came to work in the Delian sanctuary, most of them apparently staying for only a short time to complete one job before going home or moving elsewhere as other work became available;[141] the island of Rhodes attracted sculptors and bronze statuaries from many parts of the Greek world in the third, second and first centuries BC.[142]

Shortage of skilled labour and the movement of craftsmen to and fro are equally in evidence in the Roman period. According to Livy, for example, the marble roof of the temple of Juno Lacinia in south Italy, which had been stripped by one of the censors in 173 BC, could not be repaired because there were no workmen capable of doing the job.[143] The Greek sculptor Zenodoros worked in Rome and for the Arverni in Gaul.[144] A group of sculptors from Aphrodisias in Asia Minor became resident in Rome during the second century AD.[145] In Roman Bithynia at the beginning of the century, a shortage of properly trained architects meant, according to Pliny (the Younger), who had been sent out by Trajan to investigate the cities' finances, that ambitious building projects were badly executed or abandoned— an unfinished theatre in Nicaea had been built on soft soil and of poor stone, so that the structure cracked; but when he requested that an engineer should come out from Rome to inspect an aqueduct, the emperor replied that he had need of good surveyors at Rome himself—and his chief architect was the Syrian Greek Apollodoros of Damascus.[146] When the city of Leptis in north Africa was improved, under the auspices of Septimius Severus, masons came with consignments of marble from the far-distant quarry of Dokimeion (Synnada) in western Asia Minor.[147]

The presence of a single man might sometimes make all the difference. The engineering genius of Archimedes caused a Roman consular army considerable trouble before Syracuse in 212 BC, and also made memorable Hieron, the ruler of Syracuse, in whose service Archimedes was employed.[148]

CHAPTER III

ARTISTS AND CRAFTSMEN AT WORK

No higher wage . . . will buy for men that satisfaction which of old—until machinery made drudges of them all—streamed into their muscles all day long from contact with iron, timber, clay, wind and wave, horse strength. . . . The very ears unawares received it, as when the plane went singing over the wood, or the exact chisel went tapping in under the mallet to the hard ash with gentle sound. There ought really to be a little fun in work, for the workman's sake.

George Sturt, *The Wheelwright's Shop* (1923), 202, 203

INTRODUCTION

THE CRAFTSMAN EARNED HIS LIVING by performing activities to which the rest of the population rarely if ever turned its hand.[149] By his skilled use of tools he changed matter from its raw and unformed state into objects with a well-defined shape and function—the tanner and shoemaker converted soft hide into durable leather, stitched and nailed shoes; the carpenter trimmed the tree trunk into squared beams or planed boards, and joined them in well-fitted roofs or ships' hulls; the sculptor worked a rough block of marble into a human form, its surface so finished with hammer, chisels and abrasives as to resemble smooth flesh, hair, pleated linen or diaphanous draperies; the potter modelled a mass of damp, soft, grey clay into a well-proportioned pot, hard and waterproof, glassy smooth in texture and patterned black and red by the careful adjustment of glaze and the fire in the kiln. The excellence of finish which so many surviving products of the workshops display was a kind of achievement to which, in the nature of things, no one who had not been trained as a craftsman could attain, however knowledgeable his enthusiasm for the craft. Nor could this excellence of craftsmanship be applied in the final stages only. It had to be instilled into the raw materials from the first moment of handling. The foundation courses in the platform of the Apollo temple at Delphi were no less carefully dressed and joined than the superstructure (Pl. 60); it was at this level that the slight convexity of horizontals and the inward tilt of verticals in Classical Doric architecture had to be introduced (Pl. 58).

All craftsmen, whatever the refinements of their particular craft, had to undergo long and thorough training. Constant application was required of a man if he was to become fully acquainted with his craft. Once he had learned it, he must continue to exercise his skill, otherwise it would decay and die on him—just as an elderly wheelwright working towards the end of the last century found that he had forgotten how to make a certain type of axle which, familiar to him in his youth, had not been required again until late in his life.[150] Particular skills in certain crafts had been lost as a result of falling into disuse (owing to lack of opportunity) after the fall of the Mycenaean Greek palaces c. 1150 BC, but by no means in all; otherwise there was no big break in cultural continuity during the Greek and Roman period, nor any significant loss of craft secrets. It was only by constant practice, however, that living traditions could be preserved as forces promoting real development in the crafts. Not only the craftsman but his craft too depended for survival on the craftsman's full-time, professional dedication to his work. Alexander's favourite painter Apelles drew a little every day, notwithstanding the pressure of other business.[151]

The evidence, literary, epigraphic and archaeological, is, as we have seen, inadequate. For all the crafts whose products have survived in some quantity—pottery, buildings, sculptures, coins, mosaics, and some paintings, glass, and metal work, both ornamental and decorative—there are many of which we have very slight or no archaeological remains. And for all the artists and craftsmen that we know by name, either from the literature or from their personal records, for all the highly specialized crafts that are mentioned, there remain some important groups of workers who scarcely figure in the evidence at all. Various textile workers are known of, as professionals and as individuals, throughout the Greek and Roman period; there is the Athenian woolworker, for instance, who 'lived ninety blameless years', as his epitaph tells us.[152] But there is no answer to the question, who made ships' canvas? Large quantities were constantly required in every state which boasted a fleet and in every fishing village, yet there are scarcely any references to canvas weaving or sail making whatsoever. Who, and under what kind of organization, produced the two hundred thousand square feet or so needed to dress the new fleet of two hundred triremes which the Athenians built after 483?[153] Whoever they were, they and their descendants must have been able to maintain permanent workshops for the regular supply of canvas to the fleet, which was kept up on a large scale (with one or two interruptions) for generations thereafter. Nevertheless, these particular workers have left no mark upon the record.[154] A similar problem emerges in other crafts; no one can be traced out completely, none is more than partially open to reconstruction.

THE TOILS OF CRAFTSMANSHIP

The Athenian vase-painters occasionally portrayed craftsmen at work—the blacksmith, the shoemaker, the carpenter, the helmet maker, the potter, the bronze statuary, the vase-painter himself (Pl. 18). In no instance, however, has the artist really shown the scene as it must usually have been, noisy, dusty, and filled with activity which to the layman would have seemed chaotic. Workshop scenes all echo the harmonious stillness of the commoner themes of vase-paintings; the metalworker raises his hammer majestically, as his customers look on with admiration (Pl. 30); Athena applies clay to clay in a leisurely manner as she models her horse (Pl. 38); she crowns the vase-painters in an atmosphere of calm elegance (Fig. I); or two masters stand by, dignified figures in their tunics and cloaks, watching their assistants toil in the bronze foundry (Pl. 39). Naturally enough,

Fig. I *An Athenian red-figure vase of the mid-fifth century BC. Vase-painters are being crowned by winged Victories in the presence of Athena. On the right is a rare representation of a female vase-painter working on a large volute crater.*

the same idealized view of the craftsman's lot is reflected in the dedicatory and funeral reliefs—the potter Pamphaios and the shoemaker Xanthippos sit at ease holding in their hands a clay cup and a shoe respectively (*Pl.* 6), while the Gallic stonemason Amabilis, hammer and chisel in hand, is shown seated at his work (*Pl.* 85). But there are more realistic portrayals of artists and craftsmen at work which suggest something of the dirt and apparent confusion, the physical effort required to get things right.

Potters

Pottery demanded more than the manual dexterity of shaping and painting.[155] Forming the wet clay on the wheel and painting the vase when it had dried out constituted only half, and by far the more restful half, of the process of making painted pottery (*Pl.* 14). The Penteskouphia *pinakes* (*Pl.* 15) show the potters stoking and adjusting their kilns, clambering over them, running the risk of being scorched or even blinded if they opened the vent too far or piled in too much fuel. Building a large kiln was no doubt difficult and dangerous enough firing it (*Pl.* 16); called for precise judgment in order to maintain the right temperature for the right length of time. To achieve a true contrast between the red paste and black glaze of Attic pottery, for example, the heat in the kiln had first to be raised to a very high temperature with a good draught so that the iron content of both clay and glaze oxidized and became red. Then the fire must be reduced with green wood, and the draught cut off, so that lack of oxygen turned the red ferric oxide into black ferrous oxide. The third and most difficult stage entailed the reheating of the kiln, just for long enough to allow the porous clay to turn red again, while the denser clay remained black—if too much air were let in, the whole vase turned red, while if the kiln were damped too much, the pot lost its shape. The potters' problems are vividly portrayed in a unique example of Greek industrial literature, the so-called Homeric Hymn of the potters.[156]

Miners and smiths

Metalworkers were far more prone than potters or indeed any other group of craftsmen to physical deformity and disability from the effects of their craft. The scorn expressed by the rest of society for the *banausoi* is seen in the traditional picture of Hephaistos, lame, a buffoon and a laughing-stock—even if he was also an Olympian god.[157] Men might be crippled or crushed to death in the mines, suffocated in pit fires, poisoned by the fumes of the smelting furnaces; and in the smithy, hands, feet and eyes must have been all too vulnerable as molten metals were poured into moulds, red-hot bars shifted from fire to anvil, and hammers swung (*Pl.* 30), while the muscular development of the smith could be and was considered a deformity in itself, as the Homeric description of Hephaistos suggests.[158]

The occupation which most clearly reflects the brutality prevalent at certain levels of ancient society is mining. Ancient accounts of such work probably exaggerate its horrors very little; some bad features were inherent in the nature of the process itself, but undoubtedly the workers' sufferings were often increased by their status—slave, prisoner of war or criminal— and by the harsh discipline imposed on them in consequence. There is reason to suppose that conditions varied from one period to another; the most oppressive were those prevailing in the mines and quarries controlled by the Hellenistic kings and imperial Rome. Nevertheless, even the following description of mining in Nubia under the Ptolemies should be read with this consideration in mind, that while large gangs of unskilled labour could be driven by incessant cruelty to shift material from the mine-gallery to the surface, or to smash up ore for smelting, considerable skill as well as firm organization was required to cut the shafts and open up the galleries. There must then have been many workers in the mines who were free at least of shackles, and some who belonged to small work-gangs not unlike the workshop units of potters and stonemasons, a few of whom would have graduated by their skill from the ranks to become foremen.[159] But there can be no doubt that the majority endured conditions similar to those described by Diodorus:

The kings condemn to the mines all criminals and prisoners of war. . . . They work unceasingly—a great multitude, all bound in chains—both night and day, with no respite, and cut off from all means of escape. . . . The operations are under the charge of a skilled worker who picks out the gold-bearing rock and directs the labourers to it; . . . the physically strong break the rock with iron hammers, applying no skill to the task, but only force, cutting tunnels through the rock wherever the gold may lead. Now these men, working in darkness as they do . . . carry lamps on their foreheads . . . they throw the blocks of stone on the ground as they cut them, and they labour ceaselessly beneath the sternness and blows of the overseer. The boys . . . go in through the tunnels into the galleries

formed by the removal of the rock, and take out the pieces.
The men over thirty years old take this stone from them, and
pound it with iron pestles; then the women and older men
take it and grind the stone in mills to the consistency of flour.
And since no opportunity is afforded them to look after themselves, and they have no clothes to cover their nakedness, no
one can look upon the unfortunate wretches without feeling
pity for them. . . . They labour without respite . . . until
through ill-treatment they die in the midst of their tortures.[160]

The sufferings of Christian martyrs in the Numidian quarries
were no less, according to St Cyprian:

The body . . . has not the ease of a well-made bed in which to
rest. . . . The tired limbs are stretched out on the ground. . . .
The body becomes squalidly dirty for want of a bath. . . . Bread
is only given out in small quantities. . . . It is cold, one lacks
clothes.[161]

No references survive to similar hardships among the workers
in the Athenian mines; but harsh treatment of what was predominantly a slave-labour force would scarcely have given
cause for comment in contemporary literature. The nature of the
job made mining unpleasant, whatever the reason for one's
employment. In the Athenian mines the galleries measured about
$1 \times \cdot 75$ m. For the most part the miners worked on their hands
and knees or on their backs. Underground work of any kind
was, and is, uncomfortable; Theophrastos says of tunnelling for
fuller's earth, 'It is not possible to stand upright while digging in
the pits of Samos, but a man has to lie on his back or his side.'[162]
Yet despite the lack of space in the Athenian mines, and the fact
that they had to cut through pretty solid rock, the miners' work
was of a high standard (Pl. 27).[163]

Ventilation was a problem; in the Athenian mines, shafts and
galleries were constructed in pairs, and doors set between the
galleries to be opened or shut as a draught was required. Fires
were lit to help circulate the air. The Athenian mining regulations

included not only prohibitions on the carrying of weapons, but a clause forbidding the making of smoke to annoy one's neighbour in the next concession—for this might have killed as well as irritated him. As for the possibility of being poisoned by natural gases, Pliny for one asserted that certain silver ores exuded noxious fumes which were bad for men and particularly hazardous for dogs. The fumes from the smelting furnaces were probably both unpleasant and harmful; Xenophon comments on Laureion as 'an oppressive place', most likely referring to the pollution of the air, and according to Strabo the silver-melting furnaces in Spain required tall chimneys to take off the fumes.[164]

Collapsing galleries were another hazard. Safety regulations from Vipasca (Aljustrel) in Spain, dating from Hadrian's time, specify that all 'diggings shall be carefully propped and reinforced, and the tenant of each digging shall replace rotten materials. It shall be forbidden to damage . . . or render unsafe . . . pillars or props.'[165]

The emphasis in all these regulations is of course on the rights and obligations of the lessees and the protection of property, not on ensuring the safety of the workers (often a secondary consideration even today).

Quarrymen

Work in the stone quarries too was arduous, and not without its dangers. The worker's lot may well have been particularly cruel in the Roman imperial quarries, where convicts were often employed; but the nature of the process and often the very location of the quarry meant that everyone would have found it hard going, whatever his status. It is rather a commonplace to suppose that, as in the case of minerals, the hundreds of thousands of tons of stone (twenty thousand for the Parthenon alone, on a conservative estimate) which were used in antiquity were obtained by myriads of slaves, prisoners of war, convicts and martyred Christians. Quarries were certainly used on occasion as convenient places of detention, and quarrying as a convenient punishment, particularly by the persecuting Roman emperors; certainly, too, large labour forces were often required for the many vast building programmes of antiquity. Yet quarrying stone, like mining and smelting metal ores, demanded considerable skill. It was no use drafting five thousand untrained convicts or slaves into a quarry and hoping that by the light of nature they would produce the right amount of correctly cut stone; for the practice throughout antiquity was not to take rough-cut stone from the quarry to be trimmed by trained stonemasons elsewhere, but to cut the blocks, often to within an inch or two of the final specifications, straight from the quarry-face—not only rectangular blocks but cylinders for column drums as well—leaving only enough surplus stone to protect the blocks from irreparable damage in transit (*Pl.* 63). Instructions to the quarry masons in fourth-century Attica required that Pentelic marble be delivered to the sanctuary 'whole, white, and unflawed'.[166] Even statues were often roughed out in the quarry before being delivered *en bloc* to the sculptor's studio. One of the earliest and largest of the Naxians' experiments in marble, the abandoned statue of Dionysos (*Pl.* 75), was modelled quite extensively before the block was detached from its bed; and there are many other later examples of sculptures being started in the quarry.[167] Unskilled labour therefore had limited value.

The Pannonian quarry workers in the Emperor Diocletian's time included five particularly skilful masons, four of whom, Claudius, Castonius, Simpronianus and Nicestratus, secretly professed the Christian faith. The fifth, Simplicius, was converted and baptized by Cyril, Bishop of Antioch, one of the Christian convicts also working in the quarry, but in fetters. It was these five workers whom Diocletian commissioned to do several fine pieces, including a colossal statue of the sun god in his chariot and some richly ornamented columns of porphyry, for which he commended them highly. The *philosophi* or quarry supervisors became intensely jealous, and eventually denounced the masons as Christians and magicians. They were martyred, not for this reason, but for disobeying the emperor by refusing to work on a statue of Aesculapius and by denying the supremacy of the sun god. The account of their career and ultimate martyrdom leaves no doubt that these were highly skilled men, able to find new seams of good stone and to execute complicated designs in the block as they cut it from the rock face.[168]

It is reasonable to suppose that most if not all of the masons who worked in the quarries were also capable of working on the building site, just as the masons who quarried blocks for statues may have been the ultimate sculptors of the statue as well—for if Michelangelo and Henry Moore quarried their own stone in the Carrara quarries, why not Myron or Praxiteles on Mount Pentele? Roman legionaries both quarried and built.

A military accountant in Egypt noted, 'I give thanks to Sarapis and Good Fortune that while all are labouring in the quarry the whole day, I as an officer move about doing nothing.'[169] Some mutinies are attributed to the Roman soldier's dislike of having to do such work, a reflection of which may be seen in an inscription on a rock face near Hadrian's Wall: 'I, Apollonius Daminius, did not want (to do this work).'[170] Professional quarrymen five hundred years earlier, in Ptolemaic Egypt, made various complaints to Kleon, the architect and engineer in charge of their work; one was that the stone they had been directed to cut was far harder than they expected, which meant that their tools wore down faster. On another occasion they were annoyed at not being supplied with enough iron for the wedges used to pry away blocks from the quarry face; in addition their food and pay had not arrived. These were free workers, they could expect better treatment than convicts or slaves; but obviously they did not always get it.[171]

One of the chief disadvantages of many crafts was the noise they created, a factor which must have worn down the workers as much as it irritated the general public. The city of Sybaris ordained that noisy crafts should be excluded from the city, but otherwise we know little of the reaction to industrial noise, apart from Aristophanes' comparing, in the *Birds*, the sound of their beaks chopping the material for the construction of Cloudcuckooland with that of shipwrights in the Piraeus yards.[172]

Tanners, dyers and fullers

Certain crafts were afflicted with yet another disadvantage, which sometimes led to their exclusion from the city. Tanneries especially were noted for their smell, and not surprisingly tanning was regarded as one of the most banausic crafts. Its mere mention could be guaranteed to raise a laugh, and Aristophanes for one did not hesitate to capitalize on the democratic statesman Kleon's connection with the craft, commending in the *Peace* his 'Heraclean valour in braving the stenches of his trade'.[173] A much later writer remarks that 'the tannery annoys everybody, for the tanner has to deal with dead animals; he has to live far from town, and the stench reveals his presence, even when he is hiding.'[174]

Two of the processes involved in textile manufacture, dyeing and fulling, must also have smelt vile, but they do not seem to have been excluded from the city as a general rule. Dyers used various vegetable, insect and mineral dyes, while the purple dyers' application of juices from a certain shellfish made Tyre in particular as remarkable for its smell as for its wealth. Burning sulphur and urine among other things were essential to the fulling process, by which woollen fabrics were made soft and white. There is no doubt that both processes demanded skill of a high order; but like many other crafts they made life hard for the craftsman.[175]

The workshop

In a sense this is a misnomer, since what counted for most was the workers, not the plant; there was no plant worth speaking of, so that, when a workshop owner transferred his workshop from one place to another, he simply took his workmen along. Kilns, furnaces and forges could always be built anew, and as for the rest of his equipment, the skilled worker had only to take along a bag of tools and he was ready to get on with the job anywhere, as long as there were materials for him to work on. The structure in which work was done was, often enough, the backroom or courtyard of the craftsman's dwelling-house; such was the situation in the industrial district of Athens. Occasionally workshops were built specially for the purpose, as at Olympia for Pheidias' statue of Zeus (*Pl.* 32), at Epidauros for the sculptor of the pediments for the Asklepios temple, and on the Athenian acropolis for the Parthenon pediment sculptors; all three examples were substantial constructions.[176]

The workshop unit was generally small. Attic vase-paintings of the late fifth and sixth centuries suggest that between six and a dozen men were employed in the workshops of fine pottery makers and bronze statuaries, for example. Literary references also indicate that workshops remained small, on the whole, throughout antiquity; that large-scale organizations were exceptional in the Greek period; and that when they occurred during the Hellenistic and Roman periods they resulted not from new developments in industrial production so much as from distortions of the patterns established in the small workshop. In each case, the nature of the work, not some other arbitrary or extraneous consideration, had from the beginning dictated the number of workers, minimum and maximum, that could usefully be employed—one man per loom, last, or carpenter's bench, with an assistant or two and half a dozen men per mining gang, pottery, stoneyard, brickyard or smithy—and the nature of the work changed little throughout antiquity (*Pls.* 3, 4, 7, 11).[177]

There is at least one other craft in which somewhat larger working units would regularly have been required—the shipbuilder's. Though this is an assumption which cannot be verified, it is clear that a wide variety of skills was required to build and fit a vessel; we can, however, never know for certain whether it took ten, twenty or thirty men to saw and join planks, fashion oars and masts, caulk the hull and so on.

Larger groups of labourers were occasionally required for such things as public works, but in the Greek period these usually consisted of temporary combinations of several work units; six groups of stonemasons each comprising from five to seven men were employed simultaneously on the east front of the Erechtheion, each group fluting one of the six columns according to exactly the same specifications, but each independent of the rest.[178] In the Delian sanctuary, the Delian carpenter Phaneas joined temporarily with a woodworker from Paros, Peisiboulos, to make fifteen ceiling coffers for the temple of Apollo; another temple's roof was worked on by carpenters from three different islands—Deinokrates of Delos, Theophantos of Karystos in Euboea and Xenophanes of Syros.[179]

Not only public works but house building too would have drawn together several normally independent craftsmen for the duration of the job, after which they would have separated and returned to their smaller operations of manufacture and repair. About the only permanent building forces that we hear of are the imperial slaves who saw to the drains of Rome and the maintenance of aqueducts, and the five hundred builders belonging to Crassus who rushed to the scene of house fires in order to demolish and rebuild for a speculation.[180] Fine craftsmanship depended on the compactness of the working unit perhaps as much as on any other circumstance. One obviously deleterious effect of the large workshop would have been to reduce the degree of personal direction in the quality of work done; whereas in a workshop of normal size each craftsman would constitute anything from a twelfth to a third or even half of the total working force, so that the relationship between master-craftsman and assistants would of necessity have been close.

Working-class districts

Some crafts were of necessity practised in isolation from the rest of the community, because the craftsman had to work near the source of his materials. Workshop communities therefore grew up in the mining district of Attica, for example (Pl. 28), in Roman Spain at Vipasca, and near the mines and quarries in the eastern desert of Egypt; these were not simply labour camps but villages or small townships—Vipasca boasted amenities ranging from barbers' and fullers' shops to bath-houses and schools—and in many such places there is ample evidence of cult activity.[181]

As suggested above, the tanner was spoken of as having to work out of town because of the unpleasantness of his craft. The strange thing is that both Kleon and some metic tanners were connected with one of the city demes of Athens; in the case of the metics it is likely that they lived near their place of work— which means there must have been tanneries right in the heart of the city. At Rome the tanneries were situated out of town, on

25, 26 Examples of signed glassware. *Above*, a cup by Ennion, Syrian from Cyprus, second-first century BC. *Below*, a mould-blown beaker with the inscription 'Neikaios made me. Let the buyer remember.' Syrian, first century AD

27, 28 The Laureion silver mines were the foundation of Athenian prosperity. *Above*, the entrance to a mine and, *below*, a washing table used by the silver refiners

29, 30 Scenes of blacksmiths at work. *Left*, two smiths smelting or preparing metal to be worked, *below*, a smith in his shop

31 A fifth-century BC armourer working on a helmet

32 A terracotta plaque from Pheidias' workshop at Olympia. It shows two craftsmen and a herm, probably an apotropaic symbol intended to protect their work (cf. Plate 17).

33, 34 *Left*, the grave relief of a Romano-British blacksmith and, *below*, the god Vulcan, with hammer and anvil, on a relief from Roman Gaul

36 Roman grave stele of the smith L. Cornelius Atimetus, seen in his workshop

35 The smith on holiday – a servant offers ceremonial cakes to his master, who stands in his best clothes by the furnace. Late fifth century BC

37 A silver cup of the Roman imperial period from a grave at Hoby, Denmark, beyond the Roman frontiers. It is signed by the imperial freedman Cheirisophos.

38 Athena modelling a horse in clay, the first stage in making a bronze statue

39 The Berlin Foundry Cup—a colossal armed figure of Achilles is being made.

40 The Berlin Foundry Cup – smiths and bronze statuaries work on a figure of Achilles the Swift-footed.

41, 42 The skill of the gold-leaf worker (*aurifex brattiarius*), *right*, also produced such delicate work as the silver wreath of myrtle, *below*.

AVRIFEX BRATTIAR

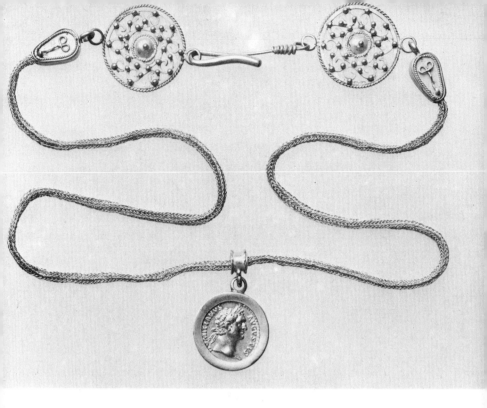

43 An intricate gold necklace with a pendant gold *aureus* of the Emperor Domitian. From Egypt, first century AD

44, 45 Engraved gems by Dexamenos of Chios, *c.*430–420 BC. *Left*, a jasper portrait of a man, *right*, a chalcedony of a flying heron

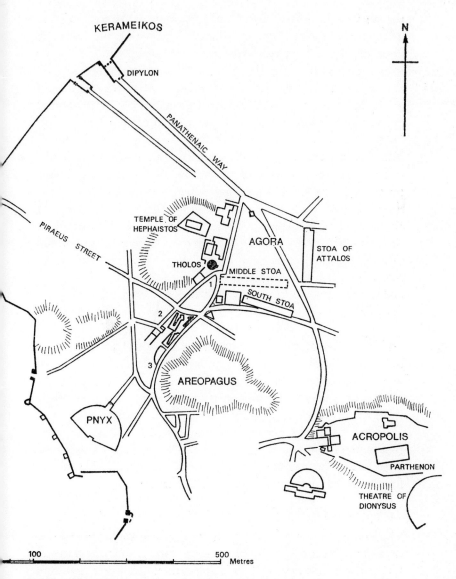

Fig. II   *Athens, the agora and its surroundings. 1 Simon the shoemaker; 2 Street of the Marbleworkers; 3 Archaic cemetery.*

the west bank of the Tiber.[182] But for most craftsmen, isolation of this kind did not arise; once cities had grown up, the craftsmen generally found their place within the city walls. Although some street names in Rome and Alexandria, for example, might suggest that each craft had its own quarter, street or alley, as in the bazaars of the Moslem world or in the medieval town, the archaeological evidence from Athens shows that craftsmen of all kinds were to be found in every street within the working-class quarter.[183] Many of the craftsmen whose domiciles we know lived in the demes immediately west of the agora—Kerameikos (early the home of potters), Kolonos Agoraios, Melite and Kollytos; the shop of Simon the shoemaker lay on the northern edge of Kydathenaion, the acropolis deme.[184] The heaviest concentrations of industrial activity found so far are the bronze foundries and potters' workshops on and round the site of the temple of Hephaistos, dating from the period before the mid-fifth century, and the various workshops in the valley between the Hill of the Nymphs and the Areopagos.[185] One section in this area, called the Street of the Marbleworkers by the excavators, contained several stone-working establishments, a smith's and at one period or another various terracotta figurine makers'. Some houses were continuously occupied for some time by workers in the same craft; the house of Mikion was inhabited by marbleworkers from c. 475 to the end of the fourth century, when what must have been a family business died out. Mikion was perhaps the first master; he is known from a tool made of bone, on which he scratched his name. Menon, whose name appears on some late fourth-century pots, may have been the last.[186]

Training and tradition

The handing down of craft secrets within the family from generation to generation always remained the most important factor in the craft's development. This is apparent in the genealogies not only of various mythical craftsmen—Daidalos (Well-wrought) was the son of Metion (Forethoughtfulness) and grandson of Eupalamos (Skilful-handed), and the Homeric shipwright Phereklos came of a family of skilled woodworkers, for his

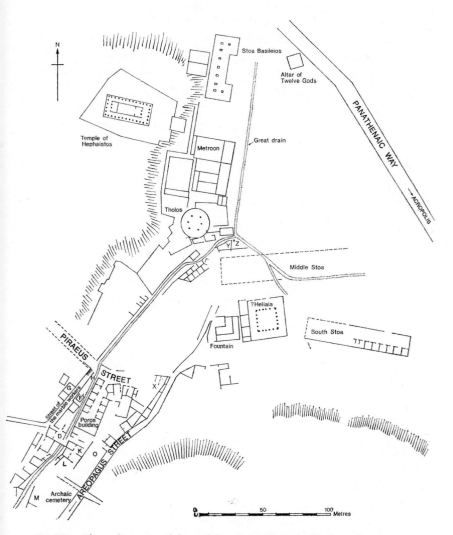

Fig. III *Athens, the agora and the workshop district. Poros building, marble masons,*
fifth and fourth centuries BC; D Aristaichmos' smithy (see p. 163); F unidentified
industrial process; G, H, K marble masons; L terracotta factory, until the first century
AD; M Roman marble workshop; O Hellenistic bronze-workers; X Mikion and
Menon; Y Simon the shoemaker; Z agora boundary marker.

father was Tekton (Carpenter) and his grandfather Harmonides (Joiner)—but of mortal craftsmen too.[187] Literary references and, more important, numerous personal records show that throughout antiquity fathers trained their sons, who trained their sons after them in the practice of the craft into which they had been born. By far the most numerous records showing the handing down of skills for several generations are those of sculptors and painters, but there is no doubt that family interest pervaded every other craft.

A remark of Plato's indicates that this was as true of the pottery industry as of sculpture or painting: 'If a potter is very poor and lacks tools, his work will be of poor quality (because he won't be able to give full attention to his work), and he will teach his sons and whoever else he happens to be instructing to be so much the poorer craftsmen.'[188] In another dialogue he states as if it were the most natural thing in the world that 'the sons of *cheirotechnai* (men skilled with their hands) learn the craft from their fathers'.[189] Very often craftsmen's signatures include their fathers' names; and there are enough sons known for certain from the literary records to have followed the same trade as their fathers to make it reasonably likely that when the sculptor Kallonides of Athens signed as 'Kallonides the son of Deinios', he meant that his father had also been a sculptor, and by giving his father's name he was presenting his own credentials as a properly trained worker, one trained by Deinios.[190] One of the earliest sculptor's inscriptions, on a seventh-century stele, stated that 'the sons of Brentes made me'; some Parian sculptors of the sixth century also signed their work, 'the sons of Charopinos'.[191] Since the remains of their statue demonstrate fine workmanship, they too were clearly well trained, by Charopinos, regard for whom both as father and teacher is expressed in their self-effacing 'signature'.

Paros remained one of the main sources of fine marble and of sculptors too. Skopas, one of the greatest of the fourth-century sculptors, was himself the son of a sculptor, Aristandros; among their descendants must be counted the later Skopas and *his* son Aristandros.[192] Another fourth-century Parian, Satyros, was the father of one sculptor, Lykos, and most likely the son of another,

Isotimos.[193] At Sikyon, another great centre of the arts, we find the brothers Aristokles and Kanachos in the fifth century, and Lysippos, whose pupils included his brother Lysistratos and his sons Daippos and Boedas.[194] In Argos, a concentration of artists and craftsmen in the fifth and fourth centuries was headed by Polykleitos I, his brother or son Naukydes, and the younger Polykleitos in the fourth century.[195]

Athenian sculptor families are known in some numbers. Antenor's father and brother were both sculptors, and Kritios and Nesiotes may have been younger relatives;[196] Myron, one of the greatest early Classical sculptors, was followed by his son Lykios;[197] and the family of Praxiteles and Kephisodotos was in business for several generations—Kephisodotos I and Praxiteles I were perhaps brothers, at work in the late fifth century, and Kephisodotos' son, the great Praxiteles II, was followed by his sons, descendants of whom can be traced to Pergamon *c*. 200 BC and even later.[198] In the Hellenistic and Roman period family tradition remained as strong—to take just one example, Eucheir, son of Euboulides, was the father of another sculptor Euboulides.[199] The late sixth-century Chiot sculptor Archermos had an artist son, Boupalos.[200] In the island of Rhodes, where sculptors from many places were active in the third and second centuries, one or two sculpting dynasties were founded; one may be traced through four generations,[201] and another through six.[202] Many other fathers and sons are known from the Rhodian evidence, including the sculptors of the Laocoon group (*Pl.* 81).

Family concern in the lower levels of the craft can also be detected; the stonemason's business of Neokleides of Kephisia in fourth-century Athens was continued by his son Antimachos,[203] and the Argive sculptors were backed in their profession by quarrymen and stonemasons like Polyxenos and his sons Chremon and Lysiadas, who quarried stone for the *tholos* at Epidauros, and worked on the superstructure too.[204]

For potters and vase-painters the evidence is far less abundant, but signatures on Attic fine painted pottery suggest that family tradition was strong in their craft too.[205]

Among the painters, Euenor of Ephesos, who was perhaps a

sculptor as well, was followed by his son Parrhasios; Polygnotos, one of the greatest of them all, was probably taught by his father Aglaophon of Thasos;[206] Zeuxis of Herakleia was perhaps the son or nephew of Zeuxippos of Herakleia; and Apelles too is said to have come of a painting family.[207]

Aptitude for more than one skill was often to be found within the family. The really first-rate craftsman could generally master two or three related crafts, such as sculpture, bronze-casting, architecture and painting. Pheidias the sculptor also cast bronzes, directed the monumental building programme on the Athenian acropolis and constructed gold and ivory statues; he may have begun his career as a painter like his brother Panainos, who worked with silver and bronze too. There are various instances of painters who were the fathers or sons of sculptors.[208] Versatility of this kind is, as we would expect, only to be found at the higher levels of craftsmanship; exponents of the purely utilitarian crafts such as shoemaking or weaving could not have afforded to diversify.

Sculpture and architecture were often practised within the same family or even by the same man, so that family tradition seems to have played an equally important part in the transmission of both.[209] In the matter of the transmission of architectural practices we may compare Vitruvius' remark that 'formerly the architects themselves would teach none but their own sons or kinsmen, and trained them to be good men, who could be trusted without hesitation in matters of such importance'.[210] So we find that Chersiphron and his son Metagenes were associated with the construction of the sixth-century temple of Artemis at Ephesos; at Delphi the post of official architect was held for a while by Agathon in the mid-fourth century, then by his son Agasikrates, and then again by his son Agathokles c. 230 BC; the architect of the Roman theatre at Aspendos signed as Zenon, son of Theodoros (Pl. 73). [211]

It is clear that some architects were first and foremost carpenters by trade. The Delian carpenter Kaikos had three sons, all of whom worked in wood, and two of whom were appointed architect to the sanctuary.[212] In the Roman period Ti. Claudius

Vitalis and his son were both carpenters and architects, just as P. Cornelius Thallus, one of the leaders of the carpenters' *collegium* in Rome *c.* AD 130, was the son of an architect.[213] In the ship-building craft, too, family relationships may be detected among the names of the fourth-century shipwrights in Athens— Archeneos, Archeneides, and Archenikos were probably members of the same family, as were perhaps Lysikles, Lysikrates, Lysi-kleidas and Lysistratos, and Amphinomos, Amphidemos and Amphikrates.[214] Of other examples of family concern in the crafts, it is enough to mention the miner Xanthippos and his son Charinos from Thasos, who worked at Laureion in the fourth century BC, and the weavers Akesas of Cyprus and his son Helikon, who made the special shoulder-cloak commissioned by the people of Rhodes as a present for Alexander.[215]

But, as Plato remarked and as anyone could see for himself, the sons of great fathers very often failed to fulfil the promise of their heredity and upbringing. Polykleitos' sons, for example, were notable for being less talented than their father; and though Pheidias' descendants were supposed to have had the duty of keeping his chryselephantine statue of Zeus at Olympia oiled and in sound condition, none of his immediate family is known to have followed in his footsteps.[216] In all crafts it is more than likely that many craftsmen were childless, and they themselves only sons, so that they had no young relatives to bring into the workshop as assistants and eventual successors. The mortality rate in antiquity was generally high, and those who had children may have lost them or have died young themselves.

Apprentices

To make up for the lack of talent or inclination within their own families, or to fill the want of a family at all, craftsmen working mainly for themselves could do one of three things. They could adopt a young relative or friend as their heir; they could take on as apprentices the sons of free men who lacked other means of making a living, or slaves whose owners wished them to get a good training from a good master so that they could make money for the owners thereafter; or the master craftsman could buy his own slaves and train them. For the only way of acquiring a skill was to learn it in the workshop. Rarely in the ancient world did any government sponsor training for its youth apart from military and physical education and the elements of reading, writing and numbers; indeed it was not until the later Roman Empire that there was any question of the state's trying to increase the number of skilled workers in any craft by directing them to special training provided by the state, even when labour was painfully short. Nor did private academies at any period, as far as we know, profess to teach technical subjects in an academic way, as distinct from the practical experience gained in a workshop. It was clearly recognized that theoretical training could not take the place of practice; as Xenophon said, 'the observation of even the cleverest bystander is not enough to give a man a proper working knowledge of the craft.'[217]

While natural aptitude for a *technē* was appreciated as a necessary quality of the greatest craftsmen, it could be improved on by good training. Aristotle remarked that 'the crafts are teachable; otherwise, good craftsmen would be born, not made.'[218] Plato laid emphasis on the need for early training within a craft, which would generally have meant learning in the family:

> Everyone who wants to be good at any pursuit must practise it from infancy, by using all the tools of his occupation in work and play. . . . A man who wants to be a good builder must play at building toy houses. . . . A carpenter should have elementary instruction in the use of the rule and measure. . . .[219]

Admission of the craftsman's dependence on the traditions of his craft is made most clearly in the signature of two Argive sculptors who worked together on the statues of a family of Olympic victors: 'Eutelides and Chrysothemis of Argos accomplished these works, having learnt the art from their forebears.'[220]

Few details are known of the apprenticing system in Greece or Rome. Indeed we know little beyond the fact that it existed, as it had in earlier urban (and to that extent industrialized) societies. There is a reference to 'competent *didaskaloi*'—instructors—for 'the lowest mechanics' in Xenophon's *Memorabilia*, and Plato makes a comparison between the master of rhetoric and his fee-paying pupil, and the sculptors Pheidias and Polykleitos and their fee-paying pupils; a little further on he refers to Zeuxis of Herakleia who gave painting lessons.[221] A formal agreement of some kind was made between the parents or guardians of the prospective apprentice and the master-craftsman who had consented to take him on; the only surviving records of such agreements, from Hellenistic and Roman Egypt, suggest that the terms would have been of the simplest; although the political and economic organization of Egypt differed in many ways from that of the rest of the ancient world, the conditions of apprenticeship cannot in the nature of things have varied much. To be sure, we know of apprentice contracts in only a restricted number of crafts—nail making, flute playing, weaving, shorthand, hair-dressing and hieroglyph carving—so that we can only assume that the same practice prevailed in other crafts.[222]

There seem to have been two kinds of contract, one concerned with the teaching of a pupil for a fee, and the other by which, far from receiving a fee, the master was supposed to teach his apprentice for nothing, and to keep him too. The first operated in the teaching of shorthand and flute playing; the distinction between the two types rested on the fact that while an apprentice shorthand writer or flute-player could be of no profit to his master or anyone else until he had learnt the craft thoroughly, an apprentice nail-maker, weaver, or even hieroglyph-cutter could usefully be put to do the simplest tasks in the workshop from the beginning of his training. His teacher would not then be training him for nothing, but would get the use of his labour during the time of apprenticeship.

The Egyptian documents only refer to minors and slaves; it would always have been advantageous to start apprentices young, for then they would learn quickly and retain what they had learnt. Training probably began at an earlier age than in modern times; for what they are worth, the Athenian vase-paintings of workshop scenes show a fair proportion of youths and boys at work, and not only at the most menial tasks (*Pl.* 17). Epitaphs reveal that

L. Arrius Secundus, who died when he was seventeen, could already be spoken of as a sculptor, and Eutychides, who died at the age of sixteen, was compared to the great Praxiteles, which he could scarcely have been if he were not at least reasonably well trained in the rudiments of the craft by the time he died. A jeweller, Pagus, who was described as highly skilled in working with gold and gems, died at the age of twelve; and C. Valerius Diophanes, spoken of as a fully-fledged silver engraver, was only eleven-and-a-half at his death.[223]

The only test of an apprentice's competence in his craft lay in the quality of the things he made; and the only proof of a master-craftsman's ability to teach could be given by the workers he trained. There is some evidence in the Egyptian records of an examination by other master-craftsmen of the work done by an apprentice, but as far as we can tell none of the craftsmen's organizations which flourished especially in the Roman period, the *collegia*, took any steps to protect the standards of the craft by laying down rules for the way in which work should be done and apprentices trained, as the medieval gilds did. Standards were set by the workshop masters, as they saw fit. If the master did not teach his apprentice properly he was guilty of a breach of contract, as we know happened in the case of an Egyptian weaver; if an apprentice missed sessions and also failed to learn within the time fixed, he was bound to stay with the master until he had made up his time; but if he learnt more quickly, then he could leave the master before his time was up. The length of an apprenticeship depended on a variety of factors, for example, the kind of work to which the pupil was apprenticed, his ability and the efficiency of the teacher; a weaver might learn his trade in two or three years, but a smith, carpenter or sculptor might take five, seven or ten years to become fully adept.

Many workshops were of course entirely manned by slaves; but when a craftsman is described in the literature as someone's pupil, there is often no means of distinguishing whether he was a freeborn worker or a freedman or slave. Even when there were differences of status this surely had no significance for the quality of the work done. So long as each had reached the same degree of skill, having been trained in the same way, no distinction whatsoever was made between the work done by slaves and that of free men. Some of the teams of masons who fluted the columns on the east front of the Erechtheion (*Pl.* 61) were led by citizens, others by metics; some included metics and freedman workers, others slaves. All did the same work, all according to the same very high standards, and all received the same pay.[224] So far as his skill is concerned, there is absolutely nothing inherently impossible in Demetrius, the architect of the fourth-century Artemision at Ephesos, having been a temple slave, as Vitruvius says.[225]

Most of the evidence for the importance of the teacher-pupil relationship in the transmission of the crafts comes, once again, from the top flight. Pheidias, of course, was taught by and taught in turn several other sculptors;[226] the same can be said of every other great sculptor and painter. One or two examples are also provided by the humbler crafts—the mosaic-worker T. Sen. Felix of Puteoli signed one of his floors jointly with his pupil 'Amor, citizen of Carthage, *discipulus*';[227] and the Syrian metal-worker T. Ascharenos Eutyches made a joint dedication with his pupil Paulos to Baal.[228] As for slave pupils, one of Pheidias' teachers, Hagelaidas of Argos, owned a slave named Argeias who signed a joint effort with Atotas, presumably another member of Hagelaidas' workshop and an ex-slave himself.[229] The Sicyonian painter Nealkes' slave assistant Erigonos began as a colour-mixer, but eventually became a painter too.[230] The Roman architect L. Cocceius Auctus was the freedman of the citizen architect Postumus, and no doubt his pupil.[231] Professionally speaking, slave and free started on the same footing, used similar tools and dealt with precisely the same kind of materials. Learning a craft was as difficult for a free man as it was for a slave; conversely the slave's pride of craftsmanship could be just as great as that of a free man.

Discipline in the workshop

What evidence there is on this point presents a picture of un-relieved severity—first, the fourth-century Boeotian vase-painting of atrocities in a potter's workshop; second, the accounts of conditions in the quarries and mines; and then this spine-chilling illustration of a legal point arising out of lawsuits concerning personal injury, quoted in the *Digest*. The example taken is that of a craftsman-workshop owner who

> wounds or kills a slave when disciplining him—is the master liable for loss caused contrary to the law? . . . The man who put his pupil's eye out when disciplining him *is* liable. . . . A shoemaker who had a free 'son of the family' as apprentice struck him with a last for not doing properly what he had shown him, and knocked the boy's eye in. . . .[232]

Somehow or other, the Roman jurists had obtained a rather grim impression of what went on in the workshop.

How far can it have been the case that harshness of this kind prevailed in the crafts? An unwilling or harassed worker would surely have produced less excellent manufactures than one who was allowed to establish his own pattern and keep to it. The armourer Pistias, when Socrates interrogated him as to the nature of his craft, showed that he made breastplates which were minor masterpieces, in his own time and more or less at his own pleasure.[233] Liberty of this kind was denied to armourers working for the Roman government under the later Empire, as the following instructions suggest:

> Six helmets are bronzed by the metalworkers in thirty days at Antioch and at Constantinople, and cheekguards also with wrought metal. At Antioch, eight helmets and cheekguards are silvered and gilded, but at Constantinople only three, in thirty days. Therefore the workers at Constantinople are to gild and silver six helmets in that time.[234]

As the imperial system became more rigid and times more difficult, it was decreed that armourers be branded to prevent desertion. The ultimate sanction was imposed for bad or 'incorrect' workmanship; the weight of a finished article was checked against the weight of metal supplied, and the Emperor

Valentinian is said to have condemned to death a worker who burnished a breastplate so highly that he slightly reduced its weight.[235]

Designers and executants

The strength of tradition in the design, techniques and materials used was in all crafts so strong that, once trained, a good craftsman needed very little close guidance from anyone else thereafter to maintain his competence. A new vase shape, developed by one Rhodian or Athenian potter though it might have been, did not spring from the imagination of the potter unaided, but stemmed directly from the inherited traditions of design shared by all properly trained potters in his district, so that to reproduce the shape was no problem for any other. One sculptor would have no difficulty in communicating to any other sculptor in his circle the ideas he might have of modifying the inherited canon of sculptural method, because both were raised on the same basic concepts and neither was going to take more than a small step away from them in any direction. Masons on a building site could well understand what the architect's plan required them to do without his having to draw out in simplified terms all the relationships between one part and another, or the precise mathematical concepts he might have introduced into the proportions of his design.[236]

But in architecture there had always to be someone who designed the structure—a temple did not just grow. And it was the designer, not the masons, carpenters, or decorators of the temple, who gave it whatever distinction from other structures it might have in the way of greater refinements, modified proportions and so on; the architect's role as designer and, if he chose, innovator in his craft was recognized in the title *architekton*, whereas in the other crafts the individual who introduced a new form or started in a new direction would on the whole influence his fellows *informally*. The prefix *archi*-, 'chief' or leading carpenter or builder as distinct from the ordinary *tekton*, does not in its root sense imply any kind of overall supremacy in craftsmanship, for if it did we would expect to find self-confident potters, sculptors, bronze workers, weavers laying claim to titles like *archikerameus, archilatypos, archichalkourgos, archhyphanteus*—which we do not.[237] The *architekton* was so designated for the purely practical reason that the building of temples, fortresses or ships required larger numbers and a greater variety of workers than any other project. It was the one activity which always required a director and co-ordinator; but he need not be a brilliantly audacious innovator at the same time.[238]

Tradition in the crafts was not so strong, however, that individuality of style and technique could not exist. One very clear example is the experimentation of the potter Andocides which resulted in the complete changeover throughout the fine potteries of Athens from black-figure to red-figure during the late sixth century.[239] The rivalry in the workmanship of Euphronios and Euthymides indicates concern for the new concept of foreshortening. Shapes, styles and signatures all give some hint of relationships in the potteries, suggesting that the potter was in charge, and employed the painter; but whether the potter had any say with regard the subject-matter or style of the decoration of his pots, we can never know. Some painters remained long associated with one pottery, but all potters employed several painters, and it seems that most painters moved from one pottery to another during their career.[240] The potters Nikosthenes and Pamphaios may have owned a pottery jointly; signatures show that both made pots, and that Nikosthenes painted one of Pamphaios' products, while they both employed the same ten or fifteen painters. Oltos, working in the early fifth century, painted for at least four different potters. Euphronios the potter began as a painter, but then turned very decisively away from this, for he never seems to have decorated any of his own pots; he employed at least three painters. One of these, Douris, was himself a potter and an innovator too, introducing two new shapes into the potter's repertoire; he did paint some of his own wares. Workshop relationships appear to have been fluid; there was a constant interchange of personnel, designs, and techniques. The situation was rather different in the potteries of the later period, however. For with the wide use of moulded relief ware (the so-called

Arretine ware, in vogue from the late third century BC until the second and third centuries AD) there arose a sharp distinction between the designer who made the mould and the makers who simply applied it to the clay (Pl. 21). [241]

All this is to say that, while on one hand we may detect some individuality, on the other hand no one should be surprised that many works of art were the product not of a single artist, but of two or even more working together. Some Attic vases were clearly decorated by two painters.[242] A stone-carved relief might be cut by one man and painted by another—a Rhodian example is signed by the sculptor Timokles of Knidos and the painter Protomachos of Halikarnassos.[243] Many if not all bronze statues were the work of two master-craftsmen; double signatures on a number of statue-bases, again from Rhodes in the third and second centuries BC, reveal that different individuals were responsible for the shaping of the statue and for the bronze work, while the Berlin Foundry Cup (Pls. 39, 40) shows two masters contemplating their assistants' work on the great statue of Achilles.[244] In all cases, we may suppose, both men were equally concerned with the construction and the finished appearance of the statue; the maker of the core or matrix (often of clay) created the outline and much of the detail of the figure, but the bronze-worker must have helped to determine how limbs were to be arranged, guided in his judgment by what he knew to be structurally feasible, just as it was he who would have burnished and touched up the statue when it had all been fastened together.

Not one but several sculptors and architects under Pheidias' leadership were concerned with the construction and decoration of the Parthenon.[245] The fifth-century Telesterion in the sanctuary at Eleusis was started by Koroibos, continued by Metagenes and Xenokles, and later by Iktinos, but still remained to be finished in the fourth century by Philon of Eleusis.[246] The architect of the Asklepios temple at Epidauros, Theodotos, must have worked in close consultation with Thrasymedes, the sculptor of the cult statue and decorator of the temple cella.[247] Mausolos' tomb at Halikarnassos was decorated by four sculptors, Skopas, Leochares, Timotheos and Bryaxis; while at least forty sculptors worked on the frieze of the great altar at Pergamon in the second century, some sections being worked on by two sculptors together—yet the style of the whole monument, if not uniform, is highly unified.[248] In the same way the design of Trajan's column, though no doubt roughed out and directed by one man, was interpreted by many.[249] Plagiarism was an unknown concept.

VERSATILITY AND SPECIALIZATION

Division of labour

There were professional differences among skilled workers to this extent, that many craftsmen who had been grounded thoroughly in the rules of one particular craft were still no more than just competent at it. Even to remain competent they had to stick to their job, however. Xenophon's comment, that it is impossible for a man of many trades to be proficient in them all, foreshadows the saying that the jack-of-all-trades is master of none. The essence of craftsmanship is, first and foremost, complete mastery of the technique.[250]

The truly great craftsmen, on the other hand, were those who mastered the techniques both of working in different materials and of working towards different ends. Versatility and breadth of interest were the hallmarks of Pheidias, Polykleitos, Lysippos, Pytheos, Vitruvius, Apollodoros, Archimedes and Theodoros of Samos, not to mention Daidalos, the mythical forerunner of them all. A potter expected to work full-time on pots; but the creator of colossal gold and ivory statues can never have found continuous employment on such projects, and so looked to other occupations to provide him with a living, as Pheidias certainly did.

Yet even the merely competent, who concentrated on one kind of manufacture, had to learn a fair number of processes in order to be able to understand (or to feel instinctively, as the craftsman must) what was happening at each stage to the thing he was making. Though his raw materials might be delivered to the workshop already prepared in some way, it was best if the craftsman knew something of their origins—where the timber had been cut and how it was seasoned, or where the marble had been quarried and how each piece had lain in the quarry-face. The painter's craft could be enhanced by interested investigators like the Athenian sculptor and painter Mikon, who is supposed to have discovered a new ochre in the silver mines of Attica.[251] In the ordinary business of the workshop, the apprentice would observe and then perform every process, from the preparation of the yarn to the weaving of intricately patterned fabric, if he were a weaver; or if he were a potter, from the cleaning and blending of the clay to the shaping of vases on the wheel. In a small working community such as this, all hands might at one time or another be called on to build the kiln, stoke the furnace, steady the half-finished bronze statue, or advise on the distribution of figures in a stone-carved relief. There could be no total division of labour, no absolute specialization; the scale and nature of the workshop forbade it.

Yet the statement is frequently made that specialization in the crafts increased considerably between the Homeric, Classical and Hellenistic periods in Greece, and between the time of the early Republic in Rome and the Empire.[252] What supporters of this view really mean is not clear, nor how they see this increased specialization as having come about. The assumption seems to be that not only was there a progression from the house economy, under which system each household produced most of the things it required, to the town or city economy in which the full-time professional craftsman took over more and more from the amateur worker at home; but it is argued in addition that specialization and the subdivision of labour increased outright within each craft. The first part of this assumption is undeniably valid; the second seems to me to stand on wobbly foundations, consisting largely of the specialist craft names to be found in the sources of Classical and Hellenistic Greece and imperial Rome. In the eighth and seventh centuries BC, Homer and Hesiod make references to only the simplest craft divisions—bronze-working, carpentry, shipbuilding, woodcutting, pottery, leatherwork and goldsmithing. But in the later sources we find far subtler distinctions—statuemaker, maker of eyes for statues, knife maker, knife sharpener, wagon builder, woodcarver, miner, smelter, smith, bronzesmith, ironsmith, silversmith, goldsmith, jeweller, gold-leaf worker, silver vessel maker, shield maker, helmet maker, trumpet maker, wool worker, flock worker, ragpicker, dyer, purple dyer, fuller, tanner, leather sewer, harness maker, shoemaker, bootmaker, ladies' slipper maker, spear polisher, sickle forger, wine-jar maker, key maker, glue boiler, and so on and so on.[253]

However, the fact that we do not hear of these 'specialists' at all periods, early and late, does not mean that the kind of workmanship which gave rise to them in fifth- and fourth-century Athens or imperial Rome was not known at other times too. The literary evidence is always selective if not entirely arbitrary in the economic and industrial conditions it reflects, and inscriptions likewise; neither Hesiod, Homer, Thucydides, Aristophanes, nor Plautus, Vitruvius, Cicero or even the compilers of Roman legal statutes and decrees were interested in leaving a comprehensive record of the economy and methods of production of their day. Their silence is no proof of these subjects' lack of importance. In any case, the quality of craftmanship alone suggests that however high the standards, and however varied the techniques of the best Classical Greek and imperial Roman products, they were matched by the best work of other periods too—Corinthian painted pottery of the seventh century was as fine as that of late sixth- and fifth-century Athens, and both were equalled by the earlier so-called Geometric ware. Painted terracotta temple ornaments in Etruria and Republican Rome were as striking in their way and as taxing to make as the marble pediment-sculptures of the standard Greek temple. The workmanship of a sixth-century *kouros* was no less skilful than that of a Hellenistic sculpture—indeed, the breakthrough, as it were, from rectangular block to standing figure was for the *kouros* sculptor a far greater achievement. Conversely, it need not have been the case that, in the periods when we do hear of specialist craft titles, a spear polisher spent his whole working life doing only that; that the *koniater* (plasterer) who provided plaster models for stone-carved decoration in the Epidaurian temple of Asklepios never stuccoed a limestone column or plastered a house wall in his life; or that the glue boiler devoted his whole working career to that unlovely occupation.[254] At all times, early and late, the worker's interest in his job, his own conceit even, would have given him reason enough to invent high-sounding technical terms and professional titles. It need not have been the case that each only came into existence when some new and lasting division of labour required definition. Craftsmen and the general public alike could coin phrases with the greatest of ease. How could a musical instrument maker have resisted calling himself *salpingopoios*—trumpet maker? Another of Aristophanes' 'trade titles', *torneutolyraspido-pegos*—lyre-turner-and-shield-maker—was not so much pure fantasy as Athenian phrase-making carried to its logical (or illogical) conclusion.[255] So too the many trades mentioned in Plautus' comedies may some of them have arisen out of comic exaggeration; the highly specialized occupations apparent in the decrees and laws of the later Roman Empire perhaps reflect less a realistic appraisal of the labour resources to be directed, pinned down, taxed or exempted from taxes than a bureaucratic nightmare.[256]

A basic division always existed among the crafts, in that wood-workers tended not to work in metal or stone very extensively, while metalworkers made no attempt to understand the many finer points of carpentry or stonemasonry. But distinctions cannot realistically be pushed further; an architect directing work in stone and other materials might originally have been trained as a carpenter, and a vase-painter might be the son of a sculptor, while the sculptor himself was often quarrymason as well as shaper, dresser, polisher, decorator, not to mention designer, of his statue.

The accounts for work done in the Delian sanctuary during the third century BC show that many of the woodworkers employed in the island were perfectly well able to do other jobs too. For instance, Theophantos from Karystos worked on the roof timbers of the old temple of Apollo, on a wooden cart for the ritual procession of Dionysos, on doors, and on house roofs; but he also built in brick and levelled the floor of the old temple, which presumably required some mason's work. The Delian Phaneas worked with a Parian carpenter on some ceiling coffers for the main temple of Apollo, and with his brother Antigonos on the temple doors; he too built, and plastered, a brick wall in another shrine. Another worker, Euphranor, constructed a door, sawed up a palm tree, and laid roof tiles.[257]

On the other hand the building accounts for the Erechtheion in late fifth-century Athens appear to indicate specialization of a very high order. Masons, sculptors, wax modellers, woodcarvers, carpenters, sawyers, joiners, lathe workers, painters, gilders, and labourers can all be distinguished by the very specific sort of work for which each was paid.[258] But closer examination reveals that, among the wax modellers, one was also a sculptor, and another a woodcarver; a carpenter worked as a joiner, woodcarver, and labourer; and several stonemasons also worked as labourers, shifting scaffolding for their own use on the columns of the east façade, maybe. It would have been quite impractical for these highly skilled men not to have performed related tasks of this kind.

In the painted pottery industry, as we have seen, although many workers confined themselves to either making or painting pots, some did both. Douris, a Samian at work in Athens between the 490s and the 460s, demonstrated even greater versatility; it seems that after a career as a potter and painter he returned to Samos where he took up the art of letter-cutting in stone.[259] The links between painting and other crafts within families have already been pointed out. The gulf between the vase-painter and the wall- or panel-painter cannot have been very wide; certainly vase-painters followed new developments very closely—there is nothing naïve or scaled-down in the work of Euthymides and Euphronios, for example. They liked to associate themselves with the great painters: after 475 not one but several different vase-painting hands signed themselves 'Polygnotos', obviously in imitation of the great Polygnotos of Thasos.[260] Whether he or Parrhasios would have condescended to paint pots is perhaps doubtful, but vase-painters, like ships' painters, could have risen to greater things.[261]

Many specialist titles among metalworkers are known, and there can be no doubt that mining and smelting remained at all periods the province of specialists. But, though we hear of a bronze-mixer named Sosinos in fifth-century Athens, as specialized a craftsman as might be, we also know from the accounts that the bronze for Pheidias' statue of Athena Promachos was blended specially, since the accounts list tin, copper, fuel and furnace-building among the statue's costs.[262] Then the titles of smiths appear to indicate specialization in one metal alone—thus the *chalkeus*, or bronzesmith, who appears in Homer, and the bronzesmith Sotas, of third-century Delos.[263] But these distinctions mean little; Sotas supplied tools of iron, and various other Delian smiths worked in lead, iron and bronze, while in the Athenian workshop of Aristaichmos scraps of both iron and bronze were found.[264] These scattered examples are perhaps sufficient to show that specialization and versatility in the crafts are not qualities which can be associated with one or another particular period, early or late, in the practice of Greek and Roman craftsmanship. Both Greek and Latin speakers were, to say the least, flexible in their use of technical terms, and they were influenced too by the flexibility which must have existed in the crafts themselves. The simple shoemaker must rarely have been inhibited by any consideration of what was or was not 'professional' from tackling a soldier's boot or even a piece of harness, if the occasion called for it; and the gold-leaf worker could surely have contrived a bit of filigree if pressed to do so (*Pl.* 41).[265]

The co-ordination of diverse skills

The greatest works produced by the ancient artists and craftsmen were the monumental constructions—the temples, theatres, aqueducts, fortresses and harbours of the Greek and Roman world. These were built not by specialists in the sense that the craftsmen who worked on them did nothing else in their entire working lives but build one or another of structures of this kind, or even in the sense that each of these projects was directed by a specialist in the single art of temple building or tunnel cutting, but by workers gathered for the occasion from many different fields and many levels of production. The men who co-ordinated their efforts were the *architects* or *engineers*, men experienced in the ways of many different materials and diverse crafts. Thus, even the Roman army depended not on special corps of trained engineers, but on the legionary soldiers who were expected to turn their hands to various kinds of construction in wood and stone as well as to fighting. Caesar's troops in Gaul built pile bridges across rivers, and ships too, with great speed;[266] and of course we have vivid evidence of the army's constructiveness in the scenes on Trajan's column (*Pls.* 67, 70).

Who were the architects and engineers, and how did they acquire their knowledge? There is something of a problem for us in that the modern distinction (which cannot always be applied consistently, even now) between the engineer and the architect did not exist in the ancient world; for although Archimedes himself was not particularly interested in architecture, and while many sculptor-architects cared little for engineering, there were many skilled workers whose interests did extend in both directions. Vitruvius is of course the supreme example of the architect and engineer, as the subject-matter of his treatise demonstrates. Among the less exalted workers, the carpenters working for the Delphic sanctuary built lifting devices for transferring stone from quayside to cart, and from ground level to its place in the superstructure.[267] The sculptors Kleoitas and Aristeides both modified the mechanism of the starting-gate in the stadium at Olympia;[268] fortifications, ships' arsenals and theatres all called for similar stone-working techniques and methods of construction to those used in memorial porticoes and temples. Should Sostratos of Knidos and Julius Lacer, for example, be called architects or civil engineers? Sostratos built the Pharos lighthouse at Alexandria, while Julius Lacer constructed a bridge as well as the small dedicatory shrine on the bank alongside.[269]

The training of the architect or engineer must have been undertaken on the site, in the actual execution of public works. Experience gained in a carpenter's or metalworker's shop, or in a stonemason's yard, would play its part, but there were no bridge-building or harbour-constructing workshops, and inherited family interest in such works would not have been sufficient to train an apprentice in the structural disciplines. A real problem emerges here—if practical experience on the building site was an essential part of an architect's training, where and when had the architects of the Parthenon learned their craft? Temple building in Athens was negligible if not non-existent between the time of the half-built older Parthenon's destruction by the Persians in 480 and the great programme of construction, under which a dozen temples and other works were put up, from about 450 onwards. The architects who had learnt on the original Parthenon would have been very old men in 450, and their assistants almost entirely inexperienced in architectural matters, unless it is the case that Iktinos, Koroibos, Kallikrates, Mnesikles and the other Periclean architects had all got their training by working as masons or carpenters on the temple of Zeus at Olympia, the only significant building to have been put up on the Greek mainland between 480 and 450.[270] Where had Eupalinos of Megara developed his evident skill as a cutter of tunnels through solid rock?[271] One possibility, of course, is that many such works were daring experiments which just happened to come off; Mandrokles' boat-bridge was perhaps the first and the last that he built.[272] Temple builders, however, rarely needed to experiment; whatever the interval between one temple and the next in any one place, sculptors and architects, stonemasons and roofing experts could draw on, and contribute in their turn to, an international pool of temple-building experience.

Socrates, in the course of putting down a conceited student, asked him if he wished to become an architect, 'for a man of knowledge is needed in that art too'.[273] The only surviving discussion of what the architect and engineer needed to know is that of Vitruvius, who makes this point even more clearly and at far greater length. Idealistic and unrealistic though his views may seem, they are worth considering because they stem directly from his own experience as an architect and military engineer:[274]

The architect should be equipped with knowledge of many branches of study and varied kinds of learning, for it is by his

judgment that all work done by the other crafts is put to the
test. This knowledge is the child of practice and theory. . . .
2 It follows therefore that architects who have aimed at
acquiring manual skill without scholarship have never been
able to reach a position of authority to correspond to their
pains, while those who relied only on theories and scholarship
were obviously hunting the shadow, not the substance. . . .
3 . . . (An architect) ought therefore to be naturally gifted, and
amenable to instruction. . . . Let him be educated, skilful with
the pencil, instructed in geometry, know much history, have
followed the philosophers with attention, understand music,
have some knowledge of medicine, know the opinions of the
jurists and be acquainted with astronomy and the theory of the
heavens.
4 The reasons for all this are as follows. An architect ought
to be an educated man so as to leave a more lasting remem-
brance in his treatises. Secondly, he must have a knowledge of
drawing so that he can readily make sketches to show the
appearance of the work he proposes. Geometry also is of much
assistance in architecture, and in particular it teaches us the use
of the rule and compasses, by which especially we acquire
readiness in making plans for buildings in their grounds, and
rightly apply the square, the level and the plummet. By
means of optics, again, the light in buildings can be drawn from
fixed quarters of the sky. It is true that it is by arithmetic that
the total costs of the buildings are calculated and measurements
are computed, but difficult questions involving symmetry are
solved by means of geometrical theories and methods.
5 A wide knowledge of history is required, because among the
ornamental parts of an architect's design for a work there are
many the underlying idea of which he should be able to explain
to enquirers. . . .
7 As for philosophy, it makes an architect high-minded and not
self-assuming, but rather tends to make him courteous, just,
and honest without avarice. . . . Furthermore philosophy treats
of physics. . . . So the reader of Ktesibios and Archimedes and
the other writers of treatises of the same class will not be able to

appreciate them unless he has been trained in the subject by the philosophers. . . .

11 Consequently, since this subject (architecture) is so vast in extent, embellished and enriched as it is with many different kinds of learning, I think that men have no right to profess themselves architects hastily, without having climbed from boyhood the steps of these studies and having reached the heights of the holy ground of architecture nursed by the knowledge of many arts and sciences.

The same combination of practical experiment with theory is seen in the writing of Hellenistic mechanical theorists like Heron of Alexandria:

In the following we are going to treat of the five powers by which the burdens are moved, and we shall explain their principles and natural function, and we shall treat of other matters that are of great use in the handling and lifting of burdens.[275]

And the mathematician Pappos, of the fourth century AD, refers to the wedge as a power

of great service, in large presses for perfumery and the very great joints in carpentry, but most of all when it comes to detaching the stones from the quarry face; none of the other powers can do this, . . . but the wedge does it all alone by any sort of blow.[276]

Vitruvius disagrees with an earlier architectural commentator, Pythios of Priene, on the degree of specialization attainable in each branch of the required competence. Pythios said that

an architect ought to be able to accomplish much more in all the arts and sciences than the man who, by his own particular kind of work and the practice of it, has brought a single subject to the highest perfection.[277]

Such is not and cannot be the case, says Vitruvius:

> An architect should not be such a philologian as was Aristarchos, but he should not be illiterate either; . . . nor such a painter as Apelles, though not unskilful in drawing; nor a sculptor such as was Myron or Polykleitos, though not unacquainted with the plastic art; nor again a physician like Hippokrates, though not ignorant of medicine. . . . For in the midst of all this great variety of subjects an individual cannot attain to perfection in each, because it is scarcely in his power to take in and comprehend the general theories of them. . . .
> 14 Even men who individually practise specialities in the arts do not all attain to the highest point of merit.[278]

Vitruvius' view of the architect's capabilities is thus shown to be somewhat more down-to-earth than Pythios':

> 15 It appears then that Pythios was mistaken in not observing that the arts are each composed of two things, the actual work and the theory of it. The doing of the work is proper to men trained in the individual subject, while the theory of it is common to all scholars.

He allows that a 'good working knowledge' of the various subjects will suffice, for those 'on whom nature has bestowed so much ingenuity, acuteness and memory that they are able to have a thorough knowledge of geometry, astronomy, music and the other arts go beyond the function of architects and become pure mathematicians'.

The men who directed the monumental works of antiquity, be they colossal statues in bronze, rock-cut water courses, the Claudian harbour at Ostia, temples, theatres, Pantheons or siege-engines, were always among the most versatile and most unusual members of the whole craft network. Specialization in a sense had always existed; as Vitruvius says, many men could only master the elements of a single craft. But the concept of breaking down each craft into separate processes, and the work-group into performers of one process each, was never the natural outcome of craftsmanship.

GOOD, BAD AND INDIFFERENT CRAFTSMANSHIP

The discussion so far has tended to emphasize the very high standards achieved by the best craftsmen. But there were obviously many mediocre craftsmen, and some downright poor; much which may have been of quite sound construction and workmanship lacked style. While no craftsman in the slightest degree worthy of the name, who had gone through the rigours of a workshop training and who wished to continue earning his living, would make boots which fell to pieces after a few times of wearing or a plough which did not run straight, a knife that would not cut or a terracotta figurine which crumbled to dust, there were workshops which produced objects of poor proportions, or blurred and inaccurate detail, cutting corners to the inevitable detriment of good craftsmanship. For no method was evolved in antiquity of actually speeding up production while at the same time preserving excellence of design and finish.

The clearest evidence of poor craftsmanship comes from the clay-working craft. In Corinthian ware of the late seventh and early sixth centuries B C there are several examples of short-cut work—the potter drove his vase-painters to fill an order, so that instead of doing justice to the surface of the vase with a design of six encircling animals, the painter saved time by stretching four round it, feline dachshunds rather than the trimmer lions or panthers they should have been. At all periods the majority of the terracotta figurine makers' products were squalid little pieces, whether hand-made, as in the early period, or mould-made, as they came to be by the thousand; designs were stereotyped and detail rough or lacking. For although the use of moulds for figurines, pottery—the so-called Arretine ware or *terra sigillata* which became widespread from the third century B C onwards— and clay lamps did not in itself inevitably mean dreary products, there are many examples of pieces made from worn moulds or moulds which themselves had not been produced with fresh ideas in mind but consisted of motifs and arrangements taken from earlier makers' discards; the quality of mould-made lamps, figurines and relief-decorated bowls could be maintained only if fresh moulds were constantly in use (*Pls.* 22, 23, 24).

But however indistinct the relief decoration on the lamp, it could still hold oil and give illumination when lit; however displeasing the terracotta figurine might be, it sold—and served the ritual purpose for which it had been bought quite adequately. Though refinements might be entirely lacking, the basic purpose of the craftsman, to provide something which would function, was not defeated.

What was it that determined whether the public got boots, or well-styled boots? a wooden seat with a back, or a finely turned chair? a pretty lamp, or one which looked as if it had been washing about at the bottom of a river bed? Who was responsible for the standards of workmanship, the customer or the craftsman? These are not easy questions to answer; several alternatives come to mind, but none of them is conclusive in itself, and all lead to further questions.

One determining factor may often have been that those who were willing to buy were simply not willing to pay for finely made goods, which took longer to make and therefore cost more than rough stuff; thus, at Myrina in the second century BC, while some very fine terracotta figures were made as individual pieces by Menophilos' workshop, there were numerous very bad ones from the workshop of his contemporary Diphilos—the first presumably for the rich, and the others for the poor (*Pl.* 20).[279] But sometimes that section of the public which would have been willing to pay for good quality was left unsatisfied; this was surely because there were not enough good craftsmen to satisfy the market. The Athenian cloak-maker whose wares always sold out so quickly when he came to Alexandria was not an isolated phenomenon;[280] the inhabitants of Athens in the first and second centuries AD, prosperous though the city was and embellished with new monumental architecture under the patronage of Herodes Atticus, yet had to make do with very horrid terracotta lamps. There are various instances of schemes for building temples or other monumental works which had to be interrupted or seriously delayed for lack of adequate labour to carry out the work. Why did so many sculptors and architects work in so many different places? Partly because constant employment in one place of residence was not available, perhaps; but also because there was a demand for their services in other places which altogether lacked workers of their calibre.[281] Once one can establish that there was a potential market for good stuff, then it was the presence or absence of the suitably qualified craftsmen which determined whether or not that good stuff was to be had.

But what public demand was there for finely decorated painted pottery in the Greek cities of south Italy, during the fourth century BC? And what means of satisfying it were available? Numerous examples show evidence of much hard work: the shaping is ornate, the painted decoration intricate. But the overall effect of much of it is unattractive, or at best amusing; the painting is often careless, although lavish, the designs chaotic, and the pots themselves slightly unbalanced if not actually of bad proportions. Was it that the Apulian and Campanian gentry (or whoever bought the stuff) actually liked it this way? Would they not have preferred vases closer in quality to the Athenian ware which had provided the models for the south Italian style? In which case, was this the best that south Italian potters and vase-painters could do? If so, then they lacked something—not suitable materials, knowledge of technique, or even the aptitude for hard work, but that indefinable quality which Athenian potters and painters had possessed in such abundance. Why should this necessary flair be lacking in one place and present in another?

The excellence of craftsmanship which could give distinction to an object sometimes, though rarely, flourished in isolation; a single man of outstandingly good judgment or adventurous spirit could make all the difference between mediocrity and distinguished work. The island of Melos, otherwise unremarkable for its craftsmanship, seems to have produced one clay-worker with the wit to create a series of quite unusual terracotta reliefs.[282] They portrayed mythological scenes in a very distinctive style, the background being cut out so that the figures were almost free-standing, and were specially hardened to stand wear as decorations on walls or wooden chests. The period of their production, between about 465 and 435 BC, seems to have spanned the working lifetime of one man only; nothing like them was ever made again, in Melos or anywhere else. Among the comparatively few and mediocre potters of fifth-century Boeotia, there evolved a style of considerable verve, the Kabeiran style, which has been described as 'the only truly comic school' of Greek art.[283] But it did not last long, and once again may have owed its existence to the work of a single craftsman whose sense of humour was not shared by any of his successors; echoes of the style did linger on, one example being the scene showing punishment in the potter's workshop. But for bright ideas to survive, and, in general, to permit them to emerge into the light of day at all, a *community* of craftsmen was the required environment.

Some centres of craftsmanship grew up where activity of a high order in several crafts persisted for many generations, and sometimes (with fluctuations) for centuries. At Corinth, the craftsmen of the seventh and sixth centuries excelled not only in painted pottery but also led the field in the production of terracotta revetments for temples;[284] under the Roman Empire Corinthian clay-workers were still producing very fine terracotta lamps. The Corinthian construction industry was concerned equally with ships and with monumental architecture; tradition held that Ameinokles of Corinth had built ships for the Samians, as early as 700 BC by Thucydides' reckoning;[285] Corinthian architects, carpenters and masons, together with Corinthian limestone, were employed at two important building sites during the fourth century—on the temple of Apollo at Delphi, and on various structures in the sanctuary of Asklepios at Epidauros;[286] in the third century it was the Corinthian Archias who built the monster ship for Hieron of Syracuse.[287] In other places the strength of craft traditions was less enduring; sixth-century Samos saw the rise and the passing of some of the greatest craftsmen in the Greek world at that time—the group led by the family of Rhoikos and Theodoros, who included bronze and silver workers, architects, stonemasons who could turn Ionic column-bases of marble on the lathe to achieve exact and knife-sharp mouldings, sculptors, jewellers and engineers. To what greater heights might not the Samian craftsmen have attained if the Persians had not crushed the island?[288]

From the fifth to the third century the sculptors and painters of Sikyon were internationally known, for among others they included Lysippos.[289] At Argos worked a chain of skilled men stretching from the sixth to the fourth century if not later: from Polymedes, the sculptor of Kleobis and Biton, to Hagelaidas, teacher of Pheidias, the elder Polykleitos, sculptor, bronze-caster and maker of at least one gold and ivory statue, and after him the younger Polykleitos who with various masons from Argos was responsible for, among other things, one if not two of the most striking buildings at Epidauros.[290]

At Athens, the tradition of high quality in the potter's craft can be traced from the tenth century down to the fourth century BC; fine terracotta figurines were made during the fourth and third centuries.[291] Marble working, for monumental building and for sculpture, began in the early sixth century on the slopes of Hymettos and Pentele, and continued without serious interruption down to the Roman imperial period.[292] Among the places which provided particularly congenial surroundings for the fine craftsman were Rhodes during the third, second and first centuries, and the cities of the Hellenistic monarchs—Pergamon, Antioch and Alexandria. But in these places, as at Rome itself, it was less a question of native craftsmen generating and then maintaining their own body of tradition and high standards, than of skilled workers being drawn there by the promise of patronage offered by the courts of kings and emperors.

In sympathetic surroundings, such as a community of craftsmen provided, the crafts could develop. Only where the crafts moved forward, however slightly and within however narrow confines, could the craftsman's products achieve anything beyond competent mediocrity. Sculptors worked within very clearly defined limits at all periods, yet the stylistic changes within the few generations between the earliest examples of life-size stone sculpture and the works, say, of Polykleitos and Pheidias were sufficient for Plato to be able to remark, 'Daidalos, if he were born now, and if he made statues like those by which he became famous, would be laughed to scorn'.[293] The main theme of individual sculptures as opposed to pediment groups remained basically the same—the standing human figure—but the difference in concept from one end of this period to the other may be seen first in the *kouros* of sculptors such as Euthykartides (*Pl.* 2) with its rather two-dimensional, front-view and side-view presentation, the figure stiff and formalized in detail, yet even at this stage shown not at rest but in the act of stepping forward; then in the *korē* of Antenor, still a rather formal figure, but rounded so that the three-quarter view is as convincing as front or side, and far more realistic in detail; and, perhaps eighty years later, in the winged victory of Paionios, completely true to life in proportions and disposition of the limbs, a figure in the act of floating down, the draperies almost more delicate than real silk or muslin would have been. No more than two hundred years separate the first from the third; perhaps three hundred years intervened between the victory-figure of Paionios and the Laocoon group (*Pls.* 80, 81), which demonstrates rather different concepts again of how the human figure may be presented.

In architecture one sees traditional forms undergoing slight but unmistakable changes in each new monumental structure; proportions differed subtly, but without ever straying far from the path laid down in the immediately preceding work, which in turn looked to the one before it, and so on back to the formative period of Greek architecture (whenever that was). The basic elements of Doric and Ionic were already in existence by the early sixth century. The mid-sixth-century Heraeum at Paestum and the mid-fourth-century temple of Zeus at Nemea are both of the same style—Doric—but a difference of proportions and details makes them easily distinguishable. The Roman interpretation of classical Greek architectural design can be seen in the famous Maison Carrée at Nîmes; built in the Corinthian style, it demonstrates the quite different Roman disposition of the colonnade, which was reduced to a colonnaded porch on the front, and has attached columns on the sides and back where the *cella* extended to the edge of the temple platform, instead of being completely surrounded by columns as in most Greek temples.

At first sight the Pantheon in Rome presents a totally new concept in architectural form, differing profoundly from the conventional Greek structure. But this is not altogether true; for one thing, it has a quite straightforward colonnade and pediment on the front; and for another, although the construction of the dome is something entirely foreign to Greek structural thinking, Classical Greek architecture had nevertheless extended itself to the construction of circular buildings with coffered ceilings under cone-shaped roofs, such as the *tholos* at Epidauros (*Pl.* 62).

Stylistic development in painting appears, as one would expect, to have been as swift as it was in sculpture. The vase-paintings of sixth- and early fifth-century Athens show experiment with the possibilities of foreshortening and grappling with difficulties which continued to plague graphic artists throughout antiquity.[294] In the Hellenistic and Roman period, surviving wall-paintings show that new subject-matter was taken up; landscapes were one subject, naturalistic scenes of town life another, and architectural fantasies (which were probably inspired by the theatrical scene-painters) yet another, which gave the painter cause for rethinking his techniques, and so ensured that the craft did not become static.

Stylistic change in one craft was frequently reflected in other related crafts. A good demonstration of the way in which several different crafts could take up the same idea and mull it over each in his own fashion is given by the competitive craftsmanship of the vase-painters Euthymides and Euphronios, and one of the engraved gems signed by Epimenes; all were working in about 500 BC or a little later, and all show the same approach to the problem of how to show the human leg foreshortened, and not simply in profile. It is unlikely in the extreme that these craftsmen were in direct communication with one another (apart from the two vase-painters, of course); but the similarity of workmanship cannot have been pure coincidence.

The competent, or, to put it another way, the mediocre craftsman was able to maintain the tradition in which he had been trained. It was left for the great craftsman to transform traditional concepts, not only by reinterpreting familiar styles, but also by experimenting with new materials and techniques.

ANCIENT TECHNOLOGICAL DEVELOPMENT
AND ITS LIMITATIONS

Soundness of construction, exactness of detail, complete adequacy of function, ingenuity and boldness of invention—the good craftsman's best work displayed many if not all of these qualities. With quite simple tools he could make a block of marble exactly rectangular and perfectly level on every surface, which, where necessary, would be polished smooth; he could cut minute and intricate designs in gems, without benefit of magnifying glass or the equivalent; his pots would emerge from the kiln red and shiny black, exactly where he had intended, their decoration clearly defined, and their harmonious proportions having been achieved by eye; the carpentry of the ships he built would have the quality of cabinet work rather than boat-building, so fine were the joints and so firm the resulting wall of wood;[295] his shoes would be of the best and most hard-wearing leather, well-fitting and pleasing to the eye; the purity of Athenian silver was almost proverbial—in order to make it so, the refiners needed to carry out complicated processes, not only to extract it from its ore, but to separate it from the lead which was also present (Pls. 49, 50).

Good craftsmanship under intelligent direction produced the superb combination of absolute utility and architectural grace demonstrated in almost any Roman aqueduct, of which the Pont du Gard (Pl. 74) is a prime example. The large-scale elegance of Trajan's forum or the streets of Ostia resulted from the laborious and ordered piling up of brick on brick, coupled with the extended use of the new invention of cement. The self-confidence of sculptors, bronze statuaries and architects meant that, within limits, they were willing to experiment; one obvious way in which they did so was to extend statues and buildings from normal dimensions to the colossal. An early example of an experiment which failed is the abandoned Dionysos figure in Naxos (*Pl. 75*); one which came off at much the same time— *c.* 600 BC—was the Naxians' colossal statue of Apollo, the base of which alone weighed perhaps twenty-five tons, set up in the Delian sanctuary.[296] The building of vast temples, in Ionia during the sixth century, at Athens and in Sicily during the fifth, and in Ionia again during the Hellenistic period, meant taking risks with the bearing strength of marble crossbeams, columns and retaining walls, and in roofing wide spans (though it is clear that ancient architects built well within the strength of their materials). To return to statuary, in the early sixth century sculptors had already been indulging their patrons' taste for size; in the fifth century, Pheidias alone contributed to outsize art the sixty-foot high bronze of Athena Promachos and the two gold and ivory statues, each forty feet high or more, of Athena Parthenos, and Zeus at Olympia. In the fourth century, Lysippos made a seventy-foot bronze for Tarentum; his pupil Chares of Lindos took up the Rhodians' commission for a colossal bronze sun-statue, between 292 and 280 BC, which stood perhaps 120 feet high, until it was felled by an earthquake nearly a century later.[297] The Hellenistic shipbuilders produced some monster vessels for the rulers of Egypt, Syria and Syracuse.[298] And in the Roman period not only were single monuments planned on a vast scale— architects in Roman Syria could contemplate and actually embark on the project of quarrying and shifting a limestone block weighing fifteen hundred tons for the temple of Jupiter at Baalbek —but entire cities were laid out and completed.[299]

Bold ingenuity ensured the success of Eupalinos' tunnel cutting in Samos during the sixth century, with little or no precedent to guide him in Greece itself, as far as we know, and only the simplest of surveying instruments by which to achieve the meeting of the two halves of the tunnel underground and the slope from north to south necessary to ensure the flow of water through it.[300] Various waterworks on a large scale were undertaken in antiquity —the draining of Lake Copais in Boeotia by one of Alexander's engineers;[301] the wide extension of drainage and irrigation works in Ptolemaic Egypt (especially of Lake Fayum, the area around which became a very productive district);[302] and the draining of the Fucine lake, an integral part of the Claudian scheme for the lower Tiber region, which necessitated the construction of a tunnel 5½ km. long descending from a height of 600 m. to sea level, with 42 shafts (for earth removal) ranging from 17 to 122 m. in depth.[303]

Mechanical inventions attracted considerable enthusiasm on the engineers' part, and investment on the part of the patron—when it was a question of military machines; catapults and mobile siege-towers were constructed on larger and more efficient lines, and the attention devoted to them gave rise to a whole body of mechanical theory, as well as to some limited application in ordinary life of the principle of gearing a small power in such a way that it could move a mass many times its own weight.[304] Various water-lifting devices came into use—the screw, the waterwheel, the pneumatic or vacuum pump—and eventually water power was geared to millstones for grinding corn.[305] There are many other examples of mechanical ingenuity in antiquity, such as the starting-gate for horse races (traces of which have been excavated in the Isthmian sanctuary near Corinth, and for the 'invention' of which at Olympia the sculptor Kleoitas claimed the credit);[306] the klepsydra or water clock which limited speakers' time in the Athenian Assembly;[307] the kleroterion, which selected the tribe which was to preside in the Athenian Council during a prytany;[308] mechanisms such as the automatic astronomical calculator (Pl. 57) of the first century BC, with its intricate system of small gears—by no means rare, and as fine in its way as the clocks of western Europe—and clever toys such as singing birds and water organs.[309]

The technological ability of the ancient craftsman was diverse; he could answer complicated problems with quite simple means. But there seem to have been serious shortcomings in his technological awareness.[310] For example, the Athenian silver refiners only managed to extract about seventy per cent of the silver from its ore; indeed, in no respect did ancient metallurgy advance much beyond the limits already reached during the early Iron

Age.[311] If water power was applied to the waterwheel and the mill, wind power remained the province of the sailing boat alone; the windmill did not occur to anyone until well into the Middle Ages, and the ability to sail into the wind was first mastered by the Arabs.

If wonders were achieved in siege-engines, and if (somehow or other) great weights could be lifted to considerable heights during monumental building, no attempt was made to apply this mechanical ingenuity to the problems of production in mine or workshop. The resources of power, human and animal, were exploited in a very limited way. The treadmill principle was understood and used; but other labour-saving devices, apart from water-driven grindstones and water-lifting arrangements, were not developed. Although experiments were made in the transport of heavy loads, animal harness remained suitable only for cattle; the yoke, which was universally used, did not allow horses and their kind to pull with their whole strength but choked them instead. And when it came to multiplying power to draw a load too heavy for one team of animals to take, the methods used were so inefficient as vastly to reduce the power exerted by each yoke, and necessitated the employment of whole herds of animals at once.[312]

The marked cautiousness of builders' methods meant that although they were willing to build big, they usually built far more massively than necessary, not trusting to the strength of a lighter construction, and so added to the costs of quarrying and transport, apart from anything else; the architects of the Propylaia in Athens, for instance, quite unnecessarily inserted iron strengthening beams into the marble epistyle blocks in one section,[313] and Roman builders used tremendous quantities of material in their supporting walls (*Pls.* 54, 55, 59).

Why, given their undeniable ingenuity, did not the ancient technologists push beyond the confines of what they knew so well? Why, in so many respects, did the ancient world remain, technologically speaking, in much the same state as the Bronze Age cultures of anything up to two or three millennia earlier? This question should first be turned round: why do men make technological advances at all? There has to be a need or a readily recognized use to which the new development can be put; otherwise, however much initiative the craftsman inventor shows, his bright idea may very well be totally irrelevant to the times and society in which he lives. Thus, inventiveness by itself, the capacity to take advantage of a new set of circumstances which present themselves, is ineffectual. What is needed is a receptivity to new possibilities; the patron must also be willing to see the potential of a new development. If Arkwright had lived in fifth-century Athens, Hellenistic Alexandria, or Imperial Rome, he would not have had much impact.[314]

But there was a period when new techniques met the needs of society on many fronts, when the patron's willingness to see the potential of new materials and new designs was at its peak—the period from the late eighth to the sixth century, when the Dark Age ended and, among other things, the Greeks' material culture became more sophisticated. This was the period when, for example, hoplite armour came widely into use, with all its political side-effects; when consciousness of the individual was expressed in poetry, as in gravestones and craftsmen's signatures to their work; when stone architecture and sculpture were taken up after centuries of wood, mud-brick and terracotta meannesses, and the main sources of marble discovered.

Thereafter, new developments were few and far between, or confined to one small aspect of a craft, or to one narrow interest of the patron—as, for example, siege-engines. The inventiveness and receptiveness of the seventh and sixth centuries did not herald an even bigger technological breakthrough, but instead stagnated —because none of the techniques introduced in this period of change actually affected the *basis* of society and the economy, which continued (under changing political institutions to be sure) as an agricultural society with a strongly defined social hierarchy. If in the sixth century the Samian peasant, weaver or cobbler saw a large marble temple where his great-grandfather had only a hut of timbers and mud brick, he might admire, but his way of life was very little altered by the fact.

If no one saw fit to develop steam power for use in workshop or mine, or on the quayside to drive cranes for unloading ships, it was because no one saw the need. If no one invented a widely adopted means of moving heavy loads efficiently, this was because the occasions on which loads heavier than those which a single cart could take were encountered were comparatively rare, being confined to public works and military situations.

An argument frequently offered in explanation of the ancient failure to invent more effectively and to mechanize says that the availability of slave labour obviated the need to find labour-saving devices. A related argument is that slavery depressed the crafts-men's powers of invention, and that men who might have encouraged the exploration of technological improvements disdained to do so because of the banausic, not to say slavish character of industry. To take the first possibility: the abundance of human labour available in the eighteenth and nineteenth centuries did not prevent the mechanization of industry— machine-breaking seemed the only answer to the men displaced by it.[315] As for the second, investment in the crafts, at least to the extent of owning workshops and enjoying the profits, was a feature of city life throughout antiquity; such ownership was *not* confined to the lowly, the poor or the lacking in initiative— but what was lacking was the modern form of the profit motive. The idea of making more money, not by buying more slaves and having more workshops, but by altering the method of produc-tion, simply did not occur to anyone. If there had been no slaves or other labour available the workshop owners would not have mechanized, but simply have suffered a decline in their fortunes. Otherwise, apart from anything else, considerations of style and taste meant that the craftsman was employed to use his inven-tiveness, as we have seen, within narrow limits—and on style, taste, and the innate conservatism of patrons of the crafts the existence of the institution of slavery had no effect, either for good or ill.

As tradition was the essence of the craftsman's life, so con-servatism was the enduring characteristic of the patron's reaction to the things around him. Both looked back to earlier precedents. In colossal architecture and sculpture there was nothing new; the design was the same as before, but bigger. Bound up with the attachment to the familiar and traditional was, surely, the irrational and deep-rooted feeling that it was in some sense dangerous or wrong to interfere with the orderly processes of nature; this unwillingness to 'fly in the face of Providence' is expressed often enough in modern times. The idea that the craftsman had to deal with elements which were somehow beyond mortal ken is most readily apparent in the use of stone for monumental purposes, and especially marble. Working marble presented a considerable technical problem for the mason, enhancing the initial awe he might feel at his own temerity in cutting into a mountain side to reveal the (often) brilliantly white crystalline substance. Success could easily elude him, if the break-line between block and quarry-face were not true, or if he drove his chisel into the surface at too wide an angle, so scoring it too deeply for the error to be eradicated; or a ruinous fault in the stone might be found only after the block had been extensively worked, as in the case of the abandoned figure of Dionysos in Naxos. The waywardness of stone when worked with tools could be seen as a warning from the gods: the people of Cnidus threw down their implements and refused to complete the rock-cut canal which could have strengthened their city against Persian attack, because the rock splintered in their faces—a sign, they argued, that Zeus did not intend the canal to be cut.[316]

A special regard for stone which had been intended for sacred buildings is surely part of the reason for the very prominent position given in the north wall of the Athenian acropolis to a number of half-finished column drums from the older Parthenon burnt by the Persians in 480/79. They served both a useful and a commemorative purpose.[317] There were other blocks which were not cut down later for use, but left lying about on the acropolis, a striking example of which is the column drum to the south-east of the Parthenon (Pl. 63). A particularly irrational reaction to a piece of quarried Pentelic marble is to be seen in the case of the $6\frac{1}{2}$-ton column drum which was brought to Eleusis but subsequently sent back to the quarry—in spite of the fact that the journey took forty yoke of oxen three days each way to complete.[318] If, as seems most probable, the block had been cut to the wrong dimensions, it would surely have been more economical to order another one from the quarry and to cut down this block for use elsewhere in the sanctuary. But the masons' thinking may have been something along these lines: the block had been intended for the portico of the Telesterion, but there was something wrong with it; therefore it must go back to the quarry whence it had come.

Figures of stone were certainly regarded as possessing personality. It was no charming fantasy, nor merely an unfamiliarity with the art of writing, which led sculptors in the early period to sign their works, 'so-and-so made me', or the Naxians to have the inscription on their colossal Apollo speak in its own person 'I am of the same stone, both statue and base'. Other objects of stone were invested with a certain individuality—so the gravestone declared 'I am the marker of the grave of so-and-so', and in Athens, 'I am the boundary stone of the agora'.[319]

The feeling that marble was a peculiar substance was retained and enlarged upon a little in later antiquity. Pliny records two stories, both perhaps begun or at least encouraged by marble masons, illustrating the supernatural qualities of the stone. In the Parian quarries the likeness of a Silenos was found inside a split block;[320] and of the Italian marble quarries it was said that 'the quarrymen assert that the scars (where marble has been cut) in the mountainside fill up of their own accord', a theme echoed in an epigram from the Greek Anthology.[321] According to this, a marble block was brought to Marathon by the Persians, and made into a statue of Nemesis by Pheidias; it is made to speak in its own voice, like any archaic gravestone: 'I am a white stone which the Median sculptor quarried with the masons from the mountains where rocks grew again.' There are other even more amazing accounts of stones among the epigrams—such as the block bewitched by Apollo at Megara, which took to playing the lyre.[322] These literary flights of fancy, remote from reality though they may be, surely had some basis in popular beliefs, masons' included, about the nature of stone.

Evidence for the craftsmen's fear of the supernatural in other materials is very slight, suggesting that this was a negligible factor in the craftsman's thought-world generally.[323] But the use of fire seems to have caused them anxiety which could only be assuaged by resorting to magic. The dangers to the craftsmen personally, as well as the risks their products could run, when they worked with fire, have already been pointed out. If the fire was too hot, or not hot enough, dire things could happen to both the pots in the kiln and the metal in the crucible, or to the object being annealed and worked with tongs and hammer. Even the cleverest craftsman could not be absolutely certain that things would go as they should, so some put up apotropaic signs, usually in the form of grotesque masks, such as can be seen hanging by the kiln in the scene of the potter's workshop (Pl. 17), or in the graffito from Pheidias' workshop at Olympia (Pl. 32).[324] The Potters' Hymn composed at some point between c. 525 and 350 BC in Athens may then be taken at least semi-seriously:[325]

If you will pay me for my song, O potters,
Then come, Athena, and hold your hand above the kiln!
May the cups and cans all turn a goodly black,
May they be well fired, and fetch the price asked. . . .
But if you [potters] turn shameless and deceitful,
Then do I summon ravagers of kilns,
Both Syntrips [smasher] and Smaragos [crasher] and
Asbestos [unquenchable] and Salaktes [shake-to-pieces] and
Omodamos [conqueror of the unbaked], who cause much
trouble for this craft.
Stamp on stoking tunnels and chambers, and may the whole
kiln be thrown into confusion, while the potters loudly wail.
As grinds a horse's jaw so may the kiln grind to powder all the
pots within in.
And if anyone bends over to look into the spyhole, may his
whole face be scorched, so that all may learn to deal justly.

The craftsman's boldness was tempered, probably far more frequently than the surviving evidence indicates, by irrational fear of the incalculable. Particularly when he was using fire, he faced unpredictable forces, and steps must be taken to protect his work as far as possible from their effects. One of the best ways of doing so, apart from cluttering the place up with apotropaic charms, was to continue processing things in 'the way we used to do them', the refrain to which everyone in ancient society, but especially the farmer and the craftsman, was brought up.

CHAPTER IV

CRAFTSMEN AND THEIR
PATRONS

INTERDEPENDENCE

WITHOUT A PATRON, the craftsman was literally and figuratively at a loss. For lack of a buyer of ready-made goods in the shop or market, a private customer placing special orders, or an official board commissioning works on the community's behalf, the craftsman found himself unemployed and unpaid. And if he failed to observe market trends, the tastes and needs of his clientele, then even the cleverest of craftsmen could make no headway; he could never work free of tradition and the inherited preferences. To be lucky in one's patron was all-important to the ambitious craftsman; as Vitruvius rather feelingly remarked, many excellent craftsmen languished in obscurity because they had never chanced upon rich and influential patrons.[326]

A really well-trained man who cared deeply about his work for its own sake might produce objects of excellent quality even when the public for which he was working would have been well satisfied with lower standards; yet it is unlikely in the extreme that he would or could have attempted anything new in the way of size, materials or techniques without encouragement and practical support from a patron. But given the possibility, in the shape of an extravagant and glory-seeking backer, of doing something different or on a larger scale than ever before, the good craftsman was surely willing to pander to such a man's whims.

Conversely, the buyer of cooking pots in the market, the

family ordering a special grave monument, the community desirous of a better water supply could only look to the skilled worker to satisfy their wants, and if he was unavailable they did without. The great man, the tyrant, powerful aristocrat, Hellenistic monarch or Roman emperor, sought out and encouraged the finest craftsmen he could find, to the enhancement of his own reputation, both by the association of his name with great works, and by the portraits he might commission from sculptors, painters, gem-cutters and coiners. Alexander the Great picked out the greatest of the craftsmen in his service and insisted that only they should portray him; Augustus was equally well served in the men who worked for him, as the quality of the portrait on the *aureus* (Pl. 53) suggests, while Commodus was perhaps over-ennobled (Pl. 82).[327]

The problem is to decide just how closely the craftsman had to follow his patron's dictates, and to what extent he could lay down terms, in the matter of design, size, materials and so on. Could the sculptor Paionios have foisted a winged victory onto the Messenians and Naupactians, if they were not already predisposed to approve of such a monument on the grounds that it was extremely fashionable, or, on the contrary, that by its very rarity the Messenians and Naupactians would gain renown for their perspicacity in patronizing a new trend? Given the strength of tradition in the crafts, and in what men expected to see in art, it was rather the case that Paionios could scarcely have produced a monument of any kind which actually offended his patron's taste—just as no temple architect would have broken out by introducing spires or Gothic arches into his design. At no stage did craftsman and patron start with an entirely blank page before them. The only surprise which Paionios' work would have occasioned might have been the superb workmanship with which he created a figure apparently floating down to earth, in the finest draperies yet represented in stone.

Paionios was the expert, who alone knew just what could and could not be done, stylistically and technically, and he may have suggested the subject of the monument the Messenians and Naupactians wished to dedicate; yet even so the men who actually commissioned the work may have expressed opinions which influenced Paionios' final disposition of the figure. Aristotle, of course, asserted that 'the user knows best'; that, for example, the steersman will have a far clearer idea of what constitutes a good rudder than the ship's carpenter.[328] But he vastly underrated the need for the maker to understand the function of the object he was working on if he was to make it properly. It is the craftsman who sees that the knife-handle fits closely into the hand of the user; the potter who knows how to ensure that a jug will pour properly. But obviously there could be and was discussion between user and maker, for it was a matter of practical advantage as well as a question of satisfying the layman's curiosity; a man ordering a bridle and bit for a particularly spirited horse needed to explain his problem precisely if the bit was to do its job. Cicero attempted to argue with his slave architect Cyrus about the windows in a library he was having built; he suggested that they were too narrow, but 'when I spoke to Cyrus he told me that views onto a garden through wide windows were less agreeable— for let the eye be A, the visible objects B and C, and the light-rays D and E . . . you know the rest'.[329] And presumably Cicero had to be content with narrow windows after all.

Nevertheless, if the expert tended to say, 'It can't be done', when his patron suggested new departures, such experiments as were made came about as much as the result of the patron's enthusiasm for the idea as of the craftsman's technological initiative. Naxian and Parian marble masons were perhaps responsible in the first instance for the exploitation of their island's stone; but it seems unlikely that they would have embarked on colossal figures such as the Naxian Apollo on Delos or the *kouroi* found in southern Attica if they had not been encouraged to do so by a patron, who would see them provided for even if the project turned out to be a total failure—like the robed and bearded Dionysos figure already referred to, which had to be abandoned when it had already been shifted a few inches out of the quarry bed, because of a serious fault running through the block (*Pl. 75*).

But who was responsible for the quite (though not entirely) unusual temple of Olympian Zeus built at Akragas? Temples of this size were not unknown—some vast projects had already been undertaken in Ionia, as well as in Sicily itself—but the *telamones*, the giant figures holding up the cornice, were unique in style and scale, and human figures of any kind were rare enough as an architectural feature. The ladies of the Siphnian treasury at Delphi (*c.* 525 B C) and the Maiden's Porch on the south side of the Erechtheion in Athens are quite different in character.[330] The effect at Akragas was surely striking, if not terrifying; it did not attract imitators. This does not necessarily mean, however, that the architects and sculptors employed on the temple acted against their own better judgment in deferring to what we might consider the megalomaniac fantasies of their employer. And of course the building was fundamentally a quite straightforward example of Sicilian Doric. Likewise, one might ask, who made the Pantheon in Rome possible, Agrippa or his architects? For this too was in many ways an unusual structure, filling as yet a rather unusual role in associating the Julian *gens*, Augustus' own family, with the gods, and perhaps suggesting the vault of heaven in its dome (*Pls.* 64, 65).

Craftsman and patron between them could not only use the traditional designs and decorative motifs to produce something aesthetically imposing; they could also exploit them for propaganda purposes, as in the case of the Parthenon. Alexander was portrayed wearing the lion-scalp cap of Heracles; the stone-carved relief became an important instrument of Roman imperial 'historical' record, a prime example of which is Trajan's column portraying the campaign in Dacia and the role of the army in both fighting and engineering its way to victory. The design for this monument can only have emerged from a series of consultations between the emperor or his secretaries and the sculptor in charge.

It is also possible to see a relation between the style of an object and the temper of the times in which it was made, even though the design might have nothing like the same function as a portrait of Alexander or the reliefs and the very structure of the arch of Titus (*Pl.* 66). How is it that a vase, a decorated bronze object, a terracotta figurine or a silver mirror can convey a clear echo of the cultural and intellectual activity of the age in which it was made? The craftsman who made it was a part of the society for which he worked; the good craftsman, partly instinctively, captured the feel of the times in his work, and the greater the craftsman the surer his instinct for such things—just as a great general must be both clever and lucky, blessed with an innate ability to seize the occasion.

The Alcmeonid family took on the responsibility of completing (if not building in its entirety) the sixth-century temple of Apollo at Delphi.[331] The pediment sculptures were done by Antenor towards the end of the century, at about the time that the Alcmeonid Kleisthenes was propounding his reforms for the Athenian constitution. Kleisthenes' main preoccupations were with proper balance in the make-up of society and in the wielding of political power within that society. Was it purely by coincidence or instinct that the style and composition of Antenor's pediment sculptures reflected the intellectual preoccupations of his patrons?[332] Since the *kore* which he made for the potter Nearchos demonstrates a similar grandeur and calm, it seems far more likely that he knew precisely what he was doing, and that the theme of the pediments was worked out quite carefully, perhaps in consultation with Kleisthenes himself, who could not under any circumstances have been blind to the opportunity for advertisement of his ideas, as well as of the extent of Alcmeonid generosity and influence in international affairs, with which the temple in the Panhellenic sanctuary of Delphi provided him.

THE COMMON GROUND BETWEEN THEORISTS AND MANUAL WORKERS

If Antenor was consciously following an ideological line in the design of his pediment, after consultation with his patrons, it is still very much a question whether or not he really understood the underlying philosophical thinking of late sixth-century Ionians such as Anaximander. It has been said of this great sculptor, with so fine a command of his craft, that 'it is absurd to suppose that he had read Anaximander, and that he was directly and consciously under Ionian political influence'.[333] The inference is that, as it would have been expressed in antiquity, the *banausoi* had no share in intellectual activities.[334]

Yet, as we have seen, Cicero found it possible to communicate with his slave architect on equal terms. Common ground between the skilled worker and the intellectual is not hard to find. For familiarity with the craftsman's techniques was a characteristic of the intellectual activity which attained its highest achievements in the cities where the artists and craftsmen produced work of the highest quality, and at the same time subscribed to philosophical and mathematical concepts. This was particularly true of sixth-century Ionia and fifth-century Athens. At Athens, contact among philosophers, politicians and skilled workers is seen at its closest in Pericles' friendship with the astronomer Anaxagoras and the sculptor Pheidias, among others. Socrates is the supreme example of the intellectual bridging the gulf between thinkers and manual workers, in his endless conversations with craftsmen to discover the virtue of each craft; the workshops of Athens, like the barbers', seem to have been the equivalent of the modern bar or club.[335] Xenophon recorded conversations between Socrates and Pistias the armourer, Parrhasias the painter, and Kleitophon the sculptor.[336] We even encounter one of Socrates' craftsman friends in a Platonic dialogue. The craftsman is the sculptor Apollodoros, known as the Madman for his artistic zeal and fierce self-criticism, according to Pliny, and described in the *Symposium* thus:

> You are the same as ever, defaming everybody. Your view is, I take it, that all men alike are miserable, except for Socrates, and your condition is the worst. How you got the nickname of Crazy I don't know, but you are always so, raging against yourself and everybody, apart from Socrates.[337]

Socrates' sympathy with the manual workers may have come not only from his intellectual curiosity but from his having been brought up as a stonemason; if this really was the case, and I see little reason to doubt it, then his was a two-way communication between the philosophers and the craftsmen. That he had a particular liking, not for masons, but for cobblers is suggested both by Plato's frequent use of the cobbler as an illustration of his argument, and by various other anecdotes. According to one such, Alcibiades was reproved by Socrates 'for despising shoemakers'; Plutarch preserves the following rhetorical paradigm: 'I wish I were a shoemaker in ancient Athens, so that Socrates would come to sit beside Pericles and chat with him in my house.'³³⁸ Shoe shops existed close to the agora, and one such, belonging to Simon, has been excavated. Thus the story may very well be true that Socrates and Pericles both frequented the workshop of Simon the shoemaker, who is supposed to have said, 'I admit I am a shoemaker. No one is a better philosopher than Simon the shoemaker, and no one ever will be.'³³⁹

Time and time again the sheer detail of his references to the arts and crafts show by their accuracy that Plato really understood them and was in sympathy with them in a way quite at odds with the detestation apparent in his moral judgments of *banausoi*. Metaphors taken from the crafts came to him as easily as imagery of any other kind: 'I must try, like the shipwright who lays down the keel of a vessel, to build a secure foundation for the vessel of the soul in its voyage through life.'³⁴⁰ Here were men who could achieve a kind of excellence in the absolute supremacy of the command over the raw materials they had to work, to which he, intelligent though he was, could never aspire.

There was in fact much common ground between the philosophers, mathematicians and scientists, and the craftsmen—architects, engineers, painters and sculptors especially. Pythagorean theories of harmony, musical, numerical or geometrical, were of concern to both groups, not only in sixth- and fifth-century Greece but throughout Classical antiquity. The difficulty in the way of the philosophers accepting completely the craftsmen's application of these theories was that the craftsmen had a vocational interest in the subject, and did not study them purely for their own sake.

Plato said 'There are two sorts of arithmetic, "common" and

"philosophic"; the second is better because purer.'[341] Clearly the distinction lies between applied and pure mathematics; nor would any architect, Vitruvius included, have denied that architecture is an applied science, making use of abstracts for its own ends. But in the study of these principles the architect could come very close to the philosopher; Vitruvius quotes many earlier architects who wrote on harmony and proportion, and he himself devotes considerable space to those topics. He also makes a sharp distinction between the practising architect and the philosophic opponents of the arts: 'Those few who have a thorough knowledge of geometry, astronomy, and so on advance beyond the functions of the architect into the realm of pure mathematics, hence they can readily take up positions against those arts because many are the artistic weapons with which they are armed.'[342]

The temple architect was concerned with the ratios of width to height in the various parts and the overall dimensions of the building throughout the development of monumental architecture. A particularly striking instance of the architect's application of mathematical theory to a building would seem to be the treasury of Cyrene, built in the Delphic sanctuary about the middle of the fourth century BC.[343] It could almost be called an interpretation in concrete terms of parts of the Pythagorean theory of numbers; the measurements and proportions of the structure appear to embody complex mathematical relationships —the *cella* was 17 feet square, the ratios 5:7 and 13:20 were present in the overall dimensions, some elements in the façade above the colonnade contained the ratios 3:4:3, and relations of 7, 8, 9, 10 and 11 were present in the *pronaos*, while fractions, doubles and squares of these numbers were incorporated in measurements elsewhere. The column contained the most interesting proportions; one of the fundamental harmonies in Greek architecture was that between the lower diameter of the column and its height, which in this case was 30 inches by 208 inches. At first sight there is no significant connection, such as $30:210=1:7$; but with the aid of a slide-rule, which the fourth-century architect did not have, the importance of the ratio becomes apparent, for 2·08 is the cube root of 9, while 3 is the square root.

The architect chose to quote the square root in the lower diameter, which of course determined the area of the column, and the cube root in the height, which determined its volume. The inference of these and other mathematical points of interest is that, whatever means he used to calculate, the architect could pass from abstract to solid geometry with great ease; it is not inconceivable that his stonemasons also had some idea of what was going on.

Who the architect was, we do not know for sure.[344] He may perhaps be identified with the Cyrenean Euphranor, who is known to have been an official representative at the Delphic sanctuary, with the Euphranor known for his interest in Pythagorean theory, and also perhaps with the Euphranor who wrote on harmony. Cyrene was the home of the mathematician Theodoros, a friend of Socrates who took an interest in cube roots and studied the power of numbers up to 17, where he stopped. Although Euphranor would have been far too young to know Theodorus himself, he could well have been taught by pupils of Theodoros; certainly Theodoros' particular concerns in mathematics appear to be just those demonstrated in the treasury.

Similar preoccupations are declared in the inscriptions set up by the architect Nikodemos—called for short Nikon—at Pergamon during the second century AD. Dedicating a new construction with an inscription beginning 'Nikon erected this commonshall for the benefit of the skilled craftsmen and to perpetuate his own memory', he then proceeds to remind subsequent users of the hall that solid and plane geometry, while intimately related in theory, underlie at once all intellectual apprehension and practical concern with the real world and visible cosmos—all of which geometrical-philosophical considerations he evidently thought should be impressed upon the minds of the skilled workers who were to use and frequent the new foundation.[345]

The development of the theory of harmony had great relevance for sculpture, particularly in the sixth, fifth and fourth centuries BC, when sculptors were primarily concerned with the ideal proportions of the human form. The tradition of sculptural theory only goes back to the sculptor Pythagoras of Rhegion, who worked in the early fifth century, but the interest in harmony must have existed earlier, even if it was not yet expressed in formal terms; Pythagoras was 'seemingly the first to put together the principles of harmony and proportion', and won a competition in which Myron of Athens took part.[346] Now Myron was said to be even more concerned for symmetry in his work than Polykleitos of Argos, whose theory of harmony in sculpture remained famous throughout antiquity; the fifth century thus appears to have seen the absolute high-water mark in the study of proportion.[347] An interesting cross-current, this time between the arts and literature, touched Aeschylus' *Oresteia*, in the scene where Elektra compares with her own, and recognizes, her brother's footprint; her manner of expression suggests that Aeschylus was acquainted with the sculptors' theories of harmony—Orestes is described as *symmetros*, that is, of the same proportions, as his sister.[348]

Polykleitos' *Kanon*, the written work on harmony, the principles of which he embodied in his sculptures, both reflected and influenced Pythagorean philosophy.[349] It is not surprising to find a descendant of his, the second Polykleitos, sculptor and architect, building complex monuments incorporating circles and arcs of circles in a variety of relationships one to another, in the theatre and *tholos* at Epidauros.[350]

Other sculptor theorists are known from the later fourth century, remembered and quoted well after their time, but the application of theories of proportion was very much modified in Hellenistic and Roman sculpture. In painting, attempts to show depth by foreshortening were already being made in the late sixth century BC; the pursuit of the problem of suggesting a third dimension in a two-dimensional composition continued throughout the Roman period too, in relief sculptures as well as in wall-paintings and theatrical scenery.[351] The secret of perspective was never consciously discovered. But the science of optics was studied, and began, according to Vitruvius, with the scene-painter Agatharchos of Samos in fifth-century Athens. Vitruvius says that his work inspired both Anaxagoras and the atomist philosopher Demokritos to write on the same topic, to show how, if a fixed centre is taken for the outward glance of the eyes and the projection of the radii, we must follow these lines in accordance with a natural law, such that from an uncertain object uncertain images may give the appearance of buildings in the scenery, and how what is figured on vertical and plane surfaces can seem to recede in one part and project in another.[352]

Euclid's Fourth Definition was concerned with optics. Whether or not Vitruvius is correct, it is likely that there was communication still, in the later fourth century and thereafter, between theorists and practicians of optical illusions. The poet Lucretius, too, may well have had some painting in mind when he referred to the perspective of a colonnade seen from one end, and the apparent diminution of the columns towards the other end, although they were in fact all of the same height; or perhaps he was thinking of some theoretical discussion of the painter's difficulties.[353]

Engineering also demonstrates very clearly the link between mathematical theory and practical application. The first theorists in the field of mechanics appear to have been Straton, a member of the Aristotelian school, and the practising mechanic Ktesibios of Alexander, both of the early third century BC. The greatest of all, practitioners and theorists alike, was Archimedes of Syracuse; yet, despite his brilliance as an engineer, he preferred mathematical theory and left only one work on mechanics. Thereafter the writers on mechanics tended to be theorists; but as military engineering and the problems of monumental building continued to exercise the artillerymen and the architects, so mathematicians continued to take some note of the subject; witness the various handbooks on mechanics of the later Hellenistic and Roman periods, and their Arabic successors.[354]

Between philosophers and some craftsmen there were points of contact at the highest intellectual levels. But what of the attitude of the man in the street, who was not a philosopher? Of the simple craftsman who really only understood cooking pots, ropes or fishing tackle? The popular opinion of the New

Philosophy current in Athens is nicely expressed in Aristophanes' comedies: in the *Birds*, Meton, the astronomer and geometer, is satirized for showing off just such a mixture of theory and practice as was employed by the philosopher and town-planner Hippodamos of Miletos, the architect and mathematician Euphranor, or the engineer and theorist Archimedes. Meton announces that he has come to measure out the airy acres of the birds' Cloudcuckooland:

> With the straight rod I measure out, so that the circle may be squared; and in the centre a market-place, and streets leading to it straight to the very centre, just as straight rays of light flash out from a star, even though it is circular.

To this clever-sounding nonsense someone replies, 'Get out of here . . . they've all resolved to wallop every quack'.[355] The audience which laughed at this also laughed at Aristophanes' *Clouds*, which ends with Socrates' thinking-shop being burnt down, proprietor and all. Theory was unnecessary and even dangerous; the craftsman who knew his job needed experience and a true eye to do it properly, not the rules of geometry or an ethical system.

THE WAGES OF CRAFTSMANSHIP

Without patronage the craftsman starved. But how was the value of his work expressed in realistic economic terms? How much, over and above the cost of the materials involved and the minimum necessary to keep him and his family alive, could the craftsman expect in return for the exercise of his skill? The Roman jurists enjoyed playing games with such problems as who owned a painting while it was actually being done, the painter or the man who had commissioned it, and who would own it in the end. If the patron had provided the raw material for a piece of gold or silver plate, what proportion of the finished article could be said to belong to the smith? In the first instance, it depended on whether the object was being sold to the patron, or whether the patron was hiring the labour of the artist; and in the second, the value one placed on the craftsman's handiwork.[356] As for the problem of how much the making of the object increased the value of the raw materials used, the Roman lawyers at least took a very prosaic view, illustrated in the following pronouncement from the *Digest*:

> If a vase was made of stolen silver, then the value of making it must be added to the amount of the theft; just as if a child were stolen and grew up, one would have to judge the stolen object as an adolescent, not a little child any more.[357]

This perhaps means nothing more than that the craftsman's time and labour expended in manufacturing the object must be compensated; in any case it does not help in deciding whether someone like Pheidias or Praxiteles was always paid so much more than a skilled stonemason or blacksmith for the work he put in, because of the greater degree of fine craftsmanship involved as opposed to brute strength or mere competence in the craft. The fragmentary accounts for the statues of Athena Promachos and Athena Parthenos give no hint of what Pheidias himself was paid; the Parthenon accounts, on the other hand, suggest that the pediment sculptors earned during the year little more than stonemasons and carpenters, and only twice as much as the official salary paid to architects, or the allowance given to soldiers in the field.

In fourth-century Epidauros it seems that fine craftsmanship did gain economic recognition. Thrasymedes, the Parian sculptor of the gold and ivory statue of Asklepios, also took up the contract to decorate the interior of the temple where his statue would stand. His was the largest contract price of any for the temple, three times the cost of building the whole of the outer colonnade, for example;[358] the materials—ivory and fine woods—were all provided by somebody else, even the glue required for the inlay work, so that even if he employed several assistants, it still looks as though Thrasymedes' profits would have been considerable. The architect, Theodotos, only received 1 drachma per day.[359] Zeuxis is supposed to have remarked on the *priceless-ness* of his works, while Apelles received a fee of twenty talents for a painting in gold of Alexander at Ephesos—seemingly a fantastic sum, even assuming he had to supply the gold himself;[360] Apelles is also said to have helped his fellow-artist Protogenes of Rhodes by forcing up the price of Protogenes' paintings, but by how much and with what precise effect on the Rhodian art market we are not told.[361] The painter Pamphilos took pupils for a twelve-year course at 1 talent each, which came to 500 dr. a year for each pupil; if he could teach three or four at once, then he was not doing badly, even allowing for the cost of bed and board for the students.[362] What Lysippos received for each of his sculptures is not reported, but his savings from the fifteen hundred works of art he is said to have produced were reputed to amount to 1,500 gold staters.[363]

Prices paid by Roman art collectors perhaps included decent profits for the artists themselves, but here again it is difficult to know exactly what the price covered—labour costs only, or the materials as well? How much did the silversmith Mentor take for himself of the 100,000 sesterces paid by Lucius Crassus for two engraved cups? And what was the personal gain of the sculptor Arkesilaos from the fee of 1,000,000 sesterces which Lucullus paid him to make a statue?[364] Even if a clever sculptor could con his patron into paying him vast sums, he could not depend on a high income regularly. Large rewards hung on the caprice of rich men; and from public works the craftsman could look for little more than a working wage.

The vast majority of even the owners of workshops, who were both skilled workers and businessmen, did not rise very high in society, and lived simply. The question is, how simply? What did they earn on average, and how did their income compare with the earnings of other sections of society? The state of the evidence makes it virtually impossible to say even what a single individual's earnings were over a period of any length. But there is no question of the craftsman's economic status changing drastically for better or worse, from one end to the other of Classical antiquity.

If the architect Theodotos only received 1 dr. a day, and if this were his sole income, then he would have been unable to afford gold embroidery on his clothes, as was reported of the painter Zeuxis.[365] Was there then an economic hierarchy of craftsmanship based on a scale of skills, in which architects always stood well below the painters, and were paid correspondingly less?

The whole subject poses a series of interrelated problems, none of which can be answered precisely. Greek and Roman prices and wages are not amenable to definitive discussion because the evidence is inadequate. To begin with, we require some idea of what a basic wage may have been at any given time. Some day-wages are known, but in rather special contexts, which present their own difficulties. It is by no means certain how typical Theodotos' 1 dr. day-wage was of craftsmen's wages, either in Epidauros or in the Greek world as a whole at that period, c. 370 BC. 'Standard' day-wages of this kind were not real wages, calculated according to observation of the current costs of living or market trends, but what we might call 'conventional' day-wages, approximating in only a very general way to day-to-day expenses. That prices fluctuated, and fluctuated frequently, especially prices of staples like wheat, barley, olive oil, wine, slaves, metals, is abundantly clear; some price variations, as of corn, for example, are easily explained by bad weather and so on. But we can never know exactly why the prices of two contracts, both of them for quarrying and transporting the same kind of stone over the same distance, from the Corinthian quarries to the sanctuary of Asklepios at Epidauros, differed one from the other by about 7 dr. per cubic metre, within perhaps as little as two or three months of one another.[366]

For what it is, and was, worth, Theodotos' pay of 1 dr. a day appears to correspond to the accepted 'standard' day-wage paid in late fifth-century Athens. Hoplites in the field received 2 dr. for themselves and a servant; the secretaries of state commissions got 5 obols a day; and architects, carpenters, joiners, sawyers and builders of scaffolding employed on the Erechtheion were paid 5 obols-1 dr. In 410, Athenian state maintenance for the indigent was fixed at 2 obols a day, so that 1 dr. should have covered the cost of a man's daily keep and have left something over for dependants, housing, clothing and other necessities.[367] But our evidence for day-wages comes entirely from state concerns; there is nothing to tell us what craftsmen who were working on their own for private patrons earned in a day or a year. Even supposing many of the stories of high prices paid to Greek and Roman sculptors and painters were anywhere near true, we would still have no idea what any of them earned *on average*. Many craftsmen were paid on a piece rate, so that their earnings would be higher or lower depending on their speed of work; others agreed on a price for their work under contract, and though we may know what the job was, there is never any clear indication of how long they took to complete it, or of how many assistants they employed. Moonlighting may not have been unknown; it was perhaps not infrequently one of the reasons for the heavy fines for delay recorded in some building accounts, along with the insistence in the contract regulations that work be completed within a fixed time.[368] Of the six groups of masons who fluted the six columns on the east front of the Erechtheion, those including citizen masons were paid for one prytany (the 36–37 day period in the Athenian civil calendar) less than the metic and slave masons' groups, 22–23 dr. as compared with 30 dr. and more.[369] The inference is not necessarily that the citizen workers could live more cheaply than the others, but that they supplemented this pay with other work, preferring to spread out their work on the Erechtheion over a longer period than the others. Nor were they necessarily earning more altogether than the others who put in their main working day on the Erechtheion.

What sort of prices might a skilled worker have had to pay, out of an income of at least 300 dr. a year (if we reckon for the moment on a day-wage of at least 1 dr. a day over a working period of about 300 days in the year)? The only evidence for prices of household commodities at this period are the public sales lists of property confiscated from Alcibiades and other affluent members of Athenian society for alleged impiety in 415. These do not show true market prices, but they are worth quoting if only because they are actual prices paid for identifiable goods in the very same period when we know that skilled workers could earn 1 dr. a day and more.[370]

Wheat seems to have cost $6\frac{1}{2}$ dr. a measure; seven measures, it is reckoned, were enough to last a man a year, so that the yearly cost per man, wife and children might have come to 90–100 dr. This would have been the biggest item on the food bill.

As for other commodities, cattle went for 50–70 dr. a beast, and goats for about 10 dr.; what the price of butchered meat was, we do not know, but it was always a rare item in the daily diet of ordinary men. Household furniture, of presumably far better quality than the workers would have used, cost as follows: chairs—2 dr.; tables—4 dr.; beds—6 or 8 dr.; but it is not clear if they were plain or richly decorated, and there are no other contemporary prices with which to make comparison.

Slave prices are not necessarily any more realistic than the rest. A skilled Carian goldsmith was sold for 360 dr.; what was probably an untrained child for 50 dr. Even this would have been quite an outlay for a craftsman dependent entirely on his earnings and with no capital behind him, for a young slave assistant might turn out ineducable or susceptible to the first epidemic.

Agricultural and workshop tools are listed, but no prices survive. Accounts from Eleusis for the year 329 show that drills, picks, and borers each cost what was at that period a day-wage (2–$2\frac{1}{2}$ dr.) and this was probably what they had cost a hundred years earlier.

Large storage jars with a capacity of 250 gallons or more, for instance, of the kind only necessary in really big households, cost from 30 to 50 dr.; small pots could be picked up for an obol or two, however, and Panathenaic amphorae were allowed to go at about $2\frac{1}{2}$ ob. each. Baskets cost more; a large basket suitable for the storage of dry goods—wool, flax or even grain—went for $3\frac{1}{2}$ dr., six or seven times the price of a painted Panathenaic vase.

Little more than this can be said of the probably cost of living for a skilled worker at Athens in the late fifth century. Food for some may have been supplemented, in the case of citizen craftsmen, by a share of the vegetables from the ancestral farm or kitchen garden; and even metics may have rented an allotment and worked it in their spare time. Housing costs constitute another unknown; they need not have been very high, for again some citizen workers might have been able to live on the edges or in the cellar of a relation's house, rent-free; or, if they were obliged to rent, then it is clear that many workers made do with one room as workshop and living space combined, while others lived in modest houses of which the workshop was part.[371] Standards of living were low for the majority of the population. Or, to put it another way, a man could exist quite tolerably with very little.

There were some craftsmen who lived well above the level of life suggested here, those known to have come of good families, and to have had private means.[372] Architects and engineers who were hired for fixed periods by city-states and sanctuaries at a fixed day-wage need not always have depended on their earnings from the state alone, because they might either work at something else at the same time, or be able to fall back on inherited wealth.[373] Be that as it may, what did the architect's day-wage really represent? I have suggested that it was a conventional payment, not closely related to market conditions, a monetary acknowledgment of services rendered which was not necessarily calculated according to real costs or in comparison with the wages of other kinds of craftsmen, even of other architects. Nevertheless, marked differences in the pay given to the official sanctuary architects appear in the accounts for work in fourth-century Delphi and third-century Delos; it is possible therefore that variations in professional competence were closely gauged, and related to the day-wage paid to each individual.[374]

At Delphi in 345 BC, Agathon received 2 dr. a day, and Kallinos, termed 'under-architect'—an apprentice, perhaps—one-third of this, or 4 ob. So Xenodoros received $\frac{1}{2}$ dr. in 356, but by 345 he was considered deserving of 2 dr. 2 ob. (yet in 344 he only got 2 dr.—there is no obvious explanation for this decrease). The Delian accounts show less rationality in the different rates paid to the architects; some received 4 dr. and others 2 dr., while yet others were fobbed off with a mere $1\frac{1}{2}$ dr., all within the same few years. It may be that the size of some architects' reputations affected the size of their pay-packets, but perhaps the whole matter was decided by considerations quite other than those of economic rationalism. The architect's pay may often, as suggested above, have been an honorarium, not part of a living wage; and architectural services to city or sanctuary may have been considered by some a public duty rather than a means of earning a living. Hence the payment would be based not on established professional or union rates, but on what the administration thought suitable and the architect acceptable. In some cases this would have been 4 dr., in others 2 dr., with no hard feelings on anyone's part. Whether the same motives prompted architects under the Roman Empire to accept mere token payments or not is not ascertainable. Probably those employed in the imperial service were retained on a strictly business basis, but it may sometimes have been the case that architects called in to build by the government of their home town, especially when the cities of the empire were rivalling each other in civic glories, provided their services free or at low cost.

It is particularly difficult to estimate what sculptors earned. The literary evidence is, as we have seen, not very enlightening, and other kinds of evidence defy precise analysis. For example, on one hand the poet Simonides says that Arkesilaos was paid 200 dr. for a statue of Artemis which he made for the Parians, in the early fifth century BC—but of what size, materials, and degree of detail?[375] On the other hand, the Epidaurian building accounts show that Hektoridas and another sculptor whose name is half-obliterated each received 3,010 dr. for the pediment sculptures.[376] We cannot be sure, but they may have taken anything up to a year over the job, perhaps far less, and possibly employed three or four assistants, perhaps more and perhaps less; they and their helpers might have made anything up to 600 dr. each from the commission.[377] But it may be that the sculptors had to supply their own Pentelic marble, in which case their expenses would have been higher, and their clear profit considerably smaller, if they did not actually lose on the transaction.[378] As for Pheidias' profits from his colossal gold and ivory statues at Olympia and Athens, all we know is the story of how he was accused of embezzling the gold (or, according to some versions, the ivory) from the statue of Athena Parthenos (Pl. 79).[379]

The Roman evidence offers little on artists' and craftsmen's earning powers. It merely confirms the general impression that no skilled work of any kind, apart from the metalworkers', was consistently well paid. This is not to say that some individuals did not make a very good thing out of their craftsmanship, or that some patrons, especially members of the imperial house, did not pay well for good work. But not until the beginning of the fourth century AD is there any good basis for assessing the earning and buying powers of skilled workers. Even then we have to depend not on actual working records, but on a governmental decree which went out of date almost as soon as it had been published.[380] Diocletian's edict of AD 301 attempted to fix a maximum for prices and wages, after decades of tremendous inflation; it is something at least to be able to see what the state thought were realistic payments for services, and what skilled workers were expected to pay for food, clothing and their children's education (assuming that they could rise to such a luxury).

The day-wages were reckoned in addition to maintenance (board, but not bed). Lowest in the scale came shepherds' and farm labourers', at 20–25 *denarii* a day. A good linen-weaver was to get 40 den.; stonemasons, cabinetmakers, carpenters, lime-burners, mosaic workers, wagon wrights, blacksmiths, and ship-wrights who built river-going vessels—50 den.; workers of marble floors, wall-mosaic artists, shipwrights of sea-going vessels—60 den.; wall-painters and plaster modelmakers—75 den.; and figure-painters—150 den. Other payments are reckoned on piece rates, so that it is impossible to discern the average earnings of an armour polisher, who was paid 100 den. per scabbard or a top-ranking goldsmith who received 2,400 den. for each ounce of gold worked. As for the cost of living according to the edict, a man with 50 den. a day to spare over and above his own keep could buy, with that day's payment, a half-measure of wheat, enough for three weeks or more; or nearly a whole measure of barley; a quarter-measure of rice; or one-third of a pint of best olive oil; or two pints of good wine; or twelve pints of Gallic beer; or twenty-five gallons of Egyptian beer; or 4 lb. of pork; or 1½ lb. of pork sausage; or one-fifth of a fattened pheasant;

or a pair of chickens; or a dozen dormice; or fifty oysters; or twenty-five artichokes; or fifty eggs, or 6 lb. of cream cheese.

If he wanted a pair of workman's boots, he must give up two and a half days' pay; a pair of woman's shoes—one day's pay; a soldier's cloak of the best quality—eighty days' pay; a shirt, twelve days'; and a commoner's or slave's loin-cloth, from four to eight. If he wanted his son to learn Greek and Latin literature and geometry, he must give up four days' pay a month.

The list of day-wages indicates a certain hierarchy of skilled work as the state presumed it to be in the early fourth century. The scale of charges for teaching various subjects reflects much the same view of the matter; a teacher of gymnastics was to receive 50 den. a month for each pupil; of arithmetic or shorthand, 75 den.; of architecture, 100 den.; of Greek and Latin literature, or geometry, 200 den.; and of rhetoric, 250 den. Architecture still ranked well below literature and pure mathematics.

Skilled workers could not, as a matter of course, nor by virtue of their scarcity, utility or any other characteristic, command large salaries. If there was any work to be done, then they need not starve; a lack of employment in one place would drive them to seek it elsewhere. The painter Protogenes was said to have fed himself on soaked pulses while at work on one project, not because he was especially hard up but because 'he could thus both stay his hunger and thirst, and at the same time avoid blunting his sensibilities by too luxurious a diet'.[381] Whether or not Zeuxis owned more than one garment embroidered with gold thread it would be hard to say. He need only have indulged in such an extravagance once, as the result of one particularly large commission, and the fame of the gold thread would have lasted the rest of his life.

STATE INTERVENTION

There are various ways in which the state could have affected the craftsman at work. It occasionally passed sumptuary laws, setting limits to the amount that should be spent on luxuries; it sometimes legislated on working methods, and imposed taxes on the

46 The grave stele of the freedman Demetrius and his son Philonicus. Demetrius appears to have been a die-sinker for the mint official P. Licinius Stolo (whose freedman he was), while his son held the office of lictor. Rome, late first century BC

47, 48 *Above*, a terracotta plaque from the grave of a mint employee at Alexandria, showing his tools. On the relief, *right*, a coin-striker (*malleator*) is seen in action, supervised by a mint official

49, 50 Obverse and reverse of a late sixth-century silver tetradrachm of Athens showing the head of Athena and her owl

51, 52 A silver tetradrachm of Syracuse, late fifth century BC. The obverse, a charioteer, is signed 'EYO', and the reverse, the hand of Arethusa, 'EYMENOY.'

53 A very fine portrait of the emperor on a gold *aureus* of Augustus.

54, 55 Mechanical lifting devices. *Right*, a detail of the sarcophagus of the Haterii showing slaves working a treadmill to raise a sepulchral column by crane. *Below*, a modern solution to the problem of hoisting marble blocks, in use on the Athenian acropolis; it owes much to ancient methods.

56 The first-century AD grave stele of C. Vedennius Moderatus, a Roman military architect specializing in catapults, one of which is shown here, head-on.

57 An automatic calculator for taking bearings at sea, first century BC

58,59 The Hephaisteion seen from the west with the acropolis behind, and, *below*, Athena directing the building of the acropolis

60 Carefully joined and clamped foundation courses beneath the pavement of the temple of Apollo, Delphi

61 The Erechtheion seen from the east. Most of the accounts for the fluting of these columns survive. Late fifth century BC

63 An early fifth-century Pentelic marble column drum on the Athenian acropolis. Dressing of the lower edge has been completed, while the remainder of the drum was to have been finished off in the final stages of construction.

62 A section of the interior of the *tholos* from the sanctuary of Asklepios at Epidauros, mid-fourth century BC. Notice the complexity of its design and the comparatively unusual use of black and white stone.

64, 65 The Pantheon, originally built by M. Vipsanius Agrippa to the greater glory of the Julian *gens*, and restored in the second century AD. *Below*, part of the interior of the dome

66, 67 The arch of
Titus at the
entrance to the
Roman forum, AD 70.
Left, Trajan's
forum and column,
early second
century AD

craftsman's products; as his employer for public works, it could set the terms of the contract under which he worked; and it might take an active interest in the availability or otherwise of the skilled worker, encouraging his presence by the grant of privileges, or preventing his absence by restricting his freedom of movement. What the state did not do in so many words was to control the craftsman's work by laws of censorship; neither public nor private morals were seen to require the protection of the law as far as the visual arts were concerned.

Sumptuary laws were framed with economy as the chief concern, but they also reflected the moralists' anxiety about the social good. Excessive show of wealth was corrupt and corrupting, whether in personal adornment or offerings to the gods, temples or funeral monuments. Plato's seemingly very severe limitations which he set up at the end of the *Laws* were not altogether an exaggeration of the kind of law actually put on the books. For grave monuments, he prescribed that 'the mound should be no higher than would be the work of five men in five days; nor shall the stone over it be larger than enough to take four lines of praise of the dead in heroic couplets.'[382] Solon is said to have included in his legislation an ordinance 'abolishing the practice of lacerating the flesh at funerals. The sacrificing of an ox at the grave side was forbidden, together with the burial of more than three changes of clothes with the dead.'[383] There is nothing here which specifically concerns the gravestone, but the later Athenian law-giver, Demetrius of Phalerum, who consciously modelled his legislation on what he thought had been Solon's aims, forbade altogether the setting up of grave reliefs, in 316 BC.[384] By this means he dealt a death-blow to what had been until then a very flourishing arm of the stone-working craft in Athens, which had produced many fine works.

The laws of early Rome also prescribed limits for funerals. The tenth of the Twelve Tables stated that ceremonial and offerings alike must be restricted, to

three veils, one small purple tunic, ten flute players . . . no costly sprinkling of perfume . . . no long garlands . . . no incense boxes. No more than one funeral for each of the dead, and one bier. . . . No gold to be added to the burial (unless it is in the teeth of the dead man). . . .

Attempts were made to limit other kinds of expense, on jewellery, gold and silver plate, and rich fabrics; sumptuary laws of this kind may temporarily have caused setbacks for the gold-smiths, silk-weavers, jewellers, house decorators and furniture makers, but on the whole they were ineffective. Solon limited the ornaments that women should wear, and the amount of luggage that they could take with them. The Roman state tried repeatedly to cut down personal expenses; the *lex Oppia* of 215 BC restricted the amount of jewellery a women might own, and the surplus was gathered in to supplement funds in the war against Hannibal, while dresses of variegated dyes were forbidden; the law was repealed after the war, despite energetic opposition from Cato.[385] Then in 161, when, as is clear from Cato's comments and from the totals given in the sources of the booty coming into Italy, private wealth had increased tremendously, an unsuccessful attempt was made to limit the amount spent on food for ban-quets, and the gold and silver plate to be used at table was not supposed to weigh more than 100 lb.[386] Similar sumptuary laws were passed by Augustus and later emperors, but the hopelessness of the task is clear from Tiberius' cool reception of the Senate's request for sterner legislation:

> What am I to start prohibiting, and cutting down to the standards of old? The size of the country manors? the number of slaves of each nationality? the weight of silver and gold? the marvels in bronze and painting? the indiscriminate dress of men and women? . . . or women's luxury, jewels?[387]

Elsewhere Tiberius is said to have forbidden men to wear silk, and to have prohibited the use of golden tableware except for religious purposes.[388]

The Roman moralists picked on the extravagance and vulgarity of the *nouveaux riches*, but they did not condemn artists for the subject-matter of their works. The nearest that anyone came to censuring the content of a work of art was the comment made on the painter Arellius, who 'was well-thought of but for the fact that he corrupted his art with one shameful practice . . . that of painting goddesses to look like his mistresses'.[389] So Pheidias had been accused of engraving the name of a friend on the thumb of the Athena Parthenos, and also of incorporating a portrait-head of Pericles in its decoration.[390] But this was neither bad art nor pornography; it was impropriety, not to say impiety, pure and simple (*Pls.* 78, 79).

As for control of working methods, the state had some say in how the job was to be done insofar as it was a party to contracts for public works.[391] Once the decision to build had been taken, an official architect was appointed; he was the planner and technical director of the project, advising the building commissioners who in theory were both employers and work-organizers on the state's behalf, but who would not in general have had sufficient understanding of the problems to organize work on their own. The quality of work was kept under constant review, for payments of the contract price could only be made after the architect's inspection and approval; sometimes it was specified in the contract how many men must be employed—'not less than four', according to a Delian record of the early third century —at what speed they should work—'all day and every day'—and exactly what tools and other materials the craftsman must use (apart from the stone, which would generally have been provided under a different contract). A time limit and other penalty clauses were set, the infringement of which would of course have affected the craftsman if he were himself the contractor, and not simply hired for the job by the man who had taken up the contract. In the latter case he was answerable only to his immediate boss, and not to the building commission; in turn, the contractor transmitted to the craftsman only such directions as he thought fit. The state's refusal to honour the contract affected the craftsmen concerned just as closely, if in a rather different way; the few labour disputes we hear of under the Roman Empire all appear to have arisen out of agreements broken by the state.[392]

In time of war the state commandeered skilled labour and supplies, and furthermore took over the direction of essential industries: thus, at Athens, the Assembly decreed in 408 B C that shipwrights should go to Macedon to build ships with timber made available by the king of Macedon, otherwise they would be taken to court; and earlier in the fifth century the Assembly had decreed that no less than forty men should draw ships up from the sea, and no less than twenty down again, while the minimum number to be employed in caulking and pitching hulls, and shifting or fitting sailing gear had been fixed, again by decree.[393] Otherwise, there is little or nothing to be said concerning government intervention in the workshops during the Greek period.

At Rome, a similar concern to ensure supplies in wartime meant that the government put pressure on the workers concerned. In 205 B C, the preparations for what was to be the final campaign against Hannibal, in Africa, necessitated levying contributions from all the allies in Italy: Arretium provided three thousand shields, three thousand helmets, and fifty thousand each of pikes, spears and javelins, with enough axes, shovels, sickles, buckets and handmills to equip forty warships. Thirty new ships were ordered, and 'Scipio in person so relentlessly kept the workmen at their task that forty-five days after the timber had been felled the ships were launched, fully equipped and rigged'.[394] Under the Empire, the state armouries were increasingly severely controlled, and work judged with an extremely critical eye. In peacetime pursuits the state was not particularly ready to interfere; the law on fulling of 220 B C provides the only example—by it the censors sought to protect the public's clothes from cheap and corrosive cleaning substances.[395]

The state did intervene in another way, however, which resembles the ancient governments' approach to trade. Although left entirely to private enterprise, the carrying in and out of goods did provide an opportunity to impose taxes; likewise, the crafts were the objects of the state's active attention for the most part only insofar as they too could be taxed. But it looks as if the practice was unknown in Greece itself. A tax on craftsmanship, whether based on the rate of production, or of a fixed sum to be paid by all craftsmen, is mentioned in the *Economics* attributed to Aristotle; it is listed under satrapic economy, which is to say that it was a feature of the Persian imperial administration.[396] Payments made by craftsmen for the right to exercise their craft are heard of in Hellenistic Egypt, whose economy was in many ways unlike that of the Greek states;[397] under the Roman Empire produce taxes were imposed on many professional groups, and not only the craftsmen. During the second century AD taxes for merchants were remitted at Rome, and imposed on production instead.[398] The *collatio lustralis*, a five-yearly tax levied by Constantine on all who bought or sold or took fees of any kind, fell on craftsmen too; after AD 374 rural craftsmen were exempt, but craftsmen in the towns continued to be liable. This tax, which had to be paid in silver or gold, weighed heavily, an 'intolerable tribute . . . that makes men shudder at the coming of the dread five-yearly collections'. The craftsmen came off worst—'The merchants . . . use the sea to escape, and the sufferers are those whose manual toil scarcely brings them bread. Not even the cobbler escapes. I have often seen them throwing their awls into the air, swearing that these were all they had. But that does not free them from the collectors, who snarl at them and almost bite them.'[399] Extreme measures were taken to get the money to pay the tax-man, even, it is alleged, the selling of children into slavery. Poverty was not peculiar to the workers of the later Roman Empire; continuous pressure from the state, however, was.

In times of national emergency, the state was at pains to direct skilled labour, as at Athens during the Peloponnesian War. The situation during the later Roman Empire could be described as a continuous national emergency, as a result of which not only the industries concerned with military equipment, but every productive occupation, was controlled so that it became hereditary by law, and membership of the relevant *collegium* compulsory. To some extent, these rulings merely confirmed what was already the prevailing practice—the crafts were largely handed on from father to son as a matter of course, and membership of a *collegium* at least had long been customary for many craftsmen, if not

essential to their professional and private life. But now all freedom to change one's occupation was denied; even the right to
move to another part of the country was ruled out, as the following edict makes clear:

> Competent judges shall take on the task of dragging back the
> *collegium* members, and they shall order those who have
> departed to a distance to be dragged back with all their belong-
> ings to their own municipalities. If members of the *collegium*
> depart from their municipalities, they shall be recalled to
> compulsory service of their municipality.[400]

Milder methods of retaining skilled workers in the community
were tried by both Greek cities and the Roman state. They
actively encouraged them to stay put by granting political
privileges of various kinds. Thus the city of Ephesus included
among men honoured with grants of full citizenship the two
Athenian potters, Bakchios and Kittos, for the work they had
done.[401] In the third and second centuries BC, the prosperous
island of Rhodes provided work for many sculptors and bronze
statuaries from other parts of the Greek world, and several of
them were granted civic honours—Phyles of Halikarnassos was
accorded the title of 'benefactor';[402] the versatile artist Boethos of
Chalkedon was made *proxenos*, a title only awarded to men of
good reputation and some influence;[403] and others were given
residents' privileges—Charmolas of Tyre and his son Menodotos,
Ploutarchos of Apamea, Theon of Antioch, Charinos of Laodicea,
and Epicharmos of Soloi, the last three of whom boasted of the
privilege in their signatures, to which they added the phrase 'to
whom *epidamia* was granted'.[404] The architect Epicrates of
Byzantium, who was brought to Olbia to design the city's
defences, received *proxenia* and Olbian citizenship in return.[405]

Honours of this kind were still being granted by the Greek cities
under the Roman Empire—the mosaic worker P. Aelius Harpokration was honoured by the Council and Assembly of
Perinthus;[406] at Cyrene in the second century AD the painter
Loukios Sossios became a councillor, very likely in recognition

of his work as a painter.[407] The comparative rarity of such grants, together with the evidence of the jealousy with which civic distinctions were guarded, even though they had lost most of their active political value, suggests that these were not empty honours.

In the Roman world, the painter M. Plautius Lykon did some paintings for the temple at Ardea, and was given the citizenship of the city.[408] The Roman state itself seems never to have granted honours in this way or for these reasons; but efforts were made during the later Empire, not only to force, but also to encourage craftsmen as a whole to stick to their work, by relieving them of certain public duties. Constantine urged the promotion of architectural studies in the province of Africa by exempting candidates from certain duties and giving them grants; he also granted exemptions to many skilled workers in the cities— architects, doctors, vets, painters, statuaries, marble masons, tessellated pavers, directors of water supply, potters, panelled-ceiling makers, stone cutters, stonemasons, sculptors, mosaicists, gilders, goldsmiths, glassworkers, plumbers, plasterers, silver-smiths, gilders of arms, engravers, coppersmiths, founders, mirror-makers, ivory workers, furriers, carpenters, builders, step-makers, joiners, blacksmiths, purple dyers, carriage makers, and fullers.[409] Mechanics, geometricians and architects 'who observe the divisions and members of all parts', who were skilled in the management of waterworks and could train others, were to be given encouragement. Free-born professors of painting were exempt from the poll tax, and from the trade tax, as long as they were selling only their own products; they were to have no troops billeted on them, need not provide horses for the public service, and could live in what municipality they liked. Their studios could be set up in public places without payment, so long as they used them only for their own painting. Finally, 'they shall not be forced by the judges to make sacred or imperial images or to embellish public works without pay.'[410] By this generous con-cession the law of the later Roman Empire raised the bargaining position of the craftsmen up again to that of the craftsman-contractors of Epidauros or Republican Rome, five hundred or seven hundred years earlier, when there had been no question of the state compelling craftsmen to work on such terms. Yet the whole tone of these passages from the Theodosian Code is far more reminiscent of the Near Eastern autocracies than of the (comparatively) free societies of the Greek cities and Republican Rome, in which the craftsmen had entered voluntarily into agreement with their employers.

CHAPTER V

OUT OF WORKING HOURS

IF THE CRAFTSMAN'S WORKING HOURS were completely given over to the special demands of his craft, this does not mean that his private concerns also diverged widely from those of other men. The craftsmen participated in the life of the community as far as personal inclination and status permitted, not as craftsmen banded against the rest, but as rich men or poor, citizens or non-citizens, according to the alignment of the class structure. This is not to say that professional pride and the wish to stand identified by their profession did not sometimes receive expression too, but merely to suggest that when such sentiments were uttered there was no real sense of separation between the craftsman and the rest of society.

PUBLIC AFFAIRS

Philon of Eleusis, the architect of the mid-fourth century BC who worked on the Telesterion and designed the monumental ships' arsenal in the Piraeus, also took up a trierarchy in about 340.[411] His status as a man of means (which he must have been in order to become trierarch) did not in the least inhibit his devoting himself to architecture; nor did his serious commitment to architecture prevent him, by reason of his association with banausic occupations, from contributing to the defence of the city in a highly respectable manner. Vitruvius, an architect of wide experience and considerable learning, belonged to a worthy Roman citizen family, other members of which held public office.[412] Sostratos of Knidos, the builder of the Pharos lighthouse for Ptolemy II, was honoured at Delphi and in the Delian sanctuary, partly because of his connection with the Hellenistic monarch, no doubt, but also because he was a man of some standing in his own right.[413]

The humbler craftsman had neither wealth and standing of his own nor consequence borrowed from his patrons. His contact with and possible influence on public affairs would in most places and at most times be negligible in the extreme. But in the Greek democracies and in the smaller municipalities of the Roman world, craftsmen of all sorts and conditions could take some part in politics—by joining the urban mob, if in no other way. At Athens during the later fifth century and down to 322 B C (when the democracy was brought to a halt), everyone of citizen birth, however poor, had the right to a voice in public affairs. The citizen craftsmen therefore had all the power that attendance at meetings of the Assembly could give them, with the right to vote on every issue laid before it (from the choice of a temple architect to deciding between peace and war), and the opportunity to help select the most important officers in the state, the ten generals—rights held by the richest aristocrat and the poor but honest bootmaker equally. And since the craftsmen tended to be concentrated in Athens and the Piraeus, the citizens among them very probably did make up a larger proportion of the attendance in the Assembly than they did of the citizen body as a whole; for the peasant farmer, living anything up to twenty or thirty miles away, would have found it difficult to come into town forty times a year. So there is a basis in truth for the sour remarks of Socrates and Plato that the Assembly was packed with banausic riff-raff.

The poorer men in Athens, the citizen craftsman (with a few wealthy exceptions) included, benefited from the coming into being of the democracy. There was obviously a connection between the commercial activity of Athenian society and the breakdown of the old aristocratic monopoly of power in the state, begun by Solon; the same political process went on elsewhere of course, and for much the same reasons, but as in Corinth —a commercial and industrial centre if ever there was one— it did not develop into fullblown democracy as a matter of course. In Athens the Alcmeonid Kleisthenes took the political development much further when in 508 he shifted the political power struggle out of the aristocratic faction-headquarters, and brought it into the open before the Assembly. Nevertheless it is fruitless to seek for support of Kleisthenes' policies among the craftsmen as distinct from any other section of the population inside or still excluded from the Assembly, or for a Workers' Party thereafter which looked for advantages for its members regardless of the rest of the *demos*.[414] In fact neither in Athens nor anywhere else in the ancient world do we hear of any workers' group pressing for revolutionary measures of the kind which might be exploited for the workers' benefit—measures which would have had to involve the total destruction of the old order, the economy and the most deep-rooted prejudices associated with it, the city-state and all political power as it was then understood.

The only risings which can be described as workers' revolts are the so-called slave wars in Sicily of the late second century B C, which were inspired not by the vision of some new social order in which, for one thing, slavery would no longer exist, but by the slaves' sheer detestation of their own enslavement and their desire to be free of their Roman masters.[415] Otherwise, the quarrels between workers and administration, such as occurred in the Ptolemaic quarries or on Roman imperial building projects, arose from alleged breach of contract on the administration's part, or failure to send in the proper equipment, adequate food supplies, or the pay which had been agreed on.[416]

If the craftsmen of Athens, for example, enjoyed a certain professional *esprit de corps*, then there was no question of the citizen craftsmen feeling it so strongly that they wished to have full rights extended to all craftsmen, regardless of their actual status. Workshop alliances and political privileges were two quite separate things. The citizen craftsman was no less jealous of his rights as a citizen than the great landowner or the hoplite farmer. As for emancipating slave craftsmen, the citizen craftsman would only free slave employees when convenient to himself, however much he might respect their work and persons, *not* as a matter of principle, such as 'equal rights for all skilled workers'.

If the citizen craftsman had opportunity to participate in political affairs, this still left a great many metic and slave craftsmen in Athens with no voice in politics, and often enough no interest in the subject either. But even the non-citizen could not avoid knowing something, however little, about the course of public events: for one of the most important things about political life in Athens particularly was being able to talk about it. The workshops were recognized meeting places for discussion, such as the conversations Socrates is supposed to have had in one workshop or another.[417] The remarks bandied about in a lawsuit about 400 BC make the same point: the plaintiff alleged that the defendant's workshop (perhaps a barber's or a cobbler's) was the headquarters of a gang of thugs and layabouts, to which the defendant replied that every workshop in Athens was a meeting place, and that all Athenians were in the habit of frequenting them, especially those near the agora.[418] This, of course, was precisely where Simon the shoemaker met Pericles and Socrates in philosophical debate, so the story goes (*Fig.* III).[419]

If the citizen craftsman could join in electing the highest officers in the state, if he could become a member of the council of Five Hundred (assuming that, still in the fifth century, he had means enough to qualify for hoplite status), was there any hope of his rising further and attracting enough support to gain election as a general himself? The point is worth pursuing if only because during the fifth century, and especially in the second half, there were several men in high office who did have connections of some sort with one or another of the crafts. The problem is to assess the nature of the connection, of which we know only because one of the recognized weapons in Athenian political warfare was to accuse an opponent, especially (perhaps only) if he were a democrat, of being a *banausos* himself, or the son of one. So the playwright and general Sophocles was variously described as the son of a carpenter, a smith, or a knife-maker; the statesman Kephalos as the son of a potter (and a potter Kephalos is known from his signatures, but of too early a date to be linked closely with the statesman); Kleon as a tanner; and Kleophon and Anytos, later leaders of the radical democracy, as a lyremaker and a tanner respectively (not to mention Hyperbolos the flask-maker).[420]

The reason for the nature of the insult could have been simply that each of these people merely owned workshops connected with these crafts—which is precisely what one version of the *Life* of Sophocles says; and money gained from the crafts was dirty money in contrast to pure landed wealth. But if this were so, why did not radical democrats use the same weapon against the moderate Nikias, who had political enemies enough, Kleon among them? Why was Nikias never nicknamed the Miner, given the huge investment he had in mine slaves?[421] The difference may lie in the possibility that whereas Nikias left the management of the slaves entirely to an overseer, Kleon and the rest were more closely connected with the running of their workshops, perhaps to the extent of keeping the books and visiting the works occasionally, even if they did not actually dabble in the vats or string a lyre with their own hands. Some support for the suggestion that Kleon and the rest may have been put into their fathers' businesses as managers if nothing more is given by Xenophon's account of the quarrel between Socrates and Anytos, who was one of his accusers at the trial; it concerned the education of Anytos' son, who, said Socrates, should not be put to the tanning business if his father was holding high office in the state. Kleon, Kleophon, Hyperbolos and Anytos were not craftsmen gripping with calloused hands the staff of high office, as it were; but they were perhaps businessmen and townees, in contrast to the landowner Pericles or the great *rentier* Nikias.[422]

They were wealthy men—but the wealth came from others' labours, not their own. If men like these could yet bring down on themselves the cry of '*banausos*' by their purely business interest in crafts, then, however rich a craftsman might become, even his fellow-workers could not in such a society accept him as a leader. The craftsman and the peasant still looked to the better-born for their statesmen; aristocratic ideals died hard.

There was one sphere in which a craftsman could serve the public interest by using his skill, and gain a social or even political consequence otherwise denied to him—by military service. The man whose job was of strategic importance to the state, the stone-mason or carpenter who could build fortifications, the trireme builder too perhaps, surely gained more respect among his neighbours than the potter, the jeweller, or the ladies' slipper maker. The importance, militarily speaking, which attached to masons and carpenters in the Greek city-state army is hard to assess, because citizens were levied campaign by campaign and did not make up a standing army, while mercenary soldiers have left no evidence of their involvement in the military arts and crafts. But the Greek soldier was often called upon to build fortifications in the field, and wall builders were occasionally dispatched by one city to help another in its haste to fortify; sometimes the city so served was pleased to bestow civic honours on the men who came to help.[423] What difference did it not make to a soldier-mason's life if he had been given the citizenship of another city, when he came home again?

Service in the Roman army, on the other hand, especially after Marius' reforms, was a career and a way of life in itself. It provided the status of the Roman soldier, as well as good professional prospects, for builders, engineers, bootmakers, carpenters, masons and smiths, such as would not have been available to them in most towns and villages.[424] The military engineer of course had an important function, and as a result could rise high in the army. C. Vedennius Moderatus of Antium near Rome joined a legion stationed in Germany in AD 60; his precise origins are unknown, but presumably his army career meant that he did far better for himself than he would as a civilian.[425] He eventually became *architectus armamentarius* in the Praetorian Guard, the army's crack corps, and finally transferred to the imperial arsenal at Rome, presumably as a specialist in the construction of catapults, one of which is illustrated on his grave relief (*Pl.* 56). Most of the *architecti* whose epitaphs survive appear to have been military engineers, not civilian builders; and no doubt most of the ships' architects we hear of were connected with the Roman fleet, not with private shipyards. The military man had more to say for himself than the mere civilian.

PRIVATE ASSOCIATIONS

The majority of skilled workers can have been but little touched by public life or public service. Just as men at all levels of society found satisfaction of their religious needs not so much in the state cults and civic festivals as in the performance of private ritual, whether of the household, the clan, the deme or other local division or the cult group of a new divinity, so they sought a less impersonal social context than that offered by the community as a whole. The cult associations of Classical Athens, for example, whose members might be united not only by belief, but by background or even professional concerns—such as the *thiasoi* of the Thracian deity Bendis, metic merchants in Athens from Salamis in Cyprus, and Cypro-Phoenician by nationality, to take an extreme example—are somewhat similar to the far more common and far more formal organizations in the Roman world, the *collegia*.[426]

Satisfaction of the need to belong to some identifiable group in which one could feel directly involved, as distinct from the state, which was too vast and too remote or for many non-citizen craftsmen in particular totally inaccessible and without meaning, could be found in such associations, together with some compensation for the fact that all too often the making of the decisions which decided the fate of the community in which one lived was completely beyond one's control or influence. In the *collegium*, apart from the promise of good dinners at regular intervals and a respectable funeral at one's death, every member had the comfortable assurance that even if the decisions being taken were petty, then at least he had freedom to decide for himself, and did not simply have the result forced upon him.

There seem to have been very few cult associations composed only of craftsmen in the Greek world, compared with the number of 'professional' organizations in Roman society. In an early fourth-century inscription from Cos it is described how a sacrificed animal is to be divided among four groups of specialists each of whom one assumes had some cult significance for the community—doctors, flute-players, potters and smiths.[427] The association of twelve clothes cleaners who made a dedication to Pan, the Nymphs and the river Achelous in fourth-century Athens may not have been a permanent one, and if it was, it seems to have been unusual; the same goes for the eleven mine-workers who dedicated to Herakles in the Laureion district at about the same period.[428]

The Roman *collegium*, craftsmen's, businessmen's, priests' or soldiers', was primarily a cult organization, with strong emphasis on social obligation. The craftsmen's organizations were professional only insofar as the members belonged all to the same or to a closely related craft; their main if not sole function was to serve social and funerary ends—as the epitaph of a military armourer indicates: 'Julius Vitalis, armourer of the 20th legion Valeria Victrix, of 9 years' service, aged 29, a Belgic tribesman, with funeral at the cost of the *collegium* of armourers: he lies here.'[429] And since the workshop dominated so great a part of their lives, it was natural that their workmates should be the people with whom they associated after working hours. The *collegium* did not set out to guarantee fair working conditions and fair wages for its members; nor did the members of the *collegium* take any collective interest in the methods of training apprentices, or in the standards of work of their fellows. No real political influence could be exercised by the craftsmen's associations, their members could not look for the promotion of specifically *workers'* policies, even though a desperate electioneer such as Catiline might seek their support among others'—with the result that the Senate suppressed the *collegia* altogether from this time until the reign of Augustus.[430]

Under the Empire, of course, overt political power was denied to all. The *collegia* could, however, play some part in local politics, although there was no question of their putting up their own candidates; it was simply that collective support for this or that candidate could be far more effective than shouting or writing up slogans on one's own. Thus, in the municipal elections at Pompeii, C. Cuspius Pansa was supported in his bid for the aedileship by various groups including the goldsmiths and the woodmen, not by one *collegium* alone.[431]

Yet the imperial government never felt quite easy about these organizations, for sometimes they were the focus of civil disturbances, and were often suspected of harbouring potentially dangerous enthusiasms which might turn against the central authority. Thus, under Nero a dreadful riot and massacre occurred on the occasion of a gladiatorial contest given by a political malcontent between Pompeii and the neighbouring town of Nuceria in which the *collegia* were apparently involved; they were dissolved for ten years.[432] Trajan was unwilling to allow the construction workers of Nikomedia to form an association to fight fires, precisely because he feared it would foment civil disorders.[433]

But the real 'political' importance of the *collegia* was, as I have already suggested, internal. A man could belong, and by his membership gain an importance in a group outside and larger than his family or the workshop which he would not otherwise have found. The social and office-holding significance of the *collegium* comes over clearly in the constitution of the Roman association of ivory workers and inlayers, dating from the Hadrianic period:

It is ordained that if anyone other than a *negotiator eborarius* or *citrarius* has been elected under false pretences to this *collegium*, the *curatores* or officials responsible shall have their names erased from the association's lists. . . . It is ordained that promptly on January 1st, the same officials shall pay out from the guild's funds fifteen *denarii*. . . . (At some point) a laurel-cake, dates, dried figs and pears should be presented. Eight days from the Kalends of February, there shall be presented for Hadrian's birthday fifteen grants of food, and the guild officers are to lay out bread, wine and warm water here and there for those who have come to dine together. . . . And every year there are to be four *curatores* (selected) from the list (of members) in turn. They shall divide the surplus left in the guild's treasury into equal (parts). . . . On being elected to membership of the *collegium*, each man is to give ten *denarii* to the treasury. . . .[434]

There seems to have been no fixed rule, nor even a well-established custom, as to which crafts went in for associations. The carpenters' and builders' were the most numerous, and among the largest (as far as we can tell), closely followed by the leather-workers', the dyers', and the fullers'. Some crafts seem not to have been represented at all among the *collegia*; there is none devoted to sculptors or painters, for example. And oddly enough, given the perennial usefulness of their work, there were very few metalworkers' *collegia*.

It is also impossible to tell how important membership of a *collegium* was, or how exclusive it was, because we know neither the number of craftsmen altogether in any given community, nor the number who belonged to an association; some were very large, such as the *collegium* of carpenters and builders at Ostia, which may have numbered a thousand or twelve hundred members, most if not all of the carpenters and builders in the town.[435]

Membership may have been somewhat restricted if only by the fact that an entrance fee was usually expected, to help pay for the common meals, the joint dedications and the funerals of fellow-members; further gifts to the association's treasury would bring honours to the giver. Perhaps the poor craftsman, who had little to spare from his daily earnings, was discouraged from joining as a result of this. But *collegia* were not confined without exception to the well-to-do or to the larger cities. Any group of skilled workers might decide to make its working association a formal, social unit as well. A number of slave stonemasons in the quarries at Luna (Carrara) incorporated early in the first century AD, four members being chosen yearly to act in official capacities. Hilarion, one of the officials in the sixth year after the foundation of the *collegium*, appreciated the importance of his office so much that he felt it incumbent on him to publish a list of those who had held office so far—hence our awareness of his and their existence.[436]

Holding office in the *collegium* provided, if nothing else, opportunities to be busy, and (as important) to show one's fellows that this was the case. But how widely the opportunities extended, we do not know; conceivably the holding of office was often monopolized by a small inner group—there is a little evidence of fathers and sons filling the same role. As an official of a *collegium* one was in a sense a man of affairs, and this was worth boasting. The epitaph of Ti. Flavius Hilarion quoted earlier offers proof of this and shows, incidentally, that this particular carpenter was associated with his *collegium* for at least thirty-five years.[437] The carpenter and builder Q. Candidus Benignus of Arles belonged to a *collegium* according to his epitaph;[438] Camillus Polynices, 'by nationality a Lydian, by trade a goldsmith', also belonged to a *collegium* of carpenters and builders, 'among whose members he administered every office', and his son Camillus Paulus followed him in the same trade and the same association.[439]

It was by no means the case, then, that workshop acquaintances were dropped at the workshop door and ignored until the next working day. And although there is something to be said for craftsmen's taking part in public discussion, when and where they had the chance to do so, it is obvious that they spent much if not most of their time in the company of other craftsmen, either in the craft associations or less formally. Evidence for personal relationships is virtually non-existent. We can only assume that a similarity of professional preoccupations would draw some men together; that others would in the nature of things be constantly vibrating with competitive spirit and a dislike of all potential rivals; others again solitary at work and in their private lives too. There is one illustration of the intensity of feeling which could arise in a mid-fourth-century Athenian working-class context, on a lead tablet:

> By the gods of the underworld I curse Aristaichmos the bronze-smith, and Pyrrias the bronzesmith and his work, and both their souls, and Sosias of Lamia, and his work and soul . . . and Hagesion the Boeotian woman. . . .[440]

The fact that craftsmen's workmanship was put under a curse, and that the tablet was found in a smith's shop (house D in the Street of the Marble workers, *Fig.* III) makes it almost certain that the man who laid the curse was a smith too. But the quarrel probably concerned the Boeotian woman, not workshop business.

There is, as far as I know, no other glimpse to be caught of the craftsmen's personal relationships, in the whole of the rest of antiquity. When they speak, as in the records discussed below, it is with formality and forethought.

RELIGIOUS OBSERVANCES AND PERSONAL RECORDS

On the occasions when craftsmen made dedications and had epitaphs inscribed in their memory, they were conforming to established practices. The question is, how closely the craftsmen followed the conventions, and in what respects if any they differed by reason of their specialized activities as craftsmen. Dedicatory inscriptions, statements on stone of who had dedicated what to which divinity, allow us to see something of their authors' religious beliefs, and to make tentative deductions as to their cost, and so to the dedicators' wealth. But the problem then is to establish *how widespread* the practice was of making dedications grand enough to require explanatory statements on stone; the same problem arises in the case of epitaphs, for although it would seem at first consideration that everybody who was anybody in the ancient world and who could afford a gravestone, if not some more monumental memorial, would have had one, it was not necessarily so. Was the man who dedicated the Potter's Stele on the Athenian acropolis (Pl. 19) doing something customary and well suited to his status and occupation? Did P. Longidienus' heirs follow a universal convention when they set up his handsome grave relief (Pl. 9)? The survival rate of dedicatory inscriptions and epitaphs suggests that, at the time of inscribing, they were the exception, not the rule. About three thousand dedications are known from Athens, over a period of perhaps nine hundred years, which represent something like 0·1 per cent of the total citizen population.[441] The proportion of dedicating craftsmen was much more minute. In the Roman world, the proportion of dedicators to non-dedicators was probably not much larger, although at first sight the far greater abundance of epigraphic evidence available suggests the opposite. Epitaphs were more common. But even at Athens, where by far the greatest number has survived out of the entire Greek world, only about eight thousand have turned up, accounting for perhaps 0·25 per cent of the total citizen population over the same period. And of these eight thousand, sixty at most can be associated with craftsmen. Roman epitaphs are considerably more numerous, craftsmen's included.[442] But even so, it remained a mark of some distinction to have a grave inscription. So that the question arises, to what extent these records allow us to generalize about the beliefs and conditions of craftsmen as a whole. Should we go no further than the individual whose record we can read? A few assumptions may be made: one, that if the potter Nearchos could make so fine a dedication as the *korē*, and if other potters are known to have dedicated on the Athenian acropolis at about the same period, then Athenian potters as a whole may be assumed to have been comparatively prosperous, and, given the lack of dedications from other craftsmen, the most successful of all the craftsmen at that time—though not all would have been as rich as Nearchos of course. Another assumption may be made, that making offerings to the gods was fundamental to the religious beliefs of almost all conditions of people throughout antiquity, so that craftsmen of all sorts will have subscribed to the practice, even though we may not be able to distinguish their cheaper offerings from among the accumulated rubbish of the centuries; and therefore those dedications whose intention is stated in the accompanying inscription can be used as indications of the cults to which craftsmen generally subscribed. So that, for example, if the majority of dedicatory inscriptions mentioned Hephaistos, or Vulcan (or Prometheus, or a hero-craftsman), then we could be fairly sure that most craftsmen subscribed to that cult. It seems, however, that craftsmen were by no means so specialized in their religious beliefs.

Among the earliest dedications of marble sculpture, incorporating one of the earliest known personal records in the Greek world and one of the earliest craftsman's signatures, is the piece made by the Naxian sculptor Euthykartides. Dedications known from the late seventh century are rare enough, but as a crafts-man's offering it is the only one of this kind that we know of for some time thereafter. The inference is that Euthykartides was both a sculptor and man of means, whose social status required that he fulfil a religious obligation in an expensive way. But the purpose of Euthykartides' dedication perhaps included the intention which surely prompted other craftsmen to make their offerings—gratitude for the success allowed him in his craft, and supplication for future good fortune. To whom did the craftsmen pray?

If craftsmen acknowledged a divine guidance in their work as opposed to general protection of life then it is in their dedications that they would have admitted the fact. If they had felt a particular regard for one deity as distinct from another, if there were speci-fically craft cults devoted to craft gods, then it is these characters to whom their dedications would have been made. Hephaistos, the lame, limping, ugly smith, was also one of the twelve Olym-pian gods. Prometheus, the fire-bearer who gave technical intelligence to man, was worshipped in Athens together with Hephaistos and Athena; the fire god Vulcan, worshipped in Rome from the earliest period, came to be regarded as Hephaistos' Roman counterpart, a smith-god too; and Athena was frequently associated with the crafts, especially at Athens.

And yet of the surviving craftsmen's dedications not one is devoted to Hephaistos, Prometheus or Vulcan, nor even to Athena in her role of patron of the crafts. On the other hand, the ancient sources suggest that Athenian craftsmen were particularly attached to the cults of Hephaistos in the potter's quarter.[443] Hephaistos himself was widely accepted, and real enough in the popular view to give rise to the story that he had his forge in the volcanic Lipari islands.[444] He was closely associated with the island of Lemnos, where he landed after being flung out of heaven by Hera; here he learnt metalwork.[445] The importance of Hephaistos to the Lemnians is demonstrated in the name of their city—Hephaistia—and in the nature of the yearly ritual, of bringing new fire to the island—for Hephaistos, like Vulcan, was in his earliest form a fire god and later a smith.[446]

But what is the role of Hephaistos in Athens? About the middle of the fifth century, the cult of Hephaistos was graced with a large Doric temple, almost certainly the largest structure devoted to the god anywhere in the Greek world. Before this, he was worshipped in a considerably simpler shrine on the same spot.[447]

The site of the temple occupied an area previously inhabited by potters and bronzesmiths, a fact which certainly lends colour to the idea that potters and smiths were particularly concerned in the cult of Hephaistos.[448] But perhaps the aim of the cult's promoters was not to cheer up the craftsmen, but to demonstrate that the whole community was being revitalized, and that the beneficial forces which worked for the good of society and the continuation of civilized life were present in the city. Hephaistos would then have symbolized not the utility of craftsmanship in particular, or not only that, but the fundamentals of organized society, of which fire, his element, was the first (see the Prometheus legend).

The importance of fire to the maintenance of life was acknowledged at Rome in the cult of Vesta, for one thing, and in the worship of Vulcan primarily as a fire god, for another.[449] The Volcanalia, the festival of Vulcan, appears in the oldest religious calendar of Rome, and a sacred area seems to have been devoted to the god from the earliest historical period. He had no temple; in his precinct were burnt objects which had been struck by lightning (and were therefore rather inauspicious), and arms taken from the enemy in war, a practice still carried on in the second century B C—maleficent weapons were purged by fire of their evil. The only specific reference to Vulcan's working metal comes in the poet Ovid's account of the Tubilustria, the festival concerning the sacred trumpets which were Vulcan's handiwork.[450]

Here again, it seems to be the case that the cult of the fire god related to the welfare of society as a whole, and that any connection with the crafts was incidental or secondary in importance. There is one reference to fire-using craftsmen taking note of Vulcan: it records that as potters removed fired pots from the kiln, they called on the god three times, so as to prevent the pots cracking as they cooled.[451]

Generally speaking, the craftsmen accepted whatever cult was popular in their area. Euthykartides made an offering to Delian Apollo, not because the god had any peculiar significance for sculptors and marble-working, but because the Delian sanctuary was the most important in the Cyclades if not further afield, and under Naxian patronage at the time (625 BC).[452] And although Athena was regarded as the patron of the crafts at Athens, her main role, and the one in which she appears to have been revered by the craftsmen as well as everyone else, was that of guardian of the city. The appearance of Athena in vase-paintings may be the equivalent of an amusing literary reference, perhaps, with little or no real significance for the religious feeling of the potters, vase-painters and statuaries (*Figs.* I, IV).

The religious observances of potters in Corinth were equally conventional. Several small shrines have been found in the Potters' Quarter on the western edge of the city; none, however, can be identified as the cult centre of a deity particularly concerned with clay-working, neither Hera, Aphrodite, nor the demi-goddess Erosa.[453] When Corinthian potters made offerings in the sanctuary of Poseidon at Penteskouphia to the south-west of the city, they also were conforming to prevailing practices; the painted plaques found there were deposited for the most part by merchant adventurers seeking the god's protection for their ships. Among them were several illustrating one or another stage in the manufacture of pottery, and dating to the seventh and early sixth centuries, when the Corinthian pottery industry was most active (*Pl.* 13). They are certainly unusual if not almost unique in the form they take, showing graphic views of labour in the clay pit, of stoking the kiln, and even of the pots as they lie in the kiln; but the purpose of their dedication was exactly the same as that of the other votive offerings, to obtain the god's protection for their pots during the most dangerous part of their making.

There is one group of craftsmen among whom special cult interest may be detected. In general, Apollo had nothing particular to do with quarries or marble, but there survives from Hellenistic Delos one dedication to *Apollon marmarios*—and who else could have made such a dedication but a marble mason?[454] Strabo also remarks on a shrine of Apollo *marmorarios* which was situated close to the marble quarries of Karystos in Euboea.[455] Furthermore, the Ephesian shepherd Pixodarus, who, according to Vitruvius accidentally discovered marble near the city in the sixth century BC at a time when the city authorities were proposing to send all the way to Prokonnesos for material for the temple of Artemis, and who was heroized after having various civic honours bestowed on him in his lifetime, seems to have attracted devotion which lasted down to the fourth century AD —presumably masons', for who else would be in the vicinity of a quarry long enough to take trouble with such a thing?[456]

Dedications may give some hint of the dedicators' economic

Fig. IV   *An Athenian red-figure vase-painting of the early fifth century BC. It shows, left to right, bronze-workers, statues, a vase-painter at work, a bronze seated statue of Athena and another bronze-worker, probably the master bronze-worker, with his tools and Hephaestean cap hung on the wall behind him. From the Acropolis, Athens.*

and social standing. The practice of setting up offerings on the Athenian acropolis was surely restricted to the comparatively well-to-do. The Potter's Stele was presumably the offering of a wealthy potter (*Pl.* 19), perhaps Pamphaios, the partner of the productive potter Nikosthenes.[457] Antenor's *korē* was dedicated by the potter Nearchos (p. 165). The potter Aischines offered 'one-tenth of his works' to the goddess, meaning, presumably, a fair proportion of his profit,[458] and the potters Andokides, well known from his signatures as for his innovations in the craft, and Mnesiades, otherwise unheard of, made a joint dedication.[459] Although we only know for certain of a mere half-dozen or so potters who followed this practice, a very small proportion of the five hundred or more craftsmen concerned in the fine pottery business during the late sixth and fifth centuries, they are enough to suggest that Athenian potters in general were on to a good thing, compared with other craftsmen.[460] Even when the practice had declined, by the early fourth century, the potter Kittos, perhaps the brother of the renowned Bakchios I, discussed below, could still find it appropriate to make a dedication.[461]

Some objects clearly echoed the dedicator's professional concern, such as the Potter's Stele or the one or two examples of fine painted pottery which were offered up. But often enough it seems to have been the practice *not* to dedicate a work of one's own, and, surprisingly enough, none of the vases discovered with workshop scenes, not even those showing Athena in association with the crafts, was intended for the goddess.[462]

If a few potters and painters felt in a position to join the ranks of the godly and the socially acceptable in this way, the situation was quite different for the members of the equally busy and (one would have thought) even more important craft of monumental marble-working. Virtually no dedications are known of sculptors or stonemasons, but why this should have been the case is beyond comprehension, given the unsatisfactory state of the evidence for their social and economic standing in general. All we know is that they must have had plenty of employment provided by very affluent patrons.[463]

The dedication of the sculptor or stonemason Archedemos of

Thera provides pleasing evidence of his personal individuality, but says nothing as to his status, for presumably his rock-cut self-portrait and inscriptions referring to Pan and the Nymphs cost him nothing but his time and effort.[464] However, it adds weight to the argument that in their religious observances craftsmen followed the generally accepted cults. For Pan and the Nymphs were the object of many dedications in fourth-century Athens, among which is the relief of the twelve clothes cleaners (p. 160).

Not a single metalworker's dedication is known at Athens. Smiths, like monumental stone-workers, were not as well-to-do as potters, or clothes cleaners, for some reason. And whatever their views of Hephaistos, they have left no word. The only metalworkers about whose religious practices anything can be said are some fifty or sixty miners and smelters (and dependants) of the Laureion silver mines.[465] Their records give some indication of individuals' circumstances, but of course they are scarcely representative of the tens of thousands of men who made up the labour force in the mines. Yet these dedications are of interest in themselves in that, however few they were, the dedicators, mainly non-Greek by origin and of slave or freedman status in Attica, alien in belief as well as speech, were somehow able and willing to follow the fashion of dedication prevalent in Attica by making their own, in Greek and often (but not always) to Greek deities (though, again, *not* to Hephaistos). Most are of the fourth century or later. Eleven miners made a joint dedication to Herakles; the Asiatic Azaratos, to Heros; the Phrygian Mannes, to Artemis (in one of several shrines to the goddess in the mining area).[466] Mēn, an Asiatic version of Herakles, was also the object of several dedications, and he may have been popular among the miners not only because many of them came from Asia Minor too, but because he was accepted by the Greeks, as demonstrated in the dedications at Athens and in the Piraeus to Mēn together with Pan and the Nymphs.[467]

Far fewer craftsmen's dedications survive from the whole of the rest of Greece. Such as they are, they indicate little more than a similar conformity to the generally prevailing beliefs. The sculptor Grophon was allowed to add his own dedication to the statue he made for Ekphantos: 'O child of Zeus [Athena], accept this flawless statue on behalf of Ekphantos. For Grophon achieved its completion after praying to you.'[468] In the fourth century the sculptor Pausanias dedicated to Asklepios at Stylis in Thessaly.[469] And yet another sculptor, Damophon of Messene, seems to have celebrated the completion of a project with a dedication at Megalopolis in the second century B C.[470]

Perhaps one of the most unusual dedications was that of the Samian Mandrokles who engineered the bridge across which Darius crossed the Hellespont to invade Scythia in 512 BC. Herodotus, who presumably saw the dedication himself (would that some trace of it had survived) during his stay in Samos, says:

> Darius was so pleased with the bridge that he loaded its designer with presents, and Mandrokles spent a certain portion of what he received in having a picture painted, showing the whole process of the bridging of the strait, and Darius himself sitting on his throne, with the army crossing over. This picture he presented as a dedicatory offering in the temple of Hera, with the following verse inscribed on it, to serve as a permanent record of his achievement:
>> Goddess, accept this gift from Mandrokles,
>> who bridged the Bosphorus' fish-haunted seas.
>> His labour praised by king Darius, won
>> honour for Samos, for himself a crown.[471]

Mandrokles offered up his feat of engineering to the patron goddess of Samos—just as he would if he had won a military victory, or had done something equally public-spirited, like reforming the constitution, or paying for the entire construction of a temple—not to a deity specifically connected with the craft of bridge-building. Mandrokles was a public figure, making the gesture proper to a man in his position. Similarly, the sculptor Boethos of Nikomedia made a dedication to Lindian Athena in Rhodes in gratitude for his being made a Rhodian *proxenos*.[472]

Much the same practices prevailed, impelled by very similar

motives, in the Roman world. One difference is that there are far
more group dedications, especially from the craftsmen's *collegia*.
In the Greek world most craftsmen had been discouraged, by the
cost or the weight of custom against them, from making their
own dedication; in the Roman, even if they still felt this was not
a practice for them on their own, they could share in a common
dedication. As has already been suggested, craftsmen of the
Roman world showed no more devotion to any deity particularly
concerned with their craft than the Greeks; they were quite
content to pay their respects to the likeliest divinity to hand,
whether Baal (for a Syrian Greek), Asklepios or Aesculapius
(depending on which end of the Mediterranean you were in),
Mars, the imperial name, or the wild men of the woods Silvanus
and Hercules. Indeed the making of the dedication seems to have
been as important to them as the subject of the dedication, if not
more so.

Some dedications give slight hints as to the wealth and status
of the dedicator—as in the case of C. Julius Lacer, the architect
who celebrated the construction of his bridge over the Tagus
river at Alcantara by building a small temple on the bank to
honour the imperial cult. Various other architects' or engineers'
dedications have survived, but there is little to be made of them:
examples are Q. Sevius Lupus' offering to Mars, also in Spain,[473]
or the Pompeian architect Gratus' monument put up for his own
protection—no deity is specified, for the inscription merely says,
'May you be preserved, Gratus. Gratus the architect paid for this
himself. I, Felix, made it.'[474]

A few of the Athenian dedicatory inscriptions hinted at the
cost involved, as, for example, the potters' which alleged that one-
tenth of their fortunes had been spent on the offering, but in
some Roman dedications the idea that part of the object of the
exercise was to show off one's wealth comes over much more
clearly. So the second-century AD painter, Q. Attius Messor of
Tarragona, 'repaired and painted at his own expense an *exhedra*
bearing a relief of the temple of Minerva Augusta, which had
collapsed with age'.[475] At Rome a freedman sculptor, C. Cossutius
Epaphroditus, 'applied marble veneer to an altar for Silvanus,

and dedicated the shrine and altar of Hercules, after restoring the god's statue, and the broken parts'.[476]

There is a little more evidence in the Roman period of dedications being made by the humbler craftsmen, on their own. The Nikomedian stonemason Asklepiades dedicated to Asklepios 'for the sake of virtue'; the Spanish mason P. Rutilius Syntrophus 'made the gift which he promised in the temple of Minerva'.[477] Metalworkers also figure among the dedicators. The Syrian Ascharenos Eutyches and his apprentice Paul acknowledged Baal; the British smith Cintusmus dedicated to Silvanus; and another British smith, Celatus, made and shared in the dedication of a bronze statue to Mars.[478] Here again, there is emphasis on the cost and trouble involved; Celatus took the opportunity to point out that he had added at his own expense one pound of bronze to the amount supplied by the men who had originally commissioned the piece. And among various Christian offerings is one made in the fourth or fifth century AD by Flavius Tertullus, a mason, 'to the Church, from his own artistic industry'.[479]

No special link can be seen between the craft and the deity concerned in the dedications of the *collegia*. Many so-called dedications were directed at influential mortals; the goldsmiths and the silversmiths of Palmyra, on the eastern edge of the province of Syria, put up a monument to Septimius Odenathus, 'to the prince in his honour'.[480] Much money was spent on exercises of this kind, like the dedication at Epidamnos 'to . . ., Roman *eques*, aedile, *duovir*, *flamen*, augur, patron of the *colonia* of Dyrrachium', set up by the carpenters and builders.[481]

Group dedications to the gods showed the same concern for the widely accepted cults. The silversmiths and goldsmiths of Smyrna dedicated the repair of the statue of Athena 'to Good Fortune'; in Dacia the goldsmiths dedicated to Jupiter Optimus Maximus 'for safety of the commander of the *collegium*'; and many other associations in this province alone are known to have subscribed to the cult of the healing deities, Aesculapius and Hygeia.[482]

Occasionally the *collegia* admitted the existence of a presiding genius. Two gold-leaf workers at Rome made a dedication to 'the

Concordia of the *collegium*', meaning the spirit of unity which held their organization together.[483] And M. Alfius Onesimus made an offering to 'the genius of the *collegium* of pavement workers'.[484] This practice was exactly parallel to the worship of the *genius loci* or the household gods, the *lares* and *penates*; it was meant to bring down protection not on the members' efforts in the workshop, but on the corporate life of the *collegium*.

Solidarity of professional interest is, however, more obvious in the dedications of Roman imperial quarry workers (see the remarks above on Greek quarrymasons' piety). The intention of the dedication was to ensure success at the quarry-face. So we find in the Roman quarries of Gaul the following declaration of triumph and gratitude: 'To the god Silvanus and the Numidian mountains: dedication of Q. Julianus and Publius Crescentius, who were the first to cut and extract monoliths twenty feet long from here.'[485] The appearance of the Numidian mountains as deities is at first sight surprising, but surely here is one example of a specially craft-oriented divinity, the source of some of the best stone in the Roman world.

Another dedicatory inscription celebrates the opening of a new quarry at some length:

> To Jupiter Optimus, Ammon, Chnubis, Queen Juno, under whose protection this mountain lies; because for the first time under the rule of the Roman people in this most happy age of our lords [the Severans] . . . new quarries were discovered near Philae, and many large columns and standing blocks were cut there, under the rule of Sabatianus Aquila, prefect of Egypt, and under the direction of Aurelius Heraclidas of the Moorish auxiliaries.[486]

Other quarry dedications tend to reflect anxieties which are less obviously professional and specialized in character. In the Luna quarries, 'our workshop put up (this dedication) to Hercules the Helper, for our safety'.[487] In Africa, Primus, an imperial freedman and procurator of the quarry, dedicated an altar to the *lares Augusti* and 'the sacred place', whatever that was.[488] And an

Egyptian architect or quarry supervisor of Trajan's time made an offering to Zeus, the Great Sun, and Sarapis 'for the preservation of himself and all his works'.[489] These last two were officials, and perhaps only made their dedications because of their official status, not because of any efforts exerted as craftsmen. The (presumably) votive relief from Linares in Spain showing a mining gang *en route* to the gallery may also have been dedicated by an official.[490]

The setting up of an epitaph, whatever religious significance it might have, also provided a method of demonstrating the subject's worth and worthiness. It has already been suggested that memorials on stones were less common than we might have expected, and that in Greece, even at Athens, the practice was exceptional; in the Roman world a somewhat larger proportion of the population was so commemorated, and this included within it a far larger proportion of craftsmen. The Athenian craftsmen who declared themselves in their epitaphs were exceptional among the exceptions; it was virtually unheard-of to have one's career or status mentioned in the epitaph, and yet about sixty men and women out of the eight thousand or more whose memorials survive elected to be remembered by their profession—potters, textile workers, nursemaids, actors, and an artillery man included.[491] Whereas the fashionable thing to do was to state only in the starkest terms the identity of the dead, these people were recorded for ever as professionals, and in the case of the craftsmen, of course, as *banausoi*.

Neither sculptors, masons nor architects appear in the surviving epitaphs. Only one metalworker's memorial is known from Athens itself, Sosinos', which states that he was a resident alien from Gortyn in Crete, and that his profession was copper-smelting (or perhaps alloying bronze); the grave relief itself shows him as a gentleman of leisure, and the inscription otherwise describes him in the most conventional of terms.[492] The miners of Attica, on the other hand, have left more evidence of their existence in their epitaphs as well as dedications. Of the few which survive (given the number of men who lived and worked in the mining district altogether), even fewer actually state that the

68 The fine brick front of the House of Diana at Ostia
69 A wall-painting from the tomb of Trebius Justus, showing house-builders at work

70 Detail of a relief on Trajan's column showing Roman legionaries building roads

71, 72 Acropolis wall on the island of Thasos. *below*, a mason's graffito, and, *right*, the inscription 'Parmenon made me'. Early fifth century BC

73, 74 Two feats of Roman engineering at opposite ends of the empire: *above*, the theatre at Aspendos, Turkey; *below*, the Pont du Gard aqueduct in southern France

75 An unfinished colossal statue, bearded and robed, in the marble quarry on Naxos, c.600 BC

76 Graffiti on a statue base from Persepolis. The heads of the men and lions, in Athenian sixth-century BC style, must have been executed by Greek craftsmen in Persian employ.

77 A sculptor carving a herm, mid-fifth century BC

78, 79 The Strangford
shield, a copy of the shield
of the Athena Parthenos
statue, a reconstruction of
which is seen *below left*.
The old man wielding an
axe is possibly a
self-portrait of Pheidias.

80 The Winged Victory of the
sculptor Paionios of Mende, *c.*425 BC.
It commemorates a naval victory by
the Messenians and Naupaktians
off Pylos.

81 The Laocoon group, made by the Rhodian sculptors Hagesandros and his sons Polydoros and Athenodorus. First century BC

82, 83 *below*, Two Roman busts. The flattering sculptural expertise of the bust of Commodus, *left*, compares strikingly with the austerity of the head of a lady, *right*, made a century earlier.

84, 85 Grave stelai of two sculptors. *Left*, Megistokles, son of Philomousos, Hellenistic; *right*, M. Se…Amabilis, from Roman Gaul.

86 Wall-painting of a garden from the so-called 'House of Livia', Rome.

87, 88 Examples of mosaic work; *above*, from Pella in Macedonia, signed by Gnosis, early third century BC; *below*, from the Villa of Cicero, Pompeii, signed by Dioskourides of Samos, first century BC

subject was a mine-worker; the rest are identified as such by the mere fact of their presence among the mines. The most explicit is the epitaph of Atotas, a record remarkable in other ways too:

> Atotas the miner
> Atotas the great-hearted Paphlagonian, from the shores of the Black Sea, has ceased from toil in this distant land. No one rivalled me in skill. I am from the stem of Pylaimenes, who died tamed by the hand of Achilles.[493]

The hexameter verses are Homeric in style and epic in content; Pylaimenes' death is mentioned in the *Iliad*. Furthermore, Atotas claims descent from and presumably membership of the ruling dynasty in Paphlagonia. If this was the case, how had he come to be a miner in Attica? There is some indication that Paphlagonians fell fairly frequently into enslavement at Athens, either through the operations of slave dealers in northern Asia Minor itself, or through brigands who kidnapped likely material for the slave market; perhaps Atotas had been the victim of some dynastic plot, and shunted off to slavery far away from his ancestral home. Another mine-worker, Thous, whose grave relief survives, might also have been involved in the same or a similar upset, for he bore the same name as a Paphlagonian dynast of the mid-fourth century.[494]

Thous' grave relief is perfectly conventional in form, making no reference to life in the mines, but showing him seated with his hand outstretched to a woman standing by him, a design typical of many Athenian grave reliefs. The Ethiopian Skiapos' memorial also omits mention of his mining activity; the relief shows him instead as a soldier, armed and in action, recalling no doubt the far nobler role he had in life before being captured and put on the slave market.[495]

The only other miner's epitaph which refers to the dead man's work is that of Ianibelos, a Carthaginian or Phoenician of the Roman period, the *archikamineutes* or chief smelter.[496]

The cultural aspirations of various potters who were moved to make dedications about 500 BC and later did not extend, as far as we can tell, to epitaphs—but then very few epitaphs of any kind are known from this period. Two potters' memorials of the fourth century, however, have survived—Leptines', otherwise unknown, and Bakchios', who signed many pieces of fine black-glazed ware, and whose epitaph lays considerable emphasis on his success as a potter:

Bakchios, son of Amphis —— of the Kerameikos deme. The whole of Greece judged Bakchios the first, by his innate craftsmanship, among his fellow-craftsmen in the art of compounding earth, water and fire in the competitions which the city organized. He took all the crowns.[497]

His commemorators seemingly gave a very individual account of Bakchios' achievements. But what really happened is that the professionals were establishing conventions of their own, for Bakchios' epitaph states more elegantly the sentiments of the woodman Mannes' epitaph, and echoes closely the phrasing of the memorial for the contemporary comic actor Euthias.[498] The phrase expressing primacy in his craft was also used by the painter Parrhasios in a set of boastful verses with which he accompanied the signature to one of his works.[499] The question is, how the literary style of such statements could become so standardized, whether by close contact within the craftsman group as a whole, or by the agency of some professional epitaph-writer. The first is by far the more appealing alternative.

We know of two leatherworkers, both of them shoemakers—Xanthippos, identified as such only by the shoe which he holds as he sits at ease with small daughters clustering round (Pl. 6); and Thraix, a ladies' slipper maker (and conceivably a Thracian by origin, therefore a freedman or metic at his death?).[500] No tanners' epitaphs have come to light. Several textile workers, all of the fourth century, are known: Dionysios the cloak maker; the Egyptian Hermaios 'a wool worker from Thebes'; 'most worthy Mannes, wool-plucker' and the 'wool worker who lived ninety blameless years'.[501]

Elsewhere in Greece, the proportion of identifiable craftsmen's epitaphs to the rest of the population's is virtually nil. One can be detected, that of the sculptor Theon of Antioch, but only because what is said in his epitaph repeats what he included in his signatures, the statement that he had been granted Rhodian rights of residence.[502]

Craftsmen in the Roman world identified themselves far more frequently by their profession. It was not that the *banausia* complex was less prevalent, but rather that they thus gained a necessary supplement to their identity in a society which was after all, considerably more complicated in structure than the Greek city-states'. Roman epitaphs in general included more biographical details than most Greek examples, including age, offices and honours (if not profession in so many words) and family details. The craftsmen followed suit; and almost every known craft and its subdivision appear in the funerary inscriptions.

Some included a great deal more than the formal declaration of the dead man's profession, equalling in the emphasis on his success as a craftsman the Athenian epitaphs which singled out their subject's virtuosity. Grave reliefs showing the dead man at his work in life are a little more common in the Roman period, a striking example of which is P. Longidienus Camillus' (*Pl.* 9); conditions in Gaul seem to have been quite conducive to craftsmen's being commemorated by graphic representations of activity in the workshop—that is to say, a few have survived, compared with none in most other areas.[503]

But most Roman epitaphs are remarkable only for the monotony of their formal phrases. This is true of architects' and engineers' memorials. A very few reveal anything out of the ordinary, one of which is the epitaph and relief of the military catapult-maker, C. Vedennius Moderatus (*Pl.* 56 and p. 158 above). The imperial freedman architect Phosphorus, who was attached to the Julio-Claudian household, had a memorial set up by his wife 'to the best of husbands, C. Julius P(h)osphorus, architect, son of Lucifer'.[504] Both father and son were called 'light-bearer', the one in Latin and the other in Greek; the play on words was surely intentional.

The records of sculptors and stonemasons are for the most part conventional, and not very revealing either. L. Arrius Secundus of Catania, who died at the age of seventeen, had a grave monument put up for him by his 'fellow marble workers', meaning the members of his *collegium* who were thus fulfilling one of the association's most important functions.[505] The epitaph of the imperial freedman Agrypnus reveals that he had first belonged to Maecenas, but was later transferred to the household of Augustus, becoming a member of Livia's staff with the title *a statuis*, in charge of statues—the imperial funeral monuments, no doubt.[506] There are also records of Greek-speaking masons in the Roman world—the imperial freedman Aurelius Agathias, a Syrian who died at Rome and was commemorated in Greek as *marmorarios*—marble worker; Gorgias, from Nikomedia, a marble mason who worked and died at Ostia; Pallas, a Greek-speaking Ethiopian in Egypt, 'overseer in the quarries at Antinooupolis'.[507]

Some sculptors' epitaphs laid heavy stress on their subjects' supposed virtuosity. During the second century AD a group of Greek sculptors from Aphrodisias was resident in Rome; on the tomb of the Zenon family was the following verse inscription:

Of me, Zenon, the most blessed fatherland is Aphrodisias. I have visited many cities, depending on my skill. . . . I built this tomb, and put up this grave-stone for my son Zenon who has just died; I myself cut the stone and carved the relief, achieving this remarkable work with my own hands, and within I constructed a tomb for my wife and all our descendants.[508]

The sixteen-year-old Eutychides, a Milesian who died at Athens, was commemorated thus: 'I flourished as a stone worker not inferior to Praxiteles'.[509] And the Roman sculptor Novius Blesamus had an eight-line epitaph which ended, 'This man embellished the city and the world [*urbem decoravit et orbem*] with his sculptures. The public holds the memory of his name; this is the resting place of his body.'[510]

Among the funerary reliefs from Gaul, two show the sculptor

at work; one portrays Iulius Cadgat with hammer and chisel, and the other Amabilis working away at the capital of a column in the structure which encloses him (*Pl.* 85).[511]

Painters' epitaphs are known in great numbers, but most only identify their subject by his professional title and nothing more. A fuller and far more individual statement of the painter's abilities, together with his distinction in public life, comes from the Greek-speaking world; Loukios Sossios, a great painter and generous with his skill, became a member of the city council of Cyrene.[512] Closely parallel to this is the epitaph of the mosaic worker P. Aelius Harpokration of Perinthos: 'I exercised my art in all cities outstandingly as a mosaic worker, endowed with the gifts of Pallas (Athene). I leave a son, Proklos, member of the city council and my equal in craftmanship. I now occupy this tomb at the age of eighty.'[513]

These records differ considerably in tone and content from the extremely conventional memorial at Rome of the painter C. Vettius Capitolinus who died at the age of thirteen, and who was described by his mother as an infant prodigy, in somewhat unconvincing terms.[514] The slave jeweller Pagus, who died at the age of twelve, is commemorated at length and with deep emotion: 'Weep, all passers-by . . . Pagus was the delight of his master . . . he was marvellously dexterous at working gold and setting fine jewels. . . .'[515]

A very formal record of the life of a goldsmith in Switzerland reads as follows: 'To the gods of the underworld. Camillus Polynices, by origin a Lydian, by profession a goldsmith, of the *collegium* of carpenters and builders, who held all positions of honour in the *collegium*.'[516] The memorial was erected by his son, also a goldsmith and member of the same association. In strong contrast is the very personal epitaph of the freedman M. Canuleius Zosimus, put up by his patron at Rome: 'He never spoke any evil, nor did anything against the will of his patron. . . . He always had access to large quantities of gold and silver, but never coveted any of it. He excelled in the art of Clodian engraving.'[517] This is an unusual testimonial to the character, rather than the skill, of an obviously well-liked client craftsman, comparable

in a way to the epitaph of the silver-engraver C. Valerius Diophanes in Spain: 'C. Valerius Zephirus set up this monument for
C. Valerius Diophanes, who died at the age of eleven years and
five months, his intended successor and most tractable pupil.'[518]

Various of the more utilitarian metalworkers are identified by
trade names and by the emblems of their craft in grave reliefs of
fairly simple design.[519] Comments on metallurgical virtuosity,
on the other hand, are rare in the extreme; the Gallic blacksmith
Vireus Vitalis of Lyons, was 'a young man of unrivalled genius
in the craft of ironworking, . . . and a member of the *collegium*
of builders and carpenters. He had been adopted by Valerius
Maximus Vitricus who had trained him in the craft, and placed
in him his expectations for the future.'[520]

Of shipbuilders' records the most personal is that of P. Longidienus Camillus at Ravenna (*Pl.* 9). It combines the highly
conventional—the relief of the mourning group and the record
of his social and professional status—with the individual—the
illustration of the shipwright at work, and the caption indicating
what must have been his characteristic eagerness to get on with
the job in hand. Among woodworkers in general, the Greek
P. Beitenos is identified as 'furniture maker', and shown as such
in his relief (*Pl.* 8). Two others are spoken of in more detail:
Maximus, of Roman freedman birth and Bithynian descent, is
commemorated in terms reminiscent of the miner Atotas. His
parentage and place of origin, Astakos in Bithynia, his profession
as a 'woodworking house builder', and his skill are recorded, the
last being described as 'unrivalled'; some of the phrasing is
Homeric in style, and the whole record is in Greek, despite his
Roman upbringing.[521]

The other woodworker worthy of note is commemorated in
these terms (in Latin):

To the gods of the underworld.
Q. Candidus Benignus, member of the *collegium* of carpenters
and builders of Arles. He was a builder of the greatest skill, a
student of building theory, and modest too; great craftsmen
would always call *him* master. No one was more learned than

he, no one could excel him. He knew all about waterworks and road building. He was sweet-tempered and knew how to entertain his friends—a man of gentle and studious character, and a kindly spirit.[522]

Although this sounds like an entirely personal tribute to an outstanding individual, here again (as in the case of the Athenian potter Bakchios) many of the phrases seem to be drawn from a stock of formalities such as are found in epitaphs of all kinds. Yet there is surely something peculiar to Benignus himself in the emphasis on his sweetness of temper and his professional qualification; while the fact that he warranted a memorial of this kind at all suggests that he, like all the craftsmen who were able or inclined to have epitaphs, was outstanding in one way or another among his fellows, and in society at large.

CHAPTER VI

CONCEPTS OF THE NATURE
OF CRAFTSMANSHIP

INTRODUCTION

CRAFTSMANSHIP EMBODIES the performance of techniques according to traditional practice, in such a way that the product is entirely adequate in form and function. The question is, to what extent the ancient world allowed the craftsman any individual responsibility for his work. How was he thought to have achieved the outstanding piece of sculpture, the perfectly balanced bronze bowl—the quality of which went far beyond mere adequacy? It has already been suggested that if the patron had something to say about the form of the object he required, he was nevertheless limited by the traditions which affected both his own taste and the way in which the craftsman worked. Yet there was still a little room within these limits for the great craftsman to use his own initiative and make his own adjustments, so producing something that was truly distinctive—and it is here that what we would call artistic inventiveness or genius made itself apparent. Whether or not this was a characteristic recognized by connoisseur and patron in the ancient craftsman, or by the craftsmen themselves, is another problem, to which the answer seems to be not quite. Both appear to have agreed that great work came about as the result of tremendous technical ability, and nothing more.

MAN AS TECHNOLOGIST

'The end result of *poiēsis*—making—is something other than itself; the end result of *praxis*—doing—is not, for its end is *eupraxia*—doing well.'[523] It follows that, for Aristotle, as for anyone else concerned in the pursuit of political and moral ideals, the craftsman could never achieve virtue by means of his craft, however excellent the quality of the work he did. Technological development itself was either irrelevant to the total scheme of things, or merely a nursery phase, a prelude to man's highest activity, speculation on the universals. In the view of the philosopher who was preoccupied with concepts of reality, the craftsman's activity was irrelevant because concerned with the artificial; as Antiphon bleakly remarked, 'If a wooden bedstead were buried, and it sprouted, it would produce wood not bedsteads.'[524]

For many others, whether philosophers or less deeply thoughtful members of the general public, the craftsman's activity and the nature of his work were matters of little or no account, simply to be taken for granted as part of the natural scene. There was nothing deserving of question; the craftsman followed his trade as a bee gathered honey or a spider span its web, and that was that. And if, in the course of referring to the craftsman's work as a necessary aid to the proper ordering of society, Plato or Aristotle went so far as to suggest that, in addition to good training in the best tradition of the craft, the soundest craftsmanship depended on an innate aptitude in the craftsman concerned, this did not amount to the recognition of individual talent, or of any personal satisfaction the craftsman might gain from his involvement in the work.[525] Natural ability was simply seen as the oil which made the machine run more smoothly.

But however unworthy the work of the craftsman, past or contemporary, might be in the eyes of some, the attention of many scientific thinkers was attracted by the question of how human society and the techniques necessary to maintain it had come into being. The awareness that Man had begun in a state of ignorance (or innocence, depending on one's point of view), and had gradually approached a greater sophistication, was not of course confined to the Greeks. However, they were unique in feeling the need to account for technological development in particular. The use of fire, the art of speech, the skills of metal-working, building, cooking and so on were regarded not simply as elements in a god-provided and god-ordered landscape, in which Man was just a subject of the gods, existing in and for their service, but as means to a civilized life which Man had slowly and often painfully to acquire for himself.[526] While one point of view, to which Hesiod and Plato among others subscribed, maintained that technology and its development were nothing more or less than evils made necessary as Man slipped further and further away from the original state of existence in which material needs had been perfectly provided for, the view of the Greek anthropologists held that Man's acquisition of techniques constituted not regression but cultural progress, which was to be described in historical terms as a natural process.[527]

It is another matter to estimate the degree of initiative on men's part which was considered to have made this cultural progress possible. Was it active invention, the result of forethought and a positive awareness of the problem to be solved, which had prompted technological developments? If so, what credit was given to craftsmen as the experts in technical matters? Opinions as to how civilization had arisen, and who or what had begun the process, naturally varied; for Aeschylus, it all began with the Titan Prometheus, the fire-bearer, and his action on men's behalf in defiance of Zeus; for Lucretius, and for Vitruvius likewise, it depended upon chance and the working out of a natural process; the poet Moschion was willing to see it either as the work of Prometheus, or of Necessity, or as part of a natural process.

Although the anthropologists' theories as we have them concentrate rather heavily on the technological aspects of man's cultural growth, they most likely derive from wider surveys of the human condition, among which may be counted Herodotus' history and very probably a now lost work of the fifth-century BC atomist philosopher Democritus, among many others. The impact of the anthropological thinkers of this period on the philosophical tradition is less obvious than it might be, or deserves to be, partly because their concepts clashed head-on with those of Plato and Aristotle, and were (unfairly) beaten; the basis of their argument, acceptable in the fifth century, was no longer respected in the fourth because it did not provide a sufficiently dignified explanation of the development of human institutions. Nevertheless their line of thought reappeared in the Hellenistic period and even later.

Of the five surviving versions of the anthropologists' history of technology, the most striking and the most profound is that of the Roman poet Lucretius (c. 100 BC). Vitruvius' attempt to cover the subject is of particular interest too, for its own sake, not only because he was himself a professional craftsman.[528] The situation presented by all five versions is roughly thus: at first, man lived like the beasts, his intelligence as yet unroused, knowing neither social organization, proper shelter, the means of regular food supply, nor clothes. Then came the discovery of fire in the forest, and the overcoming of initial fear through the attraction of its warmth, the gathering together of several to share it, and, with the realization of the advantages of preserving fire, the foundations of social organization. The need to communicate for this purpose gave rise to human speech, and so the advance to more and better techniques became possible. The discovery of metal suggested the possibility of tools, which in turn led to the arts of weaving, farming and carpentry; thereafter society became increasingly civil, with the rise of conventions and the fine arts to crown man's achievement as technologist.

How did Lucretius understand the process to have occurred? The discovery of fire came about as the result of a tree being struck by lightning—*accidentally*; for Vitruvius, it was the storm-wind which rubbed the branches of a tree together and so ignited them—again, *by accident*. Men responded, at first entirely naturally or instinctively, to the new situation, but eventually with intelligence, so that they became able to take advantage of the new possibilities which unfolded before them. When, as Lucretius has it, the existence of metals was revealed, again by the accidental firing of a tree by a thunderbolt, and the subsequent smelting of silver from the rocks beneath, the way in which the molten metal slopped about into the hollows of the ground suggested the shape of tools to the observant men on the spot. They were 'taught gradually by usage and the active mind's experience, as (they) groped their way forward step by step . . . (they) saw one notion after another take shape within their minds until by their arts they scaled the topmost peak.'[529] So Vitruvius also speaks of men being of 'an imitative and teachable nature'; 'with their natural gifts sharpened by emulation their standards improved daily . . . their ingenuity was increased by their dexterity' in building shelters; and so from the development of architecture— here Vitruvius shows a very natural bias—they advanced to the other sciences.[530]

Obviously the rationalists conceived of no divine being as having started the whole process.[531] Nor is any individual human, or even a clearly definable group of humans, spoken of as being *the first* to see fire, or in taking any of the other vital steps forward. Chance was the active agent; the discoverers were 'plural and anonymous'—they were certainly never specified as *craftsmen*— and although forethought and strength of mind were allowed to man in his way of *reacting* to the situation with which he was confronted in the technological steeplechase, he was never shown acting on his own initiative.[532]

Man used his ingenuity, he responded intelligently to the challenge, he was open to the suggestion of new forms, materials and ideas, but he is never described as first feeling the lack, and then going out to look for the fulfilment of it, or experimenting to see what would happen.

The point is not whether the anthropologists were right or wrong in their assessment of the technological problem—in fact, they were supremely perceptive in many of their judgments— but that no autonomy was allowed to Man in general, or crafts- men in particular, in the development of techniques. Craftsman- ship was simply one emanation of Man's ability to respond usefully to external suggestion in the context of technical re- quirements—and nothing more.

GODS, MEN AND THE CRAFTS

For the strict anthropologists, Man's cultural development started by accident, and went on from there according to his ability to take the opportunities offered him. The first step was seen by others as the intentional act of a supernatural being: so Prometheus, by his forethought and out of his concern for defenceless Man, stole fire and gave it to men together with the knowledge of the techniques essential to civilized life, for which he was most cruelly punished. The most striking presentation of the Prometheus myth was Aeschylus' trilogy, of which only the first play and fragments of the second and third have survived. It was probably produced at Athens in the mid-450s during the period when the anthropological view of Man's development was generating more and more heat among thinking Greeks. This was the time when, at Athens, thought was being given to the physical regeneration of the city's cult centres and, as suggested above, to reasserting the city's cultural values, symbolized in the rebuilding of the shattered temples and the enhancing of the cult of Hephaistos in particular.[533] It was surely not by sheer coincidence that Aeschylus presented in *Prometheus Bound* a glorification of the techniques on which civilization rested, and which Prometheus bestowed as benefits on men.

Prometheus speaks of himself and his achievements thus:

> I am the huntsman of the mystery,
> The great resource that taught technology,
> The secret fount of fire put in the reed
> And given to man to serve his need. . . .
> I made man conscious and intelligent. . . .
> Mindless was all they did until I showed
> The dubious rise and setting of the stars. . . .
> I was the first to yoke animals
> In service to the strap. . . .
> (Of) those great utilities beneath the earth,
> Copper and iron, silver and yellow gold,
> Who before me dare claim discovery
> Of these, unless a madman?[534]

The wide range of techniques which Prometheus provided was intended as the basis of civilized life as a whole, and included speech, numbers, letters, medicine, divination, navigation and farming. The crafts are not here given any special emphasis, and although the discovery of metals is mentioned, the one other craft especially connected with fire, the manufacture of pottery— still in mid-fifth-century Athens one of the most important industrial activities—is not remarked on at all. There is then no question of Aeschylus' wishing to praise craftsmen in particular; once more, craftsmanship is to be seen as but one aspect of the total cultural achievement.

Prometheus revealed fire to men, he was the forethought without which they could begin to do nothing for themselves. But he did not actually invent fire; he stole it from Hephaistos.[535] Yet it is not clear in Aeschylus' play or anywhere else that Hephaistos discovered or created fire either. Nor is he ever shown doing more than hand on various techniques to mortals which he had himself been taught by others (see below, pp. 195–6).

Another way of accounting for technological developments was to leave aside the total picture, and confine the attempt to ascribing the invention of single techniques to this or that individual or ethnic group. There are various catalogues, more or less complete, some of which may go back to fuller accounts of how the 'invention' was made, even though they themselves now include only the technique and the name associated with its discovery.[536] A curious mixture of fantasy and rationalization resulted; so Pliny's list includes the discovery of fire from flint by Pyrodes (Fiery), son of Cilix (Flint) alongside the invention of the four-wheeled cart by the Phrygians, and refers to three alternative discoverers of the techniques of mining and smelting gold.[537] There are one or two curious omissions. All Pliny says of stone-quarrying is that it was invented by Cadmus of Thebes; neither he nor anyone else refers to the marble workers of Naxos, who were almost certainly the first in Greece, or to the later and more famous workings of Paros or Mt Pentele in Attica.[538] But, for all its shortcomings, the concept of 'first discoverers' seems at least to point to some recognition that the individual had something to do with technical progress, that some men are more apt by nature to enquire into things and better able to seize the opportunity offered by new circumstances than others, so that they are indeed more inventive. This holds good even though chance and accident frequently enter in as the original prompters of a discovery; thus, the Phoenicians only stumbled on purple dye when they observed a dog which had bitten on a murex shell and stained its mouth.[539]

The 'first discoverers' are not to be dismissed as merely rhetorical figures, or creatures of folklore. They represent a certain appreciation of technological development (at a different level of thinking from the 'anthropologists', to be sure), and exist, many of them, as a result of a real admiration for craftsmanship and those exponents of their crafts who could advance to new limits of knowledge. Pride in the craftsmanship of one's own city was certainly the basis of some invention stories: 'Arms were invented in the island of Lemnos, and the Lemnian armourers were the first *demiourgoi* in Greece.'[540] There is in many of such statements a certain fundamental truth; that 'the Aeginetans were the first to take command of curved ships and sweep with winged sails across the sea' is partially supported by the evidence for early contacts between Aegina and the eastern end of the Mediterranean, in the period when trade contact was increasing after the Dark Age (*c.* 1100–750).[541] Argive patriotism gave rise to various ambitious claims—Palamedes was a local version of Prometheus; coinage, weights and measures were invented by King Pheidon, and so on.[542] So the seafaring Corinthians included among their earliest men of distinction the shipwright Ameinokles, who was said to have built a new type of ship for the Samians *c.* 700 B C.[543] Sixth-century Samos in its turn was one of the wealthiest and technically most advanced societies in Greece; the craftsmen who worked in this period and whose name are preserved were no doubt real in the historical sense, but they were accorded legendary status by the legendary achievements which were attributed to them. Rhoikos and Theodoros, father and son, or brothers (or conflations of more than two generations of the same family) built on a vast scale, being responsible for the first large temple of Hera, and also for the second large temple, which was the first in marble of that size in Samos; they discovered how to cast large bronze figures; constructed wonders like the so-called Lemnian labyrinth; cut jewels such as the emerald of ill portent which Theodoros made into a signet ring for the tyrant Polykrates; or advised the Ephesians on a tricky architectural problem arising out of their having to site the Artemision in a bog for religious reasons. Theodoros was also a marvellous silversmith, creating great bowls which King Croesus of Lydia dedicated in the sanctuary at Delphi, and working in gold to produce a tree which came into the possession of the Persians; he took the time to invent, in addition, the carpenter's square, the plummet, the lathe, and the level, rivalling that other, greater craftsman-inventor, Daidalos.[544]

Both Corinth and Athens laid claim to the invention of all the techniques of clay-working. On one hand, Hyperbios of Corinth is supposed to have invented the potter's wheel; on the other, at Athens it was the Scythian Anacharsis—or, alternatively, Koroibos, who was credited with having invented everything to do with the potter's craft.[545] How wide an appeal such stories had among the potters themselves, and whether they had any hand in promoting them, is anyone's guess. What we do know is that an aristocrat and rationalist (not to say political extremist of all kinds), Kritias, was moved to write, in the late fifth century, that Athens was 'the city which . . . devised the potter's wheel and the offspring of clay and kiln, pottery most renowned and useful about the house'.[546]

Comparatively few discoveries can be associated with real craftsmen. Rhoikos and Theodoros of Samos, for example, are somewhat larger than life, and in any case we are given no details of how they are supposed to have made their discoveries, or have achieved their marvellous works.[547] Of historical inventions, several are mentioned by Vitruvius, as one would expect; one such device is that of the sixth-century architects Chersiphron and Metagenes of Knossos, who worked on the Artemision at Ephesus, for transporting large blocks of marble undamaged from the quarry to the building site. Vitruvius does not explain how they thought of it; we simply assume that they made their invention by a process of judicious trial and error, as would any sensible craftsman with a problem to solve.[548]

But there are three instances in which Vitruvius gives away his position on the underlying cause of invention. He seems to see it as a combination of individual initiative with the promptings of pure chance, and so supports the anthropologists' view, to which he subscribes in his general account of man's technical advance. The sculptor and ornamental metalworker Kallimachos invented the Corinthian order about the middle of the fifth century BC, not out of his own head, so to speak, and not while he was on the building site or at the drawing board, but as the result of external suggestion, by accident; while in Corinth he happened to see an acanthus plant growing up from and out of the basket in which it had been set on the grave of a young girl, and he was struck by its aptness for architectural decoration. His skill and experience as a fine craftsman thereafter enabled him to make use of his chance observation; there is no suggestion that he and he alone could have devised the new order because of some special talent vouchsafed to no other craftsman.[549]

Archimedes' case is less clear-cut. It was, on one hand, recognized that he applied theoretical knowledge to the solution of practical problems with great ingenuity, and that his inventions or engineering contrivances depended on a brilliance of mind not shared by all mathematicians or every engineer. But as for the law of specific gravity, the cleverness of its discovery lay, as Vitruvius' account has it, not in thinking out beforehand the possibilities offered by the displacement of his bath water, but in being able to realize and act on the implications of the incident afterwards.[550]

The third example is the story, quoted in all seriousness, of how marble was discovered at Ephesus in the mid-sixth century BC.[551] There is no question of the craftsman's initiative or special knowledge contributing in any way to the discovery—it was the shepherd Pixodarus who noticed the marble after one of his rams had accidentally struck a rock with one of his horns during a fight, and splintered off a fragment which revealed the brilliantly white stone. Thus it is that the architect Vitruvius would have us believe that this new and, for the Ephesians, important source of material came to light—not as the result of an intentional search set on by one of the many architects and highly skilled stone masons who must have been circulating in Ionia if not at Ephesus itself at this very moment, when the temple of Artemis was already planned, but through the chance observation of a shepherd, a man who had absolutely no connection whatever with the craft of monumental stonework.

Some discoveries, fewer than we might expect, were attributed to divine action. But the god's concern in the craft he invented, or revealed to men, was often enough rather slight, so that in some cases it seems he had been credited with an invention so as to keep the record straight, or fill up gaps in the tradition. In the case of Prometheus, of course, the divinity was seen as being concerned with the quality of life as a whole, not with a specific technique only. As for Hephaistos, metallurgy was his special province, but it was the pre-Olympians, the Titans, the Daktyloi, the Telchines, the Cyclopes, or the Chalybes, who first discovered the craft; it was, for example, the Telchines who made Poseidon's trident, not Hephaistos.[552] And if Hephaistos and Athena, the only two gods who according to the traditions had any lasting commitments to the crafts, are sometimes spoken of as teaching men the techniques of metalwork, carpentry, weaving, shipbuilding, or pottery—if the craftsmen themselves believed that their training in the workshop had in some way been supplemented by divine instruction—there is little acknowledgment of the fact (Pl. 34). The mosaicist Harpokration's epitaph, which says that 'Pallas taught me my skill', may very well reflect literary usage rather than personal conviction.[553] So the few vase-paintings from fifth-century Athens which show Athena in the workshop among the potters and painters, or the bronzesmiths, may be *genre* pieces, made to amuse but not necessarily to publicize the craftsmen's own convictions as to the nature of their work (Figs. I, IV). It seems, indeed, to have been less the gods who influenced the workshops than the practices of the workshops which affected the traditions concerning the gods and their

Fig. V   *Detail from a red-figure amphora showing Hephaistos making the armour of Achilles. Boston, Museum of Fine Arts.*

connections with the crafts; for their knowledge of techniques is described as coming not of their own divine power, but *by instruction*, from some other superhuman being. So it was the Cyclopes who 'equipped Zeus with his thunderbolt, they were the first skilled manual workers, who taught Hephaistos and Athena all the techniques of fine workmanship such as is wrought beneath the sky'.[554] Neither Hephaistos nor Athena originated any of the crafts they handed on to mortal craftsmen; whatever real power they may have been thought to wield in the workshop could only have put the finishing touch on the skills which the craftsman acquired in the normal way by being trained under a good master.

It is another matter to decide the nature of the power which Hephaistos exercised as divine craftsman in his smithy. Also, how was the first human craftsman Daidalos thought to have done his work? One is tempted to look for supernatural forces in the operations of technicians like these, and to see something magical in the way they worked.[555] And to be sure Hephaistos' products had, many of them, something distinctly uncanny and a little frightening about them: Achilles' shield, decorated in gold and silver with scenes so lifelike that the earth turned by the plough in one of them grew black, as it would in a real field with a real plough; the golden tripods which ran about at their master's bidding; the bronze serving maids who came completely to life; Pandora herself, a living woman created from clay, the source of great unhappiness for mankind; Talos, the man of bronze who had a red vein running in his ankle, a figure of terror in Crete and Sicily who according to some stories stoned the Argonauts, then drew them to him and jumped with them into a burning pit; Athena's aegis, a powerful piece of work; the bronze dog from which the Molossian people were said to be descended; or the bronze temple at Delphi which succeeded one of wax and feathers.[556]

Daidalos was first and foremost a carpenter, and the inventor of the saw, the axe, the plumbline, the gimlet, glue and isinglass. He was the forerunner of all sculptors, and inventor of the ship's mast and rigging. His works also had, often enough, mysterious or frightening associations; the wooden cow constructed for Pasiphäe, wife of Minos of Crete, in her passion for the Cretan bull; the labyrinth at Knossos built to conceal the Minotaur which resulted from the affair; his escape from Crete by means of wings made of feathers joined with wax; the images of the gods which could move their eyes and walk about, although they did not come completely to life like the figures of Hephaistos, the maker of Peleus' magic knife, among other things (Pl. 12).[557]

Craftsmanship of this order could arouse not only admiration but fear in the layman, if not in the craftsman himself. Homer says of Heracles' baldric that it was 'terrible, . . . a strap of gold on which were worked marvellous designs, bears and wild boar and bright-eyed lions, battles and fights and slayings of men. Let not the maker of this baldric ever make anything like it again!'[558]

Of course, if the general public was prepared to see something a little alarming in great craftsmanship, this was partly because the layman simply did not understand how the work had been done. But a more important question is whether the craftsman themselves were impressed by the idea that they were working in a mysterious and to some extent incalculable field. Was there an element which they felt could only be dealt with satisfactorily by means other than those of competent craftsmanship? We have already seen that there is a little evidence to support the view that craftsmen, like other men, were on occasion superstitious, and that they were sometimes inclined to use charms against evil spirits.[559] But the real answer to difficulties in the workshop or on the building site, in the mine or at the kiln, was not to recite spells, but to apply the fruits of training and experience. Daidalos was able to fly, and Hephaistos to make his bronzes come alive, not by magic or superhuman powers, but by *technē*—quite simply, these were superbly clever craftsmen, like the hero Odysseus, whose many-sided cleverness also included the craftsman's skill. Daidalos flew successfully, not because he knew the right spells, but because he used his head; Ikaros fell to his death because he foolishly went too close to the sun.

The absence of magic from the workshop is made particularly clear in Plutarch's life of King Numa, which at the same time shows clearly that magic was a force in other spheres of human activity. Numa himself was in touch with the supernatural; he could summon a goddess to visit him, and he conversed with Jupiter on the Aventine. He also contrived to capture the two demi-gods Picus and Faunus, Italian equivalents of the Greek Daktyloi—wild men of the woods and primitive technologists to boot—and forced them to foretell many things; they gave him a charm against thunder and lightning, which called for the use of human hair, onions and sprats. When an epidemic struck Rome, it was into Numa's hands that a bronze shield fell from the skies, with the message that if the shield were preserved, the city would be saved, but that eleven exact replicas must be made, to confuse any potential thief. Numa summoned the craftsmen of Rome, but all refused to take on the commission except Manurius Veturius, whose excellence of craftsmanship, *and nothing else*, ensured that his eleven replicas were indistinguishable from the original.[560]

TECHNE OR THE ESSENCE OF CRAFTSMANSHIP

The secret of Daidalos' achievements lay in the combination of his own expertise, the ability to make *daidala*, or finely wrought objects, which he gained from family training in the crafts, with the skill which he had inherited from his father Metion, 'forethought', and his grandfather Eupalamos, 'skilful-handed'.[561] Thus the qualities displayed by the first human craftsman were precisely those of which *technē* was constituted. These were the characteristics which connoisseurs saw in what they considered to be great works; and although most of the surviving comments on the subject have to do with the fine arts, it is obvious that both craftsmen and customers could seek and find *technē* in the manufacture of humbler objects.

Quotation after quotation can be given to show that it was the way in which a statue or painting had been executed, and the intentional effects the sculptor or painter had achieved, which drew admiration and analytical comment from the educated public. The fascination of fine craftsmanship is made very apparent in the Homeric poems; the description of how Hephaistos made Achilles' shield concerns divine not human craftsmanship, but the difference is one of degree, not quality:

Hephaistos began by making a large and powerful shield, adorned all over and finished with a bright triple rim of gleaming metal and fitted with a silver baldric. The shield consisted of five layers, and he decorated the face of it with a number of designs, executed with consummate skill, and representing first of all Earth, Sea and Sky, the indefatigable

Sun, the Moon at the full and all the constellations with which the heavens are crowned. . . . The craftsman had achieved a miracle.[562]

Compare Odysseus on the bedchamber in his palace on Ithaca:

A great secret went into the making of that complicated bed, and it was my work and mine alone. . . . Round [an olive tree] I built my room of close-set stone work, and when that was finished I roofed it over thoroughly and put in a solid, neatly fitting double door. . . . [The bed itself] I finished off with an inlay of gold, silver and ivory, and fixed a set of purple straps across the frame.[563]

Mythical workmanship too, but with what a wealth of circumstantial detail!

Cicero emphasizes the importance for the true connoisseur of assessing accurately the quality of workmanship of the craftsman in question: 'Who, of those who pay some attention to the lesser skills, does not appreciate the fact that the statues of Canachus were more rigid than they ought to have been, if they were to imitate reality?'[564] Just as for the Homeric audience, so for the Hellenistic man of taste, the attainment of absolute realism was the artistic ideal. The methods by which the great painters made their effects is the concern of Quintilian in this passage:

Zeuxis and Parrhasios . . . contributed much to the craft of painting. Of the two, the first discovered the calculation of lights and shades while the other . . . concentrated on subtlety of line. For Zeuxis gave more emphasis to the limbs of the body; . . . Parrhasios drew all types of outlines so well that they call him 'proposer of laws', since others follow his representations. . . . [Of later painters] Protogenes was outstanding for laborious care, Pamphilos and Melanthios for theoretical knowledge, Antiphilos for ease of execution, Theon of Samos for dramatic representations, and Apelles for ingenuity and grace.[565]

His comments on sculpture reveal the same preoccupation with technique:

> Precision and appropriateness appeared above all in the art of Polykleitos, to whom the victor's branch is awarded by many, although . . . they hold that he lacked weightiness. For while he gave to the human form an appropriateness which surpassed the ordinary, he seems not to have expressed the impressiveness of the gods. . . . It is said that he shied away from representing the more mature age-level, and did not dare to undertake anything more than smooth cheeks.[566]

Polykleitos' methods were only successful in certain cases.

The tone of these comments is echoed by Diodorus when he says (of sculptors many generations before his time), 'It was not possible for even these men to be so successful in their works that they could put on display a finished product of their skill which was considered completely flawless.'[567]

The appearance, the outline, the composition of parts making up the whole, and the techniques used to achieve as perfect a representation as possible—these are the features, and the only features, which the connoisseurs picked out. So Pliny remarks, of the colossal bronze statue, the Tuscan Apollo: 'It is a question whether it is more remarkable for the quality of the bronze or for the beauty of the workmanship.'[568] Of the bronze statuary Aristonidas he says, 'When he wanted to represent the madness of Athamas subsiding into remorse after he had thrown his son Learchos over the precipice, he made a mixture of bronze and iron so that when the rust shone through the sleek beauty of the bronze, a blush of shame would be expressed.'[569] What practical steps did the craftsman take to achieve the desired effect? This is what concerns Pliny.

The preoccupation with technique preserved, or indeed even gave rise to, 'informed' anecdotes about craftsmen and their methods of working—some of which are surely literary set-pieces somewhat remote from the actualities of the workshop. One such is the story of the competition between the painters

Zeuxis and Parrhasios; Zeuxis is said to have painted a bunch of grapes so realistically that some birds flew down to peck vainly at the fruit. Parrhasios countered by painting the picture of a curtain with such verisimilitude that Zeuxis thought it was a real curtain concealing Parrhasios' competition piece.[570] What then was the most important aspect of this exercise in fine painting? The closeness to reality which either painter could achieve by sheer technical brilliance.

The connoisseur was moved by admiration for the mechanics of craftsmanship. Pliny, speaking from his own experience, says of the sculptor Zenodoros: 'in his studio we used to admire not only the remarkable likeness of the clay model (of the colossal statue of Nero), but also the frame of quite small timbers which constituted the first state of the work put in hand.'[571] This is exactly in tune with the many anecdotal details which Pliny reports, such as that Famulus kept his toga on while painting, that Protogenes lived on lentils to keep his head clear for painting, or that Pasiteles, famous for his copies of earlier sculptures, was attacked by a panther while working from life among a shipment of recently unloaded wild beasts.[572] It may be that all of these anecdotes are based on real incidents; but the reason for their passing into the literary tradition lies in the connoisseur's preoccupation with *technē* and how to identify it. But was no other factor recognized?

By his detailed knowledge of the techniques which the fine craftsman used, the connoisseur was able to identify one man's work from another's. Styles could be distinguished not only according to schools, groups or types (like the Furnian, Clodian or Gratian styles of silver-chasing) but also, indeed mainly, by personal name. Yet if Pliny and his sources, because they knew all about how Aristonidas mixed this and that to make a striking representation of the remorseful Athamas, could identify other works by the same man; if they had learnt what characterized Polykleitos' disposition of proportions in his statues; or if they could recognize at a glance the shadow effects of the painter Zeuxis—this does not mean that they allowed any part to the *personality* of the individual craftsman in the conception of his

works, or that stylistic differences were seen to depend on anything other than variations in the way of using the traditional
techniques and of applying the tools which they had been trained
to use. Just as the patron's enthusiasm for sculpture was directed
towards the surface effects, the balance, the smoothness, the
pallor, or the fineness of detail and finish—matters for *technē*—
so the sculptor, painter, or architect was seen to respond to purely
external stimuli; he was not understood to have produced a
marvellous piece of work as a result of some insight peculiar to
his character. Artistic temperament was considered irrelevant and
unnecessary to craftsmanship; the fervour with which the sculptor
Apollodoros criticized his own works seems to have drawn not
sympathy, nor any agreement that perhaps his work was improved by such extreme measures, but only the nickname
Madman.[573] If *technē* could not provide all the answers, then it
was not the artistic flair or genius of the individual which would
do so, but chance. Protogenes struggled in vain to solve a painting
problem, and was finally moved to fling a wet rag at the picture
in a fury, thus producing, entirely by accident, exactly the effect
for which he had been seeking.[574]

Yet the large number of sculptors and painters in particular
who are known by name from the literary sources, together with
the numerous anecdotes concerning their work and habits,
suggests that there did exist a certain appreciation of the fine skilled
worker as an individual, and not simply as a label to a style or a
particular product. It has even been suggested that not only did
there develop an increasing recognition of the individual personality and its power to achieve, but that craftsmen and their activity
rose in the general estimation, and that by later antiquity the
concept of craftsmanship—*technē*—had given way to the idea
of true personal genius. The evidence will not, it seems to me, bear
such an interpretation; in most cases, reference to a craftsman by
name is made to serve the purpose of moral, philosophical or
rhetorical argument, and so throws little light on the question
of how in their own times craftsmen were considered to have
achieved their works.

Named individuals were first recognized and acknowledged in

the Greek world during the seventh century BC. Thereafter, as we have seen, craftsmen of various kinds (but mostly sculptors, some painters, and a few architects) came to be remembered by name in the traditions of the places where they worked (as well as in the signatures which they affixed to their works, very often), so that, to take a single example, Pausanias writing in the first century AD could speak of the sculptor and architect Gitiadas who made an image of Athena for the Spartans in the early period.[575] Where tradition was lacking, of course, it could be amplified or even invented; the gap between their unknown forerunners and the historical sculptors was filled by such figures as Smilis, Dipoinos and Skyllis of Crete, pupils of Daidalos, on one hand, and on the other men named in all seriousness by Pausanias as being responsible for specific works still extant in his day.[576]

If the name was remembered, then in most cases very little else remained. This is still the case in the Classical period, for although more details of their lives survive, and the craftsmanship of many sculptors and painters became proverbial in later antiquity, of the painter Polygnotos it can only be said that he painted certain pictures, that he came from Thasos, that he showed his magnanimity by painting the Athenians' Stoa Poikile at his own expense (an action which distinguished him from the *banausoi*), and that he was the first to paint women in transparent dresses, and to give expression to the faces in his pictures.[577] But we have no direct impression of his own concepts of his work. So too Polykleitos of Argos became proverbial in his own day for his theories of harmony in sculptural design, and remained proverbial for the rest of antiquity; but as a personality he too is lacking. With the stories surrounding the name of Pheidias we come somewhat closer to a real person, if only because he is remembered for his connection with Pericles; however, personal views on his working methods and opinions of the work he was doing do not come through in the surviving evidence, so we have to infer from his products and the reports of the self-portraits and representations of friends he incorporated into the statues of Athena, that he was a very confident and self-assertive individual (*Pl.* 78).[578]

It is only in the fourth century that the growing appreciation of

the power of personality which had its roots in the political and
intellectual developments of the seventh and sixth centuries came
fully to flower.[579] It is in Alexander the Great that moralists,
biographers and cataloguers of the qualities of greatness saw
potentially the most striking individual in history; they began
to make the most of him well within his own lifetime. It is
hardly surprising that the craftsmen connected with him were
caught up in the same process of enhancement of personality.

Apelles, an East Greek and member of a painter's family, was
commissioned to paint Alexander's portrait. What better means
could he have had of ensuring his own standing in the eyes of
posterity? It can be no coincidence that we are told more about
his working methods and opinions of his work than any of his
predecessors'. His highest aim, of course, was perfect realism,
and to that end he laid his work open to the criticism of the
passer-by, 'preferring the common people as more careful judges
than himself'; however, a cobbler was only allowed to pronounce
on the sandal, not the leg, of the subject in the painting.[580] That
only the expert should discuss the subject in which he was trained
is the point of the anecdote of Alexander's visit to Apelles' studio;
when Alexander persisted in talking about painting, of which he
was ignorant, Apelles tactfully advised him to stop, since the
boys who mixed the paints were laughing at him.[581]

Protogenes of Kaunos, who spent much of his time painting in
Rhodes, approximates most closely to an eccentric in what we
know of the craftsmen's world. He was not closely connected
with Alexander's court, but knew Apelles well enough to be
helped out of severe financial difficulty by him. He was said to
have begun as a poor man, a ships' painter; thereafter he 'commemorated his humble beginnings by including small drawings
of warships in the gateway of the Athena temple at Athens
which he was decorating'. He is also described as 'devoted to his
craft and hence not very productive'—presumably he could not
let a painting alone until it was perfect in his eyes.[582] The story
of the paint-rag suggests that he became more easily upset by
technical difficulties than other painters; on the other hand he
could endure hardship for the sake of his work, for not only did

he live on pulses to keep his head clear, but ignored the threat of
Demetrius Poliorcetes' siege-engines outside Rhodes, refusing
to move out of the small garden on the edge of the city where
he was working. He presents a fine picture of Hellenistic Man,
high-minded, emotional, and living in stirring times, associated
with the great men of the moment.[583]

The most famous member of Alexander's group of craftsmen
was the sculptor Lysippos, 'self-taught' as it was claimed. The
story goes that he was a coppersmith in his youth, and was
inspired to take up sculpture by hearing a painter, Eupompos,
say that 'one should imitate nature, not (the works *or* style of)
another man'.[584] Of course he cannot have broken entirely with
all tradition, but the concept of the autonomous artist, making
his own rules and creating his own style, seems for a brief moment
to have existed in the person and statements of Lysippos. What
exactly it was he said, and what precisely he meant by it, are of
course entirely open to question; but surely the independence of
mind which comes through in the reported 'remarks' is grounded
in the real man—'his predecessors had made men as they really
were, but he made them as they appeared to be'.

These few are the craftsmen of whom most is said in the surviving sources. The increasing enthusiasm for biography in the
Hellenistic and Roman period does not seem to have led to an
increase in the amount of information on the lives and times of
later craftsmen; even the sculptors, architects and others employed by the Emperor Augustus remain for the most part
anonymous—his gem-cutter Dioscurides being one of the very
few exceptions.[585] And yet much very fine work was produced
throughout the Hellenistic and Roman period, no less than by the
far better reported craftsmen earlier, so that we certainly cannot
explain the comparative silence by pointing to a difference in
standards, or by assuming that no craftsman in imperial Rome
ever said anything about his work, or thought about it sufficiently
intelligently to advance his craft a little further beyond the point
at which he had begun to learn it. Expressed admiration for
contemporary craftsmen, despite all the names, works and styles
which are so minutely and frequently quoted in the literature,

would appear to come down to the single account, by the Elder Pliny, of a visit to the sculptor Zenodorus' workshop.

What then was the point of all the references to works of art and their creators? Have they any value whatsoever as indication of what anyone really thought about craftsmanship and the men who practised it? Does a single one of the thirty-five Hellenistic epigrams in the *Greek Anthology* made on the sculptor Myron and his particularly famous Cow-statue reveal a more penetrating perception of the nature of Myron's work than had been gained by observers earlier?[586] The situation seems to be that works of art and to a certain extent craftsmen who produced them had become fashionable figures of speech among literary men, rather in the way that the painter Piraeicus' 'sordid' pictures caught on, or that the epigrammatists occasionally took up quite humble subjects, to amuse and divert.[587] If the neo-Platonist philosopher Plotinus purported to describe how Pheidias had been 'divinely inspired' in a dream to create the gold and ivory statue of Zeus at Olympia, and had not used models but had sought to portray the god as he actually saw him, Plotinus was not necessarily promoting the theory that craftsmen were to be considered inspired in their works as poets always had been; he was merely making use of a vivid metaphor to further his own argument, which was not about craftsmanship but about the pursuit of the Good.[588]

Indeed Plotinus can hardly have cared very much about Pheidias' or any other sculptor's or painter's reception or execution of ideas. He himself refused to have his portrait painted (although it would seem that the painter Carteius was a personal friend), and so it had to be done by stealth;[589] but more significant of the gulf between his philosophical preoccupations and real craftsmanship is the fact that the example he took from the crafts was one which had long since become a rhetorical cliché, and which stood at seven centuries' remove from his own time.

The main purpose of the numerous quotations from the crafts was to serve rhetorical ends. If a concrete image were required, or an educated reference to the arts, to fill out an argument or provide a common touch, any number of stock figures could be trotted forth, Myron's cow included. Works and workers of the past alone would do—contemporary sculptors, gem-cutters, painters, bronze statuaries lacked the essential cultural patina.

The concept of genius, in the post-Renaissance or modern sense, never came into being in antiquity, early or late. In the early sixth century BC Solon had said, 'The sculptor works with his hands, but it is the poet who is established as the measure of much desired wisdom', and so it remained.[590] The Muses spoke to Homer, Hesiod, Vergil; but no divine voice prompted Onatas, Pheidias, Parrhasios, Protogenes or Pasiteles. Only the poet worked in the realm of *sophia*—inner wisdom, insight—and only the poet was truly inspired.[591] The craftsman worked with *technē*, skill instilled from without, skill by which surface effects could be achieved. One of the fundamental elements in the educated public's attitude towards the craftsmen was not the gradual awakening of a deeper appreciation that they were intimately involved in their work, but the enduring distinction made between the maker and his product, succinctly expressed in Plutarch's remark that 'if the works of Pheidias and Polykleitos were admired, then, even so, no right thinking young man would want to emulate either Pheidias or Polykleitos'. So Homer had presented the Olympian gods as admiring Hephaistos' craftsmanship, while laughing at the limping god himself.

THE CRAFTSMAN'S SENSE OF IDENTITY WITH HIS WORK

The point of view of the craftsman, explicit in only a handful of personal statements, is implicit in the numerous signatures put not only to sculptures but to a wide variety of works, from building blocks to plastered walls. Evidence of this kind is barely adequate for discussion of the skilled worker's own concept of how he worked, and of what precisely he thought he was doing; but it is just sufficient to permit the inference that, just as there was no dramatic alteration during antiquity in the patron's or connoisseur's evaluation of craftsmanship, so the craftsman's view remained more or less the same, once he can be said to have formulated one.

For although we may argue that only in the intellectual climate of the fourth century BC could Lysippos have made such self-assertive remarks about his work—that only then was individual expression of this kind given its head, and that only by this stage in the development of sculpture could a craftsman think in terms of breaking away from previous practices—when all is said and done, there really seems to be very little difference in the intensity of personal involvement or in the intention of the statement, between Lysippos' pronouncements as mentioned earlier and what the Naxian sculptor Alxenor had said about 150 years before.[592] In his signature to a relief which displays the results of experimenting in the newly appreciated field of foreshortening, he declared, 'Alxenor the Naxian made this. You have only to look and see!'

Just as it was *technē* which was seen as the essence of craftsmanship by the connoisseur, so it was *technē* which the craftsman considered the vital part of his activity as a skilled worker. During the second century AD, the painter Loukios Sossios of Cyrene had it declared ,in his epitaph that his *technē* surpassed (sc. that of any possible rival):

> In case you, wayfarer, know by hearsay of Loukios Euthykles the figure painter—I who made the palace at Cyrene glorious among the nations for my surpassing *technē*—I who brought forth as a great benefice to my paternal city the likenesses of the divinities—here at that place where I figured prominently among the members of the Council do I lie.[593]

In the sixth century BC, the Chiot sculptor Archermos had said, in his signature to a dedication made by Mikkiades of Paros: 'Far-shooting Apollo, receive this beautiful statue, one of the works accomplished by Archermos in his wisdom [meaning here "technical know-how"].'[594] The joint signature of the Argive sculptors Eutelidas and Chrysothemis, *c.* 500 BC, says that 'they knew their *technē* from their forebears'.[595] With these pithy statements may be compared the sentiments of the epigrams attributed to the self-confident painter Parrhasios, such as:

A man who lives in elegant style and at the same time honours virtue has written these lines—Parrhasios, from Ephesus, his glorious fatherland. Nor have I left my father forgotten, Euenor who begot me, his own son, to carry off the prize in craftsmanship [*techne*] among the Greeks.

Another of his compositions reads:

Even if they hear unbelievingly, yet I say to them: I declare that at last the limits of this *techne* have been reached by my hand. Insurmountable is the boundary that I have fixed. Yet nothing that mortals have done is without blame.[596]

Somewhat similar thoughts are expressed in the epitaph of the potter Bakchios who died *c.* 370/60 BC, perhaps a late contemporary of Parrhasios:

Bakchios, son of Amphis ——, of the Kerameikos deme. In the competitions which the city staged, of those who combine earth and water and fire [i.e. make pottery], Greece judged Bakchios the first both in character and in achievement. He took all the crowns.[597]

At about the same time the miner Atotas was commemorated thus: 'No one rivalled me in *techne*.'[598] Considerably later, in Rome, the Greek carpenter and housebuilder Maximus was also remembered as being 'unrivalled in *techne*'.[599] In southern Asia Minor, the sculptor or stonemason Paion signed a grave relief, 'Paion, son of Mousaios of Perge, the finest in his *techne*'.[600] And at Perinthos, a sculptor, Kapiton, and a mason, Ianouarios, signed a small temple by the city gate with the statement accompanying it, that the temple had been set up by 'men wise in craftsmanship [*sophotechneies*]. They wrought it with carving and fine incising. Your [the god's] Kleitos Kapiton did the sculpture, assisted by Ianouarios, dear to you, and he engraved, in pious respect. . . .'[601] It was at Perinthos too, and at about the same time —the mid-second century AD—that the mosaicist Harpokration had comment made on his expertise.[602] The sculptor Zenon, who belonged to the group from Aphrodisias which settled at Rome stated his case in these terms: 'I journeyed through many cities, relying on my *technai*. . . . I made this tomb with my own hands, thereby accomplishing a marvellous work.'[603]

All these were Greeks. The few surviving statements from Latin-speaking craftsmen demonstrate the same point of view. According to the epitaph of the carpenter Q. Candidus Benignus, he was outstandingly knowledgable about his craft—'no one could outdo him'.[604] So a patron could say of his goldsmith, M. Canuleius Zosimus, that 'he excelled over all others in the art of Clodian chasing'.[605]

Few as these statements are, they suggest that at no stage in antiquity did craftsmen feel impelled to move on to another theme. *Technē* was the only quality which called for comment.

A certain anxiety on the part of lesser craftsmen as to their poverty in or lack of *technē* can be detected. By taking the name of a famous worker in their craft they hoped to attract to themselves the great man's quality of workmanship. Among Athenian vase-painters of the second quarter of the fifth century BC, it is clear that several different hands all signed themselves Polygnotos —it can only be, in emulation of the great painter of pictures.[606] Myron recurs as a sculptor's name, well after the time of the fifth-century sculptor—at Thebes, *c.* 200 BC, and at Rome later.[607] A third-century Argive sculptor Polykleitos is known, and even if he were a descendant of the well-known Polykleitos, it was still professionally helpful to be able to take his name, as in the cases of the later Praxiteles and the second-century Skopas of Paros.[608]

The Sicyonian sculptor Daidalos, *c.* 400 BC, cannot but have been named with the mythical ancestor of all sculptors in mind; but if so, it is somewhat curious that there were not more craftsmen of this name.[609] A few craftsmen seem to have taken names which expressed a quality inherent in their craftsmanship (or so they wished to imply); in addition to the mythical Daidalos, Metion and Eupalamos, and the terracotta workers reputed to have gone to Italy from Corinth with the exiled Demaratos,

Eucheir—'well- or able-handed'—, Diopus—'keen-eyed'—and Eugrammos—'well-drawing', a Corinthian sculptor, *c.* 525 BC, also took the name of Eucheir, as did an Athenian, *c.* 200 BC; his son was called Euboulides—'well-counselling' or 'well-advised';[610] Cheirisophos—'wise-' or 'skilful-hand'—was the name of a Cretan sculptor of the sixth century BC, as of an imperial freedman silversmith at work in Rome during the first century AD (*Pl.* 37).[611] The sculptor Theokosmos of Megara who is supposed to have worked on a gold and ivory statue of Zeus there in the mid-fifth century was 'god-decorator'.[612]

The clearest demonstration of one man's superiority in *technē* over another could be made in the craftsmen's competitions, such as the potter Bakchios won. How often affairs of this kind occurred we do not know, but probably the potters' contest in Athens formed part of a festival, in which the community celebrated the *technē* of its craftsmen by making them show off against one another, and by giving them the opportunity to beat rivals from elsewhere.[613]

The painters' contests—between Zeuxis and Parrhasios, Parrhasios and Timanthes, and Timanthes and Kolotes—if they occurred at all and are not simply rhetorical inventions, might have been purely private affairs. More likely, they were competing for a commission, perhaps to decorate some public building, which was awarded on the result of the competition. Such certainly seems to have been the nature of the sculptors' contest between Pheidias, Polykleitos, Kresilas and Phradmon at Ephesus; they competed with statues of Amazons, all four of which the Ephesians bought and set up in the sanctuary of Artemis.[614] It was the winning of such a competition that the sculptor Paionios chose to boast in his signature to the winged Victory he made for the Messenians and Naupactians at Olympia (*Pl.* 80).

Paionios amplified his signature by stating the evidence for his outstanding ability. So had Alxenor pointed to his own virtuosity. Grophon 'made the faultless statue, having prayed to Athena'. The sculptor and light engineer Kleoitas added this two-line verse to a statue which he had made for the Athenians: 'He who first invented the horse-starting gate at Olympia, Kleoitas, son of

Aristokles, made me.' And in the Roman imperial period Aristainetos signed the temple which he built for Hadrian at Cyzicus thus: 'The noble Aristainetos raised me from the ground with the assistance of many labourers and money from the whole of Asia.'

The craftsman's signature alone said a great deal—the difficulty is to assess how much. The earliest signatures known are symptomatic of the new sense of individualism which manifested itself during the seventh century BC, and which from then on was one of the characteristics which distinguished the Greeks most sharply from the peoples of the ancient Near East. The same intention always underlay the act of signing—the craftsman was saying in effect, 'Here is my answer to the technical and stylistic problems presented by this piece of work.' The seventh-century potter or vase-painter Chares of Corinth and the sculptor Euthykartides were already employing the formula used henceforth with very little variation until the end of antiquity: 'So-and-so made me'. Here then is evidence of perhaps the most fundamental unity of concept among craftsmen at all periods: not only did they always choose to recognize, in *technē*, the ruling virtue of their craft, but already in the seventh century, almost as soon as anyone had begun to express the personal as opposed to the public, religious or epic point of view, they felt and wished to express also a measure of personal responsibility for the works they made. So it continued to be felt, without any apparent development of concept. During the seventh century BC craftsmen had ceased to be anonymous; never again in antiquity did there occur so momentous an alteration in their status or in their thinking on the subject.

However, the practice did not become universal, but always remained commonest among the sculptors. It was almost certainly they who had initiated the idea; and the reason can only be that the origins of the craft of monumental sculpture in Greece coincided with, and were surely contingent upon, the new realization of personal identity, and the accompanying desire for personal memorials. The statues themselves were endowed with a certain personality, as the early form of the craftsman's signature,

'So-and-so made me', suggests, a concept extended not only to pots but occcasionally to building blocks such as the piece signed by the mason Parmenon (*Pl.* 72), and expressed particularly vividly in the Naxians' inscription on the base of their Apollo in the Delian sanctuary, *c.* 600 BC: 'I am of the same stone, both statue and base.'[615]

Henceforth most if not all statues intended as dedications were signed by the sculptor, whoever the patron. Dedicatory and grave reliefs, and sometimes the reliefs on public monuments, were signed too—as in the case of the friezes on the great altar of Pergamon.[616] But there were many such reliefs which were not signed, such as the dedication of the twelve Athenian clothes cleaners. Why this should have been the case is by no means clear; the poor quality of some signed works makes it clear that there was no convention which said that only works of good quality should be signed, nor is there any particular reason to suppose that some patrons simply chose not to allow credit for the execution of a fine piece.

Some sort of rationale can be detected in the anonymity of the majority of sculptures done for public monuments, that is to say of temple friezes, pediments, and Roman imperial memorials. So the sculptors of the pediments of the temple of Zeus at Olympia remain anonymous to this day; nor is there any real certainty as to who designed and directed work on Trajan's column and countless other 'historical' reliefs. In such works, the sculptor acted not as an independent designer and executant of his craft, but as an imperial archivist, not an initiator of the composition but a propagandist. Yet even in this sphere of operations, an occasional signature was added, on the whole discreetly—as, for example, that of M. Ulpius Orestes on the foot of a sacrificial bull in a relief from Trajan's Forum (*Pl.* 67); or Theophilus' on the heel of a colossal statue of an (unknown) emperor; or M. Epidius Eros', along the hem of the robe of Jupiter Ammon in Rome.[617]

Signing one's works was originally a Greek practice, and it remained primarily the concern of Greeks in the Roman world too. But craftsmen in the Latin-speaking or western half of the ancient world adopted the practice to a limited extent. Sculptors signing in Latin kept on the whole to the same formula, 'So-and-so made it', but there were one or two variant forms: Paulus at Rome and Iulius Musticus in Narbonese Gaul, for example, preferred to be more precise, and said 'sculpted'.[618] In even the remotest parts of the Roman world, craftsmen became concerned to sign their name—in Britain, Priscus and Sulinus did so at Bath.[619]

The architect's sense of personal connection with the building he had put up could not in the nature of things have been as great as the sculptor's with his statue. Moreover, the Greek temple architect was subordinate to the sculptor responsible for the sculptural decoration if not for the cult statue within the temple too. The situation was a little different in the Roman world. Architects stand much more readily identified by their works. For instance, C. Postumius Pollio signed the city gate of Formiae and a small temple at Terracina.[620] In Alexandria Pontius signed, in both Latin and Greek, one of the four bronze claws forming the base of an obelisk.[621] At Antibes, Sextus Iulius Caecilianus put his name on an arch; and at Herculaneum the work of P. Numisius on the theatre was commemorated—below the name of the official responsible for the project, and in smaller lettering, to be sure.[622] As a result, it may be, of Roman architects' confidence in this respect, some Greek architects of the Roman period were encouraged to sign their works. 'Kleon the Lacedaemonian was the architect' was inscribed on a building at Sparta. The theatre at Aspendos was signed by Zenon, son of Theodoros. While the most boastful signature of all was, of course, Aristainetos' at Cyzicus.[623]

The practice was imitated by one or two humbler members of the building trade. At Pompeii, the freedman Aemilius Crescens wrote up his name several times on a house wall, calling himself 'architect'; one of his signatures, if so they can strictly be called, comprised a rather elaborate verbal and visual pun on the word *architectus*, which could of course mean either 'architect' or 'shipwright'. A similar wit is perceptible in the signature of a fellow freedman, Aemilius Celer, on a painted sign he made for a gladiator's contest: 'Aemilius Celer [painted this sign] all alone in the moonlight.'[624] These are examples of signing for fun, of aping one's betters in the craft world. There is, however, one work-man's signature from early fifth-century Greece which was surely intended to be taken absolutely seriously; the quality of work of the limestone block which Parmenon signed (Pl. 72), as indeed of the entire wall in which it was set, in the mason's opinion merited a signature as much as would any sculpture in marble—even if the skill with which he worked the block was not matched by his ability as a letter-cutter.

If sculptors were the first to put their names to their works, and if they continued to do so in greater numbers than the members of any other craft, yet we would expect painters to have taken up the idea with equal enthusiasm. Unfortunately, no paintings, signed or otherwise, survive from the Classical period, but the number of names mentioned in the literature suggests that men such as Polygnotos, Parrhasios, Zeuxis, Protogenes and Apelles would have signed their productions. But if Greek painters of the Classical period had done so, then it would appear that the practice had for some reason become less common in the Hellenistic and Roman period; remarkably few of the surviving paintings are signed—for example, the Garden of Livia (Pl. 86) is not. Yet it cannot be that what has survived is all of it only second-rate, and that only the greatest painters signed their best works which have somehow perished, every one.

The situation seems quite otherwise in the case of the lesser craft of designing mosaics. They never attracted anything like the same admiration as the panel painters, yet more signed mosaics are known than signed paintings. The signatures of Gnosis and Dioskourides (Pls. 87, 88) clearly reflect pride in what are un-questionably superb examples of the craft; but why was Antaios moved to put his name to a very ordinary black and white pavement in the Delian sanctuary?[625] The signatures of Latin-speaking mosaic pavers demonstrate the desire to specify more exactly the nature of their work than the Greeks, who continued to say simply, 'So-and-so made it'. Thus, some 'painted', others 'tesellated', and yet others 'mosaic'd' their pavements.[626]

Examples of ornamental metalwork were occasionally signed,

but anonymity was far more common. Again, the reason why some were and some were not does not leap immediately to mind; pieces demonstrating some originality in design are nameless, while an imitative work like the imperial freedman Cheirisophos' silver cup (*Pl.* 37), which he probably based on a design for Arretine pottery, was given the benefit of its maker's signature.

The engraving of gems and seal-stones called for delicacy of touch and accuracy of eye in a higher degree than in other crafts (apart from the jeweller's). It is clear that at all periods this kind of work was very much admired. Yet once again, it is the case that only a few examples were signed, at all periods; we know from their works the names of Onesimos, Syries and Epimenes, in the late sixth century BC, and of Dexamenos in the fifth (*Pls.* 44, 45). Of others known, Menophilos' is somewhat unusual in having been cut in reverse, so that it would always be legible when the seal was used.[627] The one gem-cutter mentioned in the literature is Augustus' seal-cutter Dioscourides, of whom signed gems have survived, and of his three sons too.[628]

Cutting dies for coins required almost as much care as gem-engraving, and many ancient coins were truly works of art. But the number of signed coins is minute, and all were made within the same area and during the same period, in South Italy and Sicily during the late fifth and early fourth centuries BC.[629] It is easier to understand why most coins were unsigned than to explain the few which were; coins were issued by the state, and the main function of the design was to provide an immediately recognizable guarantee of the quality and value of the coin. The Athenians retained the same motifs virtually unaltered for nearly three centuries on their silver tetradrachm—helmeted Athena on one side, and the owl and olive sprig on the other (*Pls.* 49, 50). Roman coins carried symbols of civic solidarity or advertisement of imperial achievement. In neither case did the designer's personal involvement in his work have a chance of recognition. The very few coiners in southern Italy and Sicily who were allowed the privilege of signing their works can only have done so because the circumstances in which they worked were highly unusual; the coming to power in Syracuse, the leading state in the area, of a tyranny at the end of the fifth century may have had much to do with it—the tyrant wished to attract the best workers, and rewarded them accordingly (*Pls.* 47, 48, 51, 52).

Among the earliest surviving signatures is that of the vase-painter Timonides, who was working at Corinth in the late seventh or early sixth century. But signed vases from Corinth are rare, and many comparatively poor in quality; elsewhere, in other pottery-producing centres such as Rhodes, Boeotia and Euboea, the practice was scarcely known.[630] It is only at Athens, in the second quarter of the sixth century, that potters and painters seemed to gain the necessary confidence to begin signing their works in some number. The first known is Sophilos' portrayal of spectators at the funeral games of Patroklos, a scene unusual for its time in that it attempted to show the spectators in depth on a tiered bench. Impressed with his own expertise, it may be, he daringly did what no Athenian potter or painter had done before.[631] The signing of vases became increasingly common after *c.* 540 BC; even at this period, it seems, not all skilled craftsmen were exactly at ease with the written word, for the great potter and painter Exekias managed to misspell his name on one of the two surviving signed pieces of his.[632] Signing remained fairly standard practice throughout the later sixth and early fifth centuries, but became less so after *c.* 450 BC. Why this should have been the case is not clear—certainly the standard of pottery and painting was in no way in decline; and yet some of the finest vases produced, the white-ground ware with their finely drawn scenes in pastels, were none of them signed.

In fact there are far more vases unsigned than there are signed. Of those who did add their name, none appears to have signed every piece he made or painted, while some only signed a very few of the works which can be attributed to them on stylistic grounds.[633] It is curious too that none of the workshop scenes is signed either. Here one would have expected some expression of the vase-painter's sense of identification with the scene he was painting; yet the absence of any such association in the craftsman's mind was such that one workshop scene included vases of a type which, as far as we can tell, the workshop for which the painter worked never actually produced.[634]

The whole picture is one of inexplicable inconsistency of practice. Thus, of the south Italian vase-painters, only the later and poorer exponents of the craft signed their works.[635] Most craftsmen in the ancient world never put their name to any of their products, of course. But as I suggested at the beginning of this survey the important thing is not that only a handful of skilled workers expressed confidence in their ability by leaving lasting evidence of their pride of workmanship, but that any did so at all. Mannes, the Phrygian woodman resident in fifth-century Attica, could have it said in his epitaph, 'By Zeus, I never saw a better woodman than myself'. A Roman Republican silversmith could inscribe a cosmetics pot, 'Novios Plautios made me'.[636] All that Greek sculptors employed by the Great King of Persia could do to establish their identity was to scratch on the base of a royal statue graffiti which were unmistakably Greek in style (*Pl. 76*).

NOTES

ABBREVIATIONS

ABV   J. D. Beazley, *Attic Black-Figure Vases* (1956)
AJA   *American Journal of Archaeology*
*ARV*²   J. D. Beazley, *Attic Red-Figure Vases*, 2nd edn. (1963)
BCH   *Bulletin de correspondance Hellenique*
Bluemner,   H. Bluemner, *Technologie und Terminologie der*
  Gewerbe und Künste   *Gewerbe und Künste der Griechen und Römer*, 4 vols.
                          (1875–8)
BSA   *Annual of the British School at Athens*
Calabi-Limentani   I. Calabi-Limentani, *Studi sulla società Romana: il*
                          lavoro artistico (1958)
CIG   *Corpus Inscriptionum Graecarum*
CIL   *Corpus Inscriptionum Latinarum*
Cod. Theod.   *Codex Theodosianus*
CP   *Classical Philology*
CQ   *Classical Quarterly*
Crook, *LLR*   J. A. Crook, *Law and Life of Rome* (1967)
Dubois   C. Dubois, *Etude sur l'administration et l'exploitation*
                          des carrières dans le monde romain (1908)
FD   *Fouilles de Delphes*, vol. III, part v
FGH   F. Jacoby, *Die Fragmente der griechischen Historiker*
                          (1923–)
FHG   C. Müller, *Fragmenta historicorum Graecorum*
FIRA   S. Riccobono *et al.*, ed., *Fontes iuris Romani anteius-*
                          tiniani, 3 vols. (1951, 1943)
Frank, *Economic Survey* T. Frank, ed., *Economic Survey of Ancient Rome*, 6
                          vols. (1933–40)
GTBE   A. Burford, *The Greek Temple Builders at Epidauros*
                          (1969)
HSCP   *Harvard Studies in Classical Philology*
ID   *Inscriptions de Délos*
IG   *Inscriptiones Graecae*
IGRR   *Inscriptiones Graecae ad res Romanas pertinentes*
ILS   H. Dessau, *Inscriptiones Latinae Selectae*, 3 vols. (1892–
                          1916)

JDAI	*Jahrbuch des deutschen archäologischen Instituts*
JHS	*Journal of Hellenic Studies*
Jones, *AD*	A. H. M. Jones, *Athenian Democracy* (1957)
Jones, *LRE*	A. H. M. Jones, *The Later Roman Empire 284–602*, 3 vols. (1964)
JRS	*Journal of Roman Studies*
Lauffer, *Bergwerkssklaven*	S. Lauffer, *Die Bergwerkssklaven von Laureion* (1955, 1956)
Lindos I	*Lindos*, vol. II, part I (ed. Chr. Blinkenberg)
Loewy	Loewy, *Inschriften griechischen Bildhauer* (1885)
NH	Pliny, *Natural History*
OGIS	W. Dittenberger, ed., *Orientis Graecae Inscriptiones Selectae* (1903–05)
PA	J. Kirchner, *Prosopographia Attica* (1901–3)
Randall, *Erechtheum*	R. H. Randall Jr, 'The Erechtheum Workers', *AJA* 1953, 199–210
Raubitschek, *Dedications*	A. E. Raubitschek, *Dedications from the Athenian Acropolis* (1948)
RE	Pauly-Wissowa, ed., *Real-Encyclopädie der classischen Alterumswissenschaft*
REG	*Revue des études grecques*
SCA	M. I. Finley, ed., *Slavery in Classical Antiquity* (1960)
SEG	*Supplementum Epigraphicum Graecum*
SHA	Scriptores historiae Augustae
SIG³	W. Dittenberger, *Sylloge Inscriptionum Graecarum*, 3rd edn. (1915–24)
TAPA	*Transactions of the American Philological Association*
Waltzing	J.-P. Waltzing, *Etude historique sur les corporations professionelles chez les Romains*, 4 vols. (1895–8)
Westermann, *Slave Systems*	Westermann, *Slave Systems of Greek and Roman Antiquity* (1960)

CHAPTER I

1 *ID*, 1

2 Xenophon, *On Household Management* IV, 2–3—a point of view also expressed by Plato and, in particular, by Aristotle

3 *Dream* 1, 8. Of course Lucian derides, here and elsewhere, virtually every occupation and station in life—so that plucking this statement out of context is to a certain extent unfair selectivity

4 Plutarch, *Pericles* 2, 1

5 For Loukios Sossios' epitaph, see p. 208; Epikrates' honours—*SIG³*, 707

6 This excludes the makers of ephemera like scent, bread and sausages, even

though they were skilled too. Doctors and actors are likewise excluded from consideration, except in passing, for although they were professionals and highly skilled, there are too many other points of difference between them and the craftsmen proper to allow of a combined study which would be any more useful than separate surveys. Similarly, to have included the farmers—skilled, traditionally trained, and dependent on their own labours as they were—would have widened the scope of this book into something like a treatise on 'the ancient world at work'. But of course the sculptor, the smith and the potter played, numerically speaking, a small part in that workaday ancient world

7 Cf. Cicero's remark that 'it was more important for the Athenians to have weather-proof roofs over their heads than to possess a gold and ivory statue of Athena; yet I would have preferred to be a Pheidias rather than a master-roofer. . . . There are few competent painters or sculptors, but no danger of a shortage of porters and labourers' (*Brutus*, 257)

8 *Iliad* XXIII, 140. Hephaistos' work of course included the shield of Achilles, *Iliad* XVIII, 178–613. Odysseus is made to describe in great detail exactly how he built the master bedchamber in his palace in *Odyssey* XXIII, 190

9 Diodorus Siculus, XXVI, 1

10 Melville J. Herskovits, *Cultural Anthropology* (1966), 140–1, comments on the kind of economy in which, for example, the making of pottery was restricted to the women of the community

11 'What stranger is welcome, unless it be the seer, the bard, or the sawyer of planks?' asks Eumaios in *Odyssey* XVII, 382–5. The itinerant skilled worker was one of the few outsiders whom the early Greek community was glad to see. Itinerancy, and the consequent uncertainty as to whether or when skilled workers would be available, was a characteristic of later society too

12 The people of Bassai in Arcadia may be regarded as hapless provincials importing what they thought were the best designers to build their temple. The experimental nature of the inner colonnade, with its unusual—for the fifth century BC—Corinthian order, is perhaps due to the architect's feeling that before an awed and uncritical building authority two thousand feet up in the Arcadian hills he could get away with daring personal innovations which would not have been accepted at Athens

13 As exemplified by the career of the Greek sculptor Zenodoros, who worked on a colossal statue of Nero at Rome, and also made a statue for the Arverni in Gaul (Pliny, *NH*, 34, 45)

14 *IG* I², 1084

15 *ILS*, 7237

16 *Works and Days*, esp. 176–264

17 Archilochos (Budé), fr. 13

18 The most complete collection of the early inscriptional material is L. H. Jeffrey's *The Local Scripts of Archaic Greece* (1961)

19 The translation is taken from A. T. Olmstead, *History of the Persian Empire* (1948), 168, where further references are given

20 *IG* I², 374, 256ff, 197ff

21 B. Ashmole, *Journal of the Warburg and Courtauld Institutes*, 1956, 179–91

22 This point is observed further in ch. II

23 The picture presented here may seem over-pessimistic. But the fact is that, although much work has been done on the cost of living in the Greek and Hellenistic periods, the evidence on which calculations are based comes from widely scattered sources and varying contexts; the Athenian evidence is gathered together in A. H. M. Jones' *Athenian Democracy* (1957), ch. 1, 'The Economic Base'. There are too many unknowns, such as what prices were for privately contracted services or for goods sold on the open market, to allow of precise statements on rises or falls in the standard of living, *pace* the arguments of G. Glotz, *Ancient Greece at Work* (1926), 282–7

24 J. B. Ward-Perkins, 'Tripolitania and the Marble Trade', *JRS* 1951, 89–104

25 A definitive discussion of these and the other workers concerned in the completion of the Erechtheion is provided by R. H. Randall Jr, 'The Erechtheum Workers' *AJA* 1953, 199–210

26 Cf. the marks on Roman tiles, which have lent themselves to very detailed analysis by H. Bloch, *I bolli laterizi: la storia edilizia Romana* (1938)

27 The problem of lost identity concerns not only the more ordinary crafts. The name of the architect of four of the temples in Pericles' building programme is not known for certain; it may have been Kallikrates, who was responsible for other monuments in this period. I. M. Shear, 'Kallikrates', *Hesperia* 1963, 375–424. The sculptors of the pediments of the temple of Zeus at Olympia, *c.* 460 BC, cannot be identified at all—B. Ashmole, 'Some Nameless Sculptors of the Fifth Century BC', *Proceedings of the British Academy*, 1962

28 Athens—*IG* I², 335–74, *IG* II², 1665–85; Delos—*IG* XI², 142–287, *ID*, 288–509; Delphi—*FD*, 19–90; Epidauros—*IG* IV², 1, 102–20, and A. Burford, 'Notes on the Building Inscriptions from Epidauros', *BSA* 1967, 254–334

29 The one known example is the building contract from Puteoli, *c.* 100 BC; see T. Wiegand, 'Die puteolanische Bauinschrift', *Jahrbuch für Classische Philologie*, Supplementband, 1894

30 As pointed out some time ago by P. Guiraud, *La Main d'oeuvre industrielle dans l'ancienne Grèce* (1900), 37

31 Xenophon, *Memorabilia* II, 8, 1–5

32 An introductory survey of the ancient writers in this *genre* is made by J. J. Pollitt in the introductions to his *Art of the Greeks* and *Art of the Romans* (1965 and 1966)

CHAPTER II

33 *On Household Management* IV, 2–3

34 C. Mossé, *The Ancient World at Work* (1969), 14—from Lysias, XXXIV

35 *On Duty* I, 42, 151–2

36 In Jane Austen's *Pride and Prejudice* Mr Bingley was to purchase an estate with the money he had inherited; his sisters were particularly eager for him to do so—'They were of a respectable family. . . , a circumstance more deeply impressed on their memories than that their brother's fortune and their own had been acquired by trade'

37 Kleon—Thucydides III, 36ff; Aristophanes, *Knights, passim*; Kleon and Nikias—Thucydides IV, 21.3, 27–8; Plutarch, *Nikias*

38 Xenophon, *Ways and Means* IV, 14

39 Cato, *On Agriculture*; see also Plutarch, *Cato*

40 Cicero, *To Atticus* XIV, 9, 1

41 For further discussion and detail of what follows see A. Zimmern, *The Greek Commonwealth* (1931), 5; C. G. Starr, *The Origins of Greek Civilisation* (1962); W. G. Forrest, *The Emergence of Greek Democracy* (1966); H. H. Scullard, *A History of Rome from 753 to 146 B.C.*[3] (1961); *From the Gracchi to Nero*[3] (1970); A. N. Sherwin-White, *The Roman Citizenship* (1939); A. H. M. Jones, *The Later Roman Empire, AD 284–602* (1964)

42 A. M. Duff, *Freedmen in the Early Roman Empire* (1928), esp. 67; Suetonius, *Augustus*, 2

43 Aristotle, *Politics*, 1278 A

44 The city of Thespiae, also in Boeotia, is supposed to have limited the political activity of manual workers too (Heraclides Ponticus, *Politics*, 43). In the constitution which Ptolemy I drew up for Cyrene various prohibitions were laid on professionals of many kinds, craftsmen included (*SEG*, IX, 1)

45 Plutarch, *Agesilaus*, 26, 4–5

46 Herodotus II, 167

47 E. Preuner, *JDAI* 1920, 69–72

48 Isocrates XIX, *On Aeginetan Affairs*, shows how difficult the situation could become for a non-citizen in the law-courts

49 *RE: Metoikoi*, XV, 1413–58

50 *IG* II², 10 records some of the metics who were rewarded for their services to the democratic cause in 403 BC. Of metics in general Euripides could say that the model metic is 'neither burdensome nor in any way obnoxious to the city' (*Suppliants*, 892)

51 Philip V of Macedon made this point in an announcement to the Larissans in 214 BC when he was trying to persuade the city to expand its citizen body (*SIG*[3], 543, 29–34)

52 Crook, *LLR*, 107ff

53 *ibid.*

54 Crook, *LLR*, 51ff

55 Suetonius, *Claudius*, 22

56 Scullard, *Roman Politics* (1951), 14, 44

57 Livy, XX, 2, 25

58 *Digest*, 38, 1, 34

59 Sherwin-White, *Roman Citizenship* (1939), 220ff. See Crook, *LLR*, 223–5; Jones, *LRE*, 17–18

60 A. H. M. Jones, *The Greek City from Alexander to Justinian* (1940), 120ff

61 Libanius, *Or.* XLII, 21; Jones, *LRE*, 531

62 Optatus, Mil. *App.* V; Jones, *LRE*, 520, 131

63 Dio Chrysostom, *Or.* 34, 21–3

64 For fuller discussion of the subject given in outline here, see M. I. Finley, 'Was Greek Civilisation Based on Slavery?', *Slavery in Classical Antiquity* (1960), 53–72; W. L. Westermann, *Slave Systems of Greek and Roman Antiquity* (1955), 53–72; R. H. Barrow, *Slavery in the Roman Empire* (1928); Crook, *LLR*

65 See ch. IV, p. 126

66 The evidence for population figures is unsatisfactory, and has given rise to many different answers. See Jones, *AD*, 76–9, where he disagrees by a large margin on the size of the slave population with Lauffer, *Bergwerkssklaven* II, 150ff

67 Xenophon, *Ways and Means* IV, 14–15. Two other Athenians, Hipponikos and Philemonides, owned 600 and 300 respectively

68 See Jones, *AD*, 14–15

69 Demosthenes IX, 56; XIX, 201

70 See Finley, *SCA*, 53–72; V. Ehrenberg, *People of Aristophanes*[2] (1951), 165ff

71 As Herodotus remarks of the Thracians (V, 6)

72 'Attic Stelai' X, 9, *Hesperia* 1953, 288

73 *IG* II[2], 1672, 141, 190; 1673, 45ff; cf. references to 'sacred slaves' at Didyma in A. Rehm ed., *Didyma* (1958), 26A 7a, 27A 7

74 Pseudo-Aristotle, *Economics* I, 5, 1344a, 35

75 *IG* II[2], 1673.24

76 Pseudo-Xenophon, *Constitution of Athens* (Old Oligarch), I, 10

77 Plato, *Republic*, 563B

78 Thucydides VII, 28

79 See ch. V, 227–8, on some miners' epitaphs

80 Old Oligarch, *loc. cit.* In the Erechtheion accounts and other Athenian records some workers are described as 'so-and-so, belonging to such-and-such a deme'—metics—while others are identified by name only; these might then be freedmen who had not yet reached the status of metic

81 For a time during the fourth century, Athenian manumission involved the dedication of a silver bowl, to the value of 100 drachmae—this by quite humble workers and shopkeepers. See M. N. Tod, 'Epigraphical Notes on

Freedmen's Occupations', *Epigraphica* 1950, 3–26, discussing *IG* II², 1553–78

82 See pp. 72ff and 83ff for reference to the apparently endemic shortage of skilled labour in the ancient world

83 *Digest*, 21, 1; Crook, *LLR*, 56, comments on the sheer horror of this clause

84 Polybius XXX, 15; Frank, *Economic Survey* I, 188

85 Frank, *Economic Survey* I, 315

86 On the nationalities of slaves in Rome, see Westermann, *Slave Systems*, 61ff

87 Barrow, *op. cit.* (note 64), 179

88 Plutarch, *Crassus*, 2, 4

89 On this and what follows, cf. Barrow, *op. cit.*, 151 and 153–6

90 Barrow, *op. cit.*, 47, quoting the jurist Gaius

91 Since slavery was so much an accepted feature of daily life, it is doubtful whether slaves and freedmen treated slaves under their control any better than free men did

92 Suetonius, *Claudius*, 52, 1

93 Herodotus VIII, 144

94 *Politics*, 1252b, 8

95 *Hecuba*, 479ff; Aristophanes, *Acharnanians*, 61ff

96 This point is well made by H. D. Broadhead in his introduction to *The Persae of Aeschylus* (1960), xxxff

97 Quoted in ch. I, p. 18 (note 14)

98 The wretched Eretrians, who were settled east of Susa after their capture by the Persians in 490, were still speaking Greek in Herodotus' time (Herodotus VI, 119)

99 The slave revolts in Sicily broke out in 136 and 105 BC. These and Spartacus' revolt are discussed by J. Vogt, *Struktur der antiken Sklavenkriege* (1957). See also Peter Green, 'The First Sicilian Slave Revolt', *Past and Present* 1961, 10–29

100 Aristophanes, *Knights, passim*—on Kleon; Carians—*adesp.* (Kock), no. 548. However, Ehrenberg, *op. cit.* (note 70), 152, suggests that there was some distaste for Asiatics in Athens

101 Strabo III, 3, 6–8. See A. N. Sherwin-White, *Racial Prejudice in Imperial Rome* (1967), for further discussion of the topic

102 *Against Piso*, 53; *For Fonteius*, 37

103 As illustrated by a late sixth-century plate. The trousered rider may be Miltiades; see H. T. Wade-Gery, 'Miltiades', *JHS* 1951, 212–21

104 Scullard, *op. cit.* (note 56), 224; Plutarch, *Cato*, 22

105 *de Mercede Conductis*, 40

106 Sherwin-White, *op. cit.* (note 101), 62ff

107 There were of course exceptions—see the epitaphs of Camillus Polynices and Maximus quoted below, ch. V, pp. 181, 182

108 Pliny, *Letters* III, 14; cf. Tacitus, *Annals* XIV, 52–5

109 This is very much the tone of his comments on the subject in the *Politics*

110 Cf. the discussion of H. Frisch, *The Constitution of the Athenians* (1942), 63ff

111 Thucydides I, 80

112 Plutarch, *Pericles*, 37; on Alexander's corn grant, a gift from Cyrene, see *SEG*, IX, 2

113 G. E. M. de St Croix, 'Greek and Roman Accounting', in *Studies in the History of Accounting*, ed. A. C. Littleton and B. S. Yamey (1956), 14–74

114 Burford, 'The Economics of Greek Temple Building', *Proceedings of the Cambridge Philological Society* 1965, 21–34

115 Aristotle, *Politics*, 1253b, 33f; Homer, *Iliad* VIII, 372ff

116 A rare if not unique instance of legislation in favour of Italian products was Domitian's ordinance of AD 91 that vineyards in the provinces should be reduced by half, which surely did something to boost the export of Italian wine. See Frank, *Economic Survey* V, 141ff; Suetonius, *Domitian*, 1, 2

117 Finley, *SCA*, 53–72

118 A. H. M. Jones, 'Slavery in the Ancient World', *SCA*, 6

119 See below, pp. 141–2

120 *Letters*, 52

121 *Cyropaedeia* VIII, 2, 5

122 R. M. Cook, 'Die Bedeutung der bemälten Keramik für den grossen Handel', *JDAI* 1959, 118–21

123 Randall, *Erechtheum*, 203

124 *IG* I², 352, 34–6, a year's total of over 16,000 dr., or $1\frac{1}{2}$–2 dr. a day for 300 days in the year—assuming that the mason's year lasted that long

125 *GTBE*, Appendix III, 246ff

126 See note 114, for refs. in the article cited there

127 Thucydides VII, 28, seems to suggest this, if the 'skilled handworkers' there mentioned and who are said to have run away are correctly understood to have been mine workers

128 The figure is taken from the number of architects of ships named in the naval inventories, *IG* II², 1612–32

129 *CIL* VI, 9404—there were three centuries of members in the *collegium* of sandal makers (H. J. Loane, *Industry and Commerce of the City of Rome* (1938), 64)

130 Suetonius, *Claudius*, 20

131 R. MacMullen, 'Roman Imperial Building in the Provinces', *HSCP* 1959; R. G. Collingwood and R. P. Wright, *Roman Inscriptions of Britain* (1965–), esp. nos. 799, 852–5, 979, 1051, 1299

132 Vegetius II, 11

133 *GTBE*, 201ff

134 Cf. the palace record quoted in ch. I, p. 20, and G. M. A. Richter, 'Greeks in Persia', *AJA* 1946, 15–30

135 J. Boardman, *The Greeks Overseas* (1964), 270ff

136 The mixture of classical and Parthian styles is commented on by Wheeler, *Roman Art and Architecture* (1964), 169ff

137 *loc. cit.*

138 Diodorus Siculus XIV, 18, 3; 41.3

139 Myron—G. M. A. Richter, *Sculptors and Sculpture of the Greeks* (1930), 207f; Skopas—Richter, *op. cit.*, 269–76; Satyros—Vitruvius VII, pref., 12; *SIG*³, 225; Spintharos—Pausanias X, 5, 13; Epikrates—*SIG*³, 707

140 See note 47, above

141 M. Lacroix, 'Les étrangers à Délos', *Mélanges Glotz* (1932), 501–25

142 As the signed statue-bases indicate—many of which are published in *Clara Rhodos*, VI–VII

143 Livy XLII, 3, 1–11

144 Pliny, *NH*, 34, 45

145 M. Squarciapino, *La scuola di Afrodisia* (1943)

146 Pliny, *Letters* X, 39 and 40; on Apollodoros see Dio Cassius XLVIII, 13

147 J. B. Ward-Perkins, 'The Tripolitanian Marble Trade', *JRS* 1951, 89–104

148 Plutarch, *Marcellus*, 14–17

CHAPTER III

149 No attempt is made here to give anything like a complete survey of the crafts in the Greek and Roman world. General points concerning artistry and craftsmanship and the manner in which they were achieved are taken from whichever craft provides the clearest illustration of the matter under discussion. Old, but still among the most complete studies, is H. Bluemner, *Technologie und Terminologie der Gewerbe und Künste der Griechen und Römer* (1875–8), vols. I–IV. A still useful collection of evidence for sculptors, painters and others remains that of J. Overbeck, *Die antiken Schriftquellen zur Geschichte der bildenden Künste bei den Griechen* (1868), which fully deserves to be brought up to date. References here are only given to the actual source, since Overbeck's publication may not be easily accessible

150 Sturt, *The Wheelwright's Shop* (1923), 20

151 Pliny, *NH*, 35, 84

152 *IG* II², 13178

153 Each trireme may have needed two sets, light and heavy, of perhaps 500 sq. ft each. The evidence for the nature and extent of ships' rigging is poor

154 There seems to be no known name for 'canvas weaver' as such. *Sakkhuphantai* are usually taken to be 'sack makers'

155 For the complexities of shaping and decorating ancient pottery, see in particular J. V. Noble, *Techniques of Athenian Painted Pottery* (1965)

156 The story attaching to these verses, which are quoted in part below, p. 122, is that as Homer was going past some potters who were building a kiln, they asked him to sing for them and charm away the evil spirits from their pots. The most likely period and place for the song's composition, however, are 525–350 BC and Athens

157 Cf. the folk hero Wayland-Smith, lame, anti-social, and a magician to boot, discussed by R. J. Forbes, *Studies in Ancient Technology* (1955–), VIII, ch. 3, 'Evolution of the Smith, his Social and Sacred Status'

158 Homer, *Iliad* XVIII, 410ff

159 Lauffer, *Bergwerksklaven* II, 250–1, comments on the overemphasis laid on the single leg-shackle found in the Laureion mines

160 Diodorus Siculus III, 12.2–13.2

161 *Epistles*, 76, 2, 4

162 *On Stones*, 63

163 Lauffer, *Bergwerksklaven* I, 27, notes the high quality of the work; cf. E. Ardaillon, *Les mines du Laureion* (1897), 24ff

164 Pliny, *NH*, 33, 98; Xenophon, *Memorabilia* III, 6, 12; Strabo III, 146

165 The Vipasca mining regulations: *FIRA*, vol. I, no. 104

166 *IG* II², 1668—the delivery document relating to the Telesterion at Eleusis

167 Roughing out sculptures in the quarry and cutting down building blocks to within reach of their final dimensions reduced the weight of a piece for a statue by perhaps as much as half. See Sheila Adam, *Techniques of Greek Sculpture* (1966), 5

168 *Passio sanctorum IV coronatorum*, ed. W. Wattenbach, 'Über die Legende von den heiligen Vier Gekrönten', *Sitzungsberichte der Akademie der Wissenschaft in Wien* 1896

169 *P. Karanis*, 465 (107)

170 Collingwood and Wright, *op. cit.* (note 131), no. 1952. The whole question of the Roman army's involvement in public works takes the subject beyond the scope of this study. For some further discussion, see A. von Domaszewski, *Rangordnung* (1908); R. MacMullen, 'Roman Imperial Building in the Provinces', *HSCP* 1959, 207–361

171 See the discussion, with references, of A. Bouché-Leclerq, 'L'ingénieur Cléon', *Revue des études grecques* 1908, 121–52

172 Sybaris—A. R. Burn, *The Lyric Age of Greece* (1960), 383, with references; Aristophanes, *Birds*, 1154ff

173 Kleon—Aristophanes, *Knights*, 892; *Wasps*, 38

174 On the tanner's situation—Artemidoros, *Oneirokritos* I, 51

175 Tyre—Strabo's comment (XVI, 2; 23) is well known. Plutarch, *Pericles* I, 4, makes scornful reference to dyers and perfumers

176 Evidence for the workshop at Epidauros, used first by the sculptors employed for the temple of Asklepios, comes from the building accounts, *IG* IV², 1, 102, 27ff. See also *GTBE*, 58–9. Pheidias' workshop is discussed by A. Mallwitz and W. Schiering, *Die Werkstatt des Pheidias in Olympia* (1964). Evidence of a similar structure on the east side of the Athenian acropolis is referred to by G. P. Stevens, *Hesperia* 1946, 22 and fig. 22

177 The size of Athenian potteries is indicated by the vase-paintings of workshop scenes (Pl. 17). Potters' workshops may have been somewhat larger in the Roman period, but not necessarily so in all cases; one of the first makers

in Italy of the so-called Arretine ware, the freedman M. Perennius Tigranes, had at least six workers; P. Cornelius employed fifty-eight slaves and freedmen, and at Puteoli the freedman P. Naevius Hilarus owned at least thirteen slaves. Not all of these need have been working contemporaneously; see A. Oxé, *Arretinische Reliefgefässe von Rhein* (1933); Frank, *Economic Survey* V, 188ff. Tile marks suggest that in the Roman brickyards the actual working unit may have been six or less; the founder of the business which eventually came into the possession of the Emperor Marcus Aurelius began in AD 59 with three freedmen (perhaps as foremen) and six slaves, three working units of three each, and in AD 94 there were five freedmen and twenty-three slaves, or five units of four or five members each (Loane, *Industry and Commerce* (1938), 102ff)

178 *IG* II², 374, 194ff

179 *IG* XI², 161A, 45–6; 51–2. Cf. 150A, 10–12

180 Plutarch, *Crassus*, 2, 4. A slave gang also saw to the maintenance of the drains of Rome: see Frontinus, *de Aquae Ductu* II, 116

181 E. Ardaillon, *Les Mines du Laureion* (1897), 210ff, comments on the area, which is documented by the sketch map at the end of the book; see also Lauffer, *op. cit.* (note 66), *passim*; for the Vipasca mine regulations, see note 165; C. Préaux, *L'Économie Royale des Lagides* (1939), 253ff

182 Kleon's deme was Kydathenaion, within the city and to the south of the acropolis; his tannery need not have been located there, but it seems strange that, if their work was not also in that deme, two metics of the fourth century should have been residents of Kydathenaion (*IG* II², 1556, 34; 1576, 5–6). Tanneries at Lepros are mentioned—Schol. Aristophanes, *Acharnians*, 724. At Pompeii, both fullers and tanners appear to have had establishments in town—see A. Mau, *Pompeii*² (1907), 393–7

183 Examples of trade quarters in Rome include the street of the harness makers, the sandal makers and carpenters, and alleys of the glassblowers, smiths, incense makers, clay-statuette makers (Loane, *op. cit.* (note 177), 64, note 17). Vitruvius VII, 9.4, speaks of red lead from the Spanish mines being brought to Rome for treatment in the workshops which stood between the temples of Fortune and Quirinus. But if the crafts had at any time been in separate districts, it is pretty clear that they were not by the time of the late Republic, and that workshops were to be found fairly widely distributed throughout the city

184 The Athenian building records often included a metic craftsman's place of residence, as well as his name, as for example in the Erechtheion accounts (Randall, *Erechtheum*). Dorothy Burr Thompson discusses the evidence for Simon the shoemaker in *Archaeology* 1960, 234–40

185 R. S. Wycherley, *JHS* 1959, 153—workshops on the (later) site of the Hephaisteion. R. S. Young, 'An Industrial District of Ancient Athens', *Hesperia* 1951, 135–288

186 T. L. Shear Jr, *Hesperia* 1969, 383ff, discusses the house of Mikion and Menon

187 Daidalos—Diodorus Siculus IV, 76. Phereklos—*Iliad* V, 59–60
188 Plato, *Republic*, 412D
189 Plato, *Protagoras*, 328A
190 *IG* I², 1002. Obviously, the patronymic will not have meant in every case that the father had been in the same business; but it is a reasonable assumption that this was more often than not the case
191 The sons of Brentes are mentioned in Archilochos (Budé) fr. 115–16. Charopinos' sons—*FD* IV, 1, figs. 24 and 25
192 *RE*: Aristandros, no. 7
193 Satyros—*SIG*³, 225 and 361B
194 Aristokles and Kanachos—Pausanias VI, 9, 1; Patrokles—Pausanias VI, 3, 4; *CIG*, 2984; Lysippos—Pliny, *NH*, 34, 51; 35, 153; 34, 66
195 The relationship of the Polykleitoi and Naukydes (one or two?) is by no means clear; see Pausanias II, 22, 7; VI, 6, 2; VIII, 314. A third Polykleitos of Argos worked at Rhodes in the third century—*Clara Rhodos* VI–VII, p. 410, no. 35. Perhaps Polymedes, sculptor of the Kleobis and Biton pair about 600 BC, was the founding father of the family business; see M. N. Tod, *Greek Historical Inscriptions* (1933), I, 4
196 Raubitschek, *Dedications*, nos. 51 and 97; on pp. 482–3 he suggests that Kritios and Nesiotes were pupils and heirs of Antenor
197 Athenaeus XI, 486D
198 On the family of Kephisodotos and Praxiteles see J. Kirchner, *Prosopographiae Atticae* (1901), Kephisodotos, Praxiteles—where it is also suggested that Praxiteles VI, perhaps a ninth-generation descendant of the great Praxiteles' other son Kephisodotos II, was a sculptor too
199 Eucheir—Pausanias VIII, 14, 10; his son—Loewy, nos. 222–7; Polykles, father of Timarchides and grandfather of Dionysios and Polykles II—Loewy, no. 242, Pliny, *NH*, 36, 34, Pausanias VI, 12, 8; Adamas and his sculptor sons—Loewy, no. 243
200 Archermos and Boupalos—Pliny, *NH*, 36, 11; Schol. Aristophanes, *Birds*, 573
201 The family tree of the Timagoras and Aristonidas clan may tentatively be restored as shown on p. 231. The connection between Aristonidas I and Timagoras is entirely hypothetical. Ophelion I might have been the son of either; if Mnasitimos III belongs to this family, his father's name is of no assistance in deciding to which branch he was related
202 S. Dow, 'A Family of Sculptors from Tyre', *Hesperia* 1941, 351–60
203 Neokleides and his son—*IG* II², 1672, 52, 53, 78; 1682, 16
204 Polyxenos and his sons—*IG* IV², 1, 103, 12, 14, 53, 55, 73, 85, 87, 88, 115–16
205 Smikythos—Raubitschek, *Dedications*, nos. 349–50, 353 (made by his son Onesimos); Nearchos and sons—Raubitschek, *Dedications*, no. 32 (a tentative restoration of the sons' names); no. 197 is, it has to be admitted, only assumed to be a dedication by *the potter* of the name Nearchos

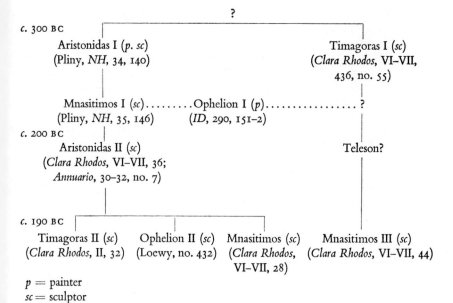

p = painter
sc = sculptor

206 Euenor and Parrhasios—Harpokration, s.v. Παρράσιος; Polygnotos—
Plato, *Gorgias*, 448B and schol. Aristeides of Thebes—Pliny, *NH*, 35, 108

207 Zeuxis and Zeuxippos—Plato, *Protagoras*, 318B. It would be strange if two
men with such similar names, both painters, and both from the same city
within the same generation, were not related. Apelles—Suidas, s.v.
'Ἀπέλλης

208 Pheidias and Panainos—Strabo VIII, 354; Euenor as both sculptor and
painter—Raubitschek, *Dedications*, nos. 496–8; Polygnotos—Pliny, *NH*, 34,
85; Antenor's family—see note 196. Parrhasios—Pausanias I, 28, 8;
Athenaeus XI, 782B; Euthymides and Pollias—Raubitschek, *Dedications*,
no. 150 and pp. 522–3; Boupalos—Pausanias IV, 30, 6; IX, 35, 6; Ophelion
I—see note 201

209 Subordination of the architect to the sculptor is to be seen in the Parthenon.
The sculptures, pediments, friezes and cult statue within the temple were
far more important than the architectural frame in which they were set,
and it was the sculptor Pheidias who held responsibility for all the Periclean
projects on the acropolis, not Iktinos or one of the other architects also
involved in the work. Cf. *GTBE*, 143–4: at Epidauros it was clearly the
sculptor Thrasymedes, responsible for the cult statue and for the interior
decorating of the temple of Asklepios, who had the final word, not the
architect Theodotos

210 Vitruvius VI, pref., 6

211 Chersiphron—Vitruvius VII, pref., 12, 16. Delphi architects—*FD*, 25, II, 22; *SIG*³, 295, 494. Zenon—*CIG*, 4342d

212 *IG* XI², 142, 43; 199C, 41

213 Vitalis—*CIL* VI, 9151-2; Thallus—*CIL* VI, 10299

214 The naval inventories, *IG* II², 1604-32, cover a period of perhaps fifty years; Greek personal names tended to run in families for several generations and to echo the same two or three types—but there was of course no hard and fast rule

215 Xanthippos—*IG* II², 12332. The bronze-workers of Capua—Frank, *Economic Survey* V, 198; Akesas of Cyprus—Athenaeus II, 48B

E. W. Marsden, *Greek and Roman Artillery: Historical Development* (1969), 72-3, asserts that certainly in the Hellenistic period (and presumably earlier too) the expert knowledge of artillery was handed on from father to son, in several clear instances

216 Plato, *Protagoras*, 328C, refers to the sons of Polykleitos; Pheidias' descendants—Pausanias V, 14, 5

217 *On Household Management* XVIII, 9

218 *Nicomachean Ethics* II, 1

219 *Laws*, 643B-C

220 For this see Pausanias VI, 10, 4; Lysippos—Pliny, *NH*, 34, 61; Silanion —Pliny, *NH*, 34, 51; Protogenes—Pliny, *NH*, 35, 101; Herakleides of Macedon—Pliny, *NH*, 35, 135. On 'teacherless' artists, see E. Kris and O. Kurz, *Legende vom Künstler* (1934) 28ff

221 Xenophon, *Memorabilia* IV, 2, 2; Plato, *Meno*, 91D

222 For what follows, cf. W. L. Westermann, 'Apprentice Contracts and the Apprentice System in Roman Egypt', *CP* 1914, 295ff

223 See below, pp. 180-2, for the epitaphs of some particularly youthful artists and craftsmen

224 Randall, *Erechtheum*, esp. 200

225 Vitruvius VII, pref., 16—Demetrios is described as 'servus' of the temple

226 Dio Chrysostom, *Orations* 55, 1, 282; Tzetzes, *Chiliades* VII, 929; Pliny, *NH*, 36, 16; 36, 17; 35, 54

227 *Inventoire des Mosaïques de la Gaule et l'Afrique* I, ii, 80, no. 1051

228 *OGIS*, 590

229 *Inschriften von Olympia*, 631

230 Pliny, *NH*, 35, 145

231 *CIL*, X, 1614, 3707; Strabo V, 245

232 The Aquilan law—*Digest* IX, 2, 5, 3. See Crook, *LLR*, 179

233 Xenophon, *Memorabilia* III, 10, 9-15

234 *Cod. Theod.* X, 22

235 Ammianus Marcellinus XXIX, 3, 4

236 Cf. the views put forward by J. A. Bundgaard, *Mnesicles, an Architect at Work* (1957). The closeness of interest of architects and their workers is as real in the twentieth century; Mies van der Rohe began as an apprentice in

his father's stone-cutting yard, and 'like many of his contemporaries he had no formal architectural training, but learnt to draw as a designer for stucco decorations. He . . . worked for two years (as a) furniture designer, to improve his knowledge of wood' (*The Times*, August 19, 1969)

237 The two exceptions are *archikamineutes*—smelter (man) (*IG* II², 11697) and *archilatomos*—quarryman (*SEG* VIII, 647)

238 On the architect's necessary versatility cf. J.-P. Vernant, 'Remarques sur les formes et limites de la pensée technique chez les Grecs', *Revue d'histoire des sciences* 1951, esp. 207–8

239 For full references to the potters and painters mentioned here, see *ABV* and *ARV²*, indices

240 J. D. Beazley, *Potter and Painter in Ancient Athens* (1944), discusses some workshop connections

241 See above, note 177, for further references to Arretine ware and its production

242 Beazley, *op. cit.* 25ff, detects the work of two potters and two painters in a single vase

243 *Lindos* I, no. 126

244 *Lindos* I, no. 84; *Clara Rhodos* II, 199, no. 31. Cf. the joint signature of Kritios and Nesiotes to the second tyrannicide group

245 The Parthenon accounts record a year's payment for work on the pediment sculptures, which would allow a day-wage of 2 dr. per man for about three hundred days in the year (allowing for bad weather, poor light, festivals and so on) to perhaps twenty or twenty-five sculptors (*IG* I², 352, 34–5). Cf. B. Schweitzer, 'Um Pheidias', *Zur Kunst der Antike* II (1963), 69; on p. 66, however, he reports that analysis of sculptural techniques reveals the work of about seventy different hands; on this, see above, p. 62

246 For the building history of the Telesterion, see F. Noack, *Eleusis* (1927)

247 Cf. note 208

248 Mausoleon—Pliny, *NH*, 36, 30; Pergamon—D. Thimme, 'Masters of the Pergamene Gigantomachy', *AJA* 1946, 345ff

249 It is not known who was the designer or chief co-ordinator of Trajan's column—perhaps the man known to have been his chief architect, Apollodoros of Damascus (*SHA, Hadrian*, 19)

250 Xenophon, *Cyropaedia* VIII, 2, 4. The demi-god Margites was acquainted with many arts, but skilled in none; he had much the same mischievous qualities as the Norse god Loki. See J.-P. Vernant, 'Travail et nature dans la Grèce ancienne', *Journal de psychologie* 1955, 18ff

251 Pliny, *NH*, 33, 160. Pliny also associates Polygnotos with its introduction

252 See, for example, V. Ehrenberg, *op. cit.* (note 70), 135; F. Heichelheim, *An Ancient Economic History* II (1964), 97ff and note 34. Glotz, *op. cit.* (note 23), 220–9, steers a middle course

253 Bluemner, *Gewerbe und Künste* I–IV, sets out the evidence for specialized trade names in detail. Heichelheim lists and refers to them as though a com-

plete division of labour were indisputably the reason for their use (*op. cit.,* notes 35–9). The fact that Xenophon refers to shoemakers who confined themselves to cutting uppers only (*Cyropaedeia* VIII, 2, 5) does not mean that all industry in Classical Athens was run on a modern factory system

254 *Koniater* is a technical title found only at Epidauros (*IG* IV^2, 1, 102, 247). Glue boilers are heard of at Athens (*IG* II^2, 1558, 10) and in the Roman world(*glutinarius: ILS*, 7675). The Parthenon accounts distinguish between the *lithotomoi*—stone-cutters—and the *peleketeis*—axemen—in the payments to quarrymen; there may well have been two kinds of stone-cutting done in the quarry, but they need not have been performed by two distinct labour forces, so that although it would seem that the Athenian accountants referred to these processes as separate jobs done by different men, this is hardly likely, in the light of the comparative infrequency of such large-scale quarrying works, and the scarcity in general of skilled masons

255 Aristophanes, *Peace,* dram. pers.; *Birds,* 491

256 *Cod. Theod.* XIII, 4, 2, distinguishes between joiners, carpenters and panelled-ceiling makers. Panelled or coffered ceilings were used in Greek buildings too, in temples especially, but no special trade name has survived in Greek

257 This evidence is of the period when specialization is supposed by some to have been very much on the increase. Theophantos—*IG* XI^2, 161A, 52; 91; 165, 15; 199A, 25; 104–7; 161A, 57. Phaneas—161A, 45; 165, 13. Epikrates—199A, 94; 165, 9, 19; 287A, 72—wooden scenery for the theatre, doors, roofing, and tile-laying. Euphranor—144A, 75; 64; 116; 163Ba, 5; 165, 23. Theodemos made or repaired doors—161A, 66; 165, 9; repaired houses—199A, 68; made wooden partitions—165, 19; and put up a platform, perhaps for block and tackle equipment, and scaffolding—203A, 33. Deinomenes cut inscriptions, 25,000 or 30,000 letters at a time, painted statues, and repaired wooden doors—159A, 66; 161A, 118; 161A, 90; 163A, 54; on his carpentry—165, 14 and 22; 203A, 35; 57 (if the same man is concerned in all instances)

258 See Randall, *Erechtheum,* 201 and Table 1, for instance; 206, Table 5, shows that rigid specialization was not maintained

259 The signature on his vases are remarkable for the form of the D in his name, Λ instead of the usual Δ. The dotted delta seems only to be found otherwise in some well-cut boundary stones on the island of Samos, dated to the 460s, at which period Douris may be presumed to have returned there; see Beazley, *op. cit.* (note 240), 39

260 Beazley, *ARV*^{2}, index

261 The painter Protogenes began as a ship's painter; see Pliny, *NH*, 35, 101

262 Accounts—*IG* I^2, 338, and *Hesperia* 1936, 362–80

263 *IG* XI^2, 204, 54

264 E.g. Artimas—*IG* XI^2, 144A, 40 etc. (nails and keys); Echemantis—199A, 32; 203A, 34; 59 etc. (bronze, lead, and perhaps iron too). Echestratos and

Dexios may be said to have specialized, in that Echestratos provided gold leaf on both appearances (287A, 114; 290, 232), and Dexios iron (158A, 81; 159A, 58; 199A, 27). Aristaichmos—R. S. Young, *Hesperia* 1951, 222–3

265 Latin specialist terms for all these occupations are known—see Bluemner, *Gewerbe und Künste*, 111

266 Caesar, *Gallic War* V, 2, discussed by J. A. Bundgaard, *Acta archaeologica*, 1965

267 *FD*, 19ff—various items are accounted for in the construction of lifting devices and scaffolding

268 Kleoitas and Aristeides—Pausanias VI, 20, 14

269 Sostratos—Pliny, *NH*, 36, 83. C. Julius Lacer—*CIL* II, 761. See F. J. Wiseman, *Roman Spain, pl.* X.

270 It is unlikely that private housebuilding would have allowed much opportunity for monumental experiment

271 Herodotus III, 60; J. Goodfield, 'The Tunnel of Eupalinos', *Scientific American*, vol. 210, no. 6 (1964), 104–12. Megara itself had tyrant-inspired waterworks (Pausanias I, 40, 1), but the Near East had surely led the way in tunnelling and other similar operations (Cf. Herodotus VII, 22, on the Phoenicians' canal-cutting for Xerxes at Mt Athos, and Pliny, *NH*, 7, 195, on the Phoenicians' invention of stone quarrying)

272 Herodotus IV, 87–8. See also below, p. 172

273 Xenophon, *Memorabilia* IV, 2, 10

274 Vitruvius I, 1

275 *Mechanics* I, 34

276 *Mathematics*, p. 1122; see A. G. Drachmann, *The Mechanical Technology of Greek and Roman Antiquity* (Copenhagen, 1963), 55

277 Pythios was the architect of the late fourth-century temple of Athene at Priene (Vitruvius I, 1, 12). His writings are known of only from Vitruvius

278 I, 1, 13–14

279 D. Burr, *Terra-cottas from Myrina in Boston* (1934)

280 See above, p. 61

281 See above, pp. 58, 61ff

282 R. A. Higgins, *Greek Terracottas* (1968), 69–70, 149–50

283 R. M. Cook, *Greek Painted Pottery* (1960), 102

284 See, e.g., H. Payne, *Necrocorinthia* (1931), and *Perachora* (1940); R. M. Cook, *BSA* 1970, 17–19, suggests that Doric architecture originated at Corinth *c*. 650 BC

285 Thucydides I, 13, 3

286 *FD*, 19, 20 *et al.*; Epidauros—see *GTBE*, 58, 65, 74, 142–3, 151, 193–4

287 Athenaeus V, 206D, 40ff

288 G. M. A. Richter, *Archaic Greek Art* (1949), 102ff

289 On Sicyonian painting, see M. Robertson, *Greek Painting* (1959), 46, 167; on sculptors, Richter, *Sculpture and Sculptors of the Greeks* (1950)

290 Richter, *op. cit.*; *GTBE*, 143ff, 172, 174

291 Cook, *op. cit.* (note 283); on the production of so-called Tanagra figurines at Athens see Higgins, *op. cit.* (note 282), 97

292 The extent of its use in Athens is indicated by W. Judeich, *Topographie von Athen* (1885)

293 Plato, *Hippias Major*, 282A

294 G. M. A. Richter, *Perspective in Greek and Roman Art* (1970), points out that throughout antiquity no one was able to represent chariots in depth. The usual solution was an uneasy combination of front and side view on one plane

295 L. Casson, 'Ancient Shipbuilding', *TAPA* 1963, 28–33

296 For the size of the Naxians' Apollo, see Richter, *Kouroi* (1960), no. 13; the weight given here is by my own estimate

297 H. Maryon, 'The Colossus of Rhodes', *JHS* 1956, 68–86. Another, earlier and more unusual, monument in bronze was the palm tree dedicated by the Athenian Nikias in or about 421 BC (Plutarch, *Nikias*, 3, 1). It was crushed by the subsequent fall of the Naxian Apollo in an earthquake. Among other monumental extravagances conceived but never in fact carried out was the not wholly incredible proposal that Deinokrates of Macedon made to Alexander of carving Mt Athos into a statue of a man holding a fortified city in his left hand and a reservoir for the mountain springs in his right (Vitruvius II, pref., 2)

298 As the Ptolemaic inscription honouring Pyrgoteles of Cyprus suggests (*OGIS*, 39), 'architect of the thirty-banker and the twenty-banker', cf. Athenaeus V, 204–5

299 One thinks especially of the Roman cities in North Africa. The scale of operations at Baalbek is indicated by Wheeler, *op. cit.* (note 136), 20, 22, illustrations 6 and 7

300 For references see note 271

301 *RE:* Kopais XXI, 1358, 29ff

302 For references see C. Préaux, *op. cit.* (note 181)

303 See M. E. Blake, *Ancient Roman Construction in Italy from the Prehistoric Period* (1947). That the whole question of controlling the water flow into the harbour was somewhat experimental is suggested by the report that the imperial party was almost washed away and drowned at the inauguration of the channel (Suetonius, *Claudius*, 32)

304 See Drachmann, *op. cit.* (note 276); E. W. Marsden, *A History of Greek and Roman Artillery* (1969); Vitruvius, *On Architecture*, Book X—devoted to mechanical devices of many kinds

305 Such as Vitruvius describes, with attributions (X, 4ff)—L. A. Moritz, *Grain Mills and Flour in Classical Antiquity* (1958)

306 On the Isthmian starting-gate see O. Broneer, *Antiquity* 1958

307 *The Athenian Agora* (American School), 163–4

308 S. Dow, 'Allotment Machines', in *Prytaneis: a Study of the Inscriptions Honouring the Athenian Councillors, Hesperia* suppl. I (1937), 198–215; E. S. Staveley, *Greek and Roman Voting and Elections* (1972)

309 Perhaps one of the most amusing and at the same time least useful experiments reported was that of the sculptor Timochares of Rhodes, who wanted to utilize the magnetic qualities of lodestone in the roof of a temple of Arsinoe, the sister and second wife of Ptolemy II. The idea was that an iron statue placed under the roof might then float in mid-air. The scheme was abandoned on the deaths of both Ptolemy and Timochares (Pliny, *NH*, 34, 148)

310 The subject is discussed by M. I. Finley, 'Technical Innovation and Economic Progress in the Ancient World', *Economic History Review* 1965, 29-45

311 Cf. R. J. Forbes, *op. cit.* (note 157), VII, 146

312 See my article 'Heavy Transport in Classical Antiquity', *Economic History Review* 1960, 1-18, with further references

313 W. B. Dinsmoor, *Architecture of Ancient Greece* (1950), 203

314 The negative attitude to technical improvement is well illustrated by the story of an engineer who offered the use of a labour-saving device he had invented for moving heavy building materials; his suggestion was rejected by Vespasian who commented that he must keep his people employed in some fashion so that they would have something to eat (Suetonius, *Vespasian*, 18)

315 However, Terry Coleman points out in his study, *The Railway Navvies* (1965), that the abundance of sufficiently skilled manpower in European railway building discouraged the use of the steam excavator for some time after its development in the US, even though the invention would have saved money from the outset

316 Herodotus I, 174

317 Cf. the story of Agathokles' misuse for his own house of stone intended for the temple of Athena in Syracuse—he and the house were struck by a thunderbolt (Diodoros Siculus VIII, 11.1-2)

318 *IG* II², 1673, discussed by G. Glotz, 'Un Transport de marbre pour le portique d'Eleusis', *REG* 1923, 26-45. See also the article cited in note 312

319 The personal style of early Greek inscriptions is best observed in L. H. Jeffrey, *Local Scripts of Archaic Greece* (1961)

320 Pliny, *NH*, 36, 14

321 Pliny, *NH*, 36, 125, and *Greek Anthology*, XVI, 221

322 *Greek Anthology*, XVI, 229; cf. 146, IX 159, 288; Pausanias I, 42, 1-2, refers to the stone which played the lyre

323 Traces of taboos against certain metals on the *dies feriae* or holy days in Rome remain in the sources, and they probably reflect a (certainly pre-Classical) state of mind when metals attracted a respect, or even inspired a fear for their strange properties, which they had almost entirely lost by the Classical age (just as smiths had little or none of the magician or wise-man character which they were endowed with in other and earlier cultures). Cf. P. Braun, 'Les Tabous des "feriae"', *L'Année Sociologique* (1959), 49-125

324 So the late lexicographer Pollux says (VII, 108): 'Near the furnaces of the copper or bronze smiths it was the custom to hang up or have around some little joke, as an apotropaic charm'

325 The translation was taken from J. V. Noble, *Techniques of Athenian Fine Painted Pottery* (1965), 71ff; see p. 72 and note 156 above

CHAPTER IV

326 Vitruvius, *On Architecture* III, pref., 2

327 Alexander and his favourite portrait-makers—Pliny, *NH* I, 125

328 *Politics*, 1281A–82B

329 *Letters to his Brother Quintus* II, 2

330 Vitruvius is able to explain the use of human figures in architecture (I, 1, 5–6)

331 The problem of what the Alcmeonids did, and at what period, at Delphi, is surveyed in *FGH* III, ib, Suppl., 328 Philochorus, fr. 115, pp. 449ff

332 For this rather subjective interpretation of Antenor's pediment see P. Lévêque and P. Vidal-Nacquet, *Clisthène l'athénien* (1964), 11–12

333 Lévêque and Vidal-Nacquet, *op. cit.*, 85ff

334 So Plato was pleased to say of manual workers that 'their stunted natures covet (philosophy), their minds being as cramped and crushed by their mechanical lives as their bodies are crushed by the manual crafts' (*Republic*, 495D–E); and 'Why do we scorn manual work? Isn't it because it indicates a weakness in our higher natures?' (*op. cit.*, 590C). Xenophon said that 'the banausic crafts spoil body and mind', especially those crafts which 'compel the workers to sit indoors, and in some cases to spend the day by the fire' (*On Household Management* IV, 2–3). So Aristophanes spoke of 'pallid shoemakers' (*Ekklesiazousai*, 385). 'Slavishness is ignorance; but not the ignorance of metalwork or carpentry. . . . No, on the contrary those who are skilled in such trades are for the most part slavish' (Xenophon, *Memorabilia* IV, 2, 22). Aulus Gellius, writing in the second century AD, reiterates these sentiments and adds another reason for disliking craftsmen: 'Those who are corrupted by avarice . . . are usually intent on indoor and sedentary pursuits, in which all their vigour of mind and body is enfeebled' (*Attic Nights* III, 1, 9–10). While Cicero, though he makes a distinction between arts and crafts, reiterates the point that 'all mechanics are engaged in vulgar trades; for no workshop can have anything liberal about it', referring elsewhere to 'craftsmen and shopkeepers, the very sewage of the state' (*On Duty*, 142, 150; *For Flaccus*, 18)

335 See ch. V, p. 156

336 Xenophon, *Memorabilia* III, 10, 9–15; 10, 1ff; 10, 6ff

337 Plato, *Symposium*, 173D; Pliny, *NH*, 34, 81–2
338 See D. B. Thompson, *Archaeology* 1960, 234–40
339 Diogenes Laertius II, 13, 122
340 Plato, *Laws*, 803A
341 Plato, *Philebos*, 57A
342 Vitruvius I, 1, 16
343 See the discussion by J. Bousquet, *Le Trésor de Cyrène* (1957), in particular pp. 77ff, for the arguments given here
344 Bousquet, *op. cit.*, 98ff. The identification of Euphranor is at best doubtful; there may have been one or more artists of that name confused one with another in the literature, as for example the Corinthian Euphranor, painter and sculptor, mentioned by Pliny and to be dated about the same period (*NH*, 34, 77; cf. 35, 128)
345 *IGRR* IV, 503, 504 (*Inschriften von Pergamon*, no. 333). Nikodemos, called Nikon for short, was probably the father of the great medical man Galen (Suidas, s.v. Γαληνός). If so, we have here a further demonstration of the close connection between the crafts and the intellectual disciplines, in this instance architecture, geometry and medicine
346 Diogenes Laertius VIII, 46; Pliny, *NH*, 34, 59. The sculptor Pythagoras or his family may have originated from Samos, and so have been related to the mathematician; whether or not this is so, he could certainly have been in contact with pupils and friends of the great Pythagoras, who could have reached Lokroi a generation earlier
347 Pliny, *NH*, 34, 57
348 This point is made by W. Burkert, *CQ* 1963, 177
349 J. E. Raven, 'Polyclitus and Pythagoreanism', *CQ* 1951, 147–52
350 *GTBE*, esp. p. 145
351 See ch. III, p. 113 and note 294
352 VII, pref., 11
353 *On Nature* IV, 426, 31. J. White, *Perspective in Ancient Drawing and Painting* (1956), 23, would have it that 'Euclid, as a mathematician, naturally shows no interest whatsoever' in painting
354 See A. G. Drachmann, *Mechanical Technology of Greek and Roman Antiquity* (1963), for discussion of mechanical theory in the Hellenistic and Roman periods
355 *Birds*, 1004ff. Cf. E. R. Dodds, *The Greeks and the Irrational* (1951), 'Rationalism and Reaction in the Classical Age', 179ff; M. I. Finley, *Aspects of Antiquity* (1968), 'Socrates and Athens', 58ff
356 Problems discussed by I. Calabi-Limentani, *Studi sulla società Romana: il lavoro artistico* (1958)
357 XIII, 1, 13
358 *IG* IV², 1, 102, 45–8—9,800 dr. as compared to 3,937 dr.; 7–8; 13–14
359 *IG* IV², 1, 102, 9–11—a year's salary of 353 dr.
360 Pliny, *NH*, 35, 63. Apelles—Pliny, *NH*, 35, 92

361 Pliny, *NH*, 35, 87

362 Pliny, *NH*, 35, 16

363 Pliny, *NH*, 34, 37

364 Pliny, *NH*, 33, 147; 34, 11; 35, 156—Lucullus made an agreement with the sculptor Arkesilaos for a statue costing one million sesterces; 35, 163—vast sums were expended on fine earthenware

365 Pliny, *NH*, 35, 62

366 Cf. *GTBE*, 164–6, on prices in general; costs of quarrying and transporting stone are discussed at pp. 168–75, 184–91

367 On the *diobelia*, see Tod, *op. cit.* (note 195), no. 83, with comment

368 For details of contracts, piece rates, and time limits, see *GTBE*, 88ff

369 *IG* I², 374

370 For what follows cf. W. K. Pritchett and D. Amyx, 'The "Attic Stelai" I', *Hesperia* 1953, 225–99 (texts); ' "Attic stelai" II', *Hesperia* 1956, 128–317 and 1957, 163–254 (discussion)

371 Cf. the housing in the industrial districts of Athens (*Figs.* II, III) and p. 82, notes 183–6, above

372 The painter Polygnotos is one such (Plutarch, *Kimon*, IV, 6); on the architects Sostratos of Knidos and Philon of Eleusis see ch. V, pp. 153–4

373 Pericles' military engineer Artemon seems to have been able to indulge expensive tastes. He is said to have gone about in a litter, and to have commissioned a portrait head of himself from Polykleitos of Argos (Plutarch, *Pericles*, 21; Pliny, *NH*, 34, 56)

374 See *GTBE*, 138–45, and M. Lacroix, 'Les Architectes et entrepreneurs à Délos de 314 à 240', *Revue Philologique* 1914, 303ff

375 Simonides, Bergk³, fr. 157

376 *IG* IV², 1, 102; 89–90; 98–9; 111–12

377 The entire temple was constructed in four years and eight months, so that work on the sculptures can certainly have gone on no longer than that

378 The spacing of the inscription simply does not allow for the restoration, at one or another of the gaps in the text, of a contract to supply Pentelic marble separately

379 Plutarch, *Pericles*, 31. The whole episode, together with all the evidence, is discussed by F. Jacoby, *FGH*, 328 Philochorus, fr. 121, with commentary, III B ii, 391ff

380 See Jones, *LRE*, 61 and 438; a convenient translation can be found in N. Lewis and M. Reinhold, *Roman Civilisation* (1951), II, 464–73

381 Pliny, *NH*, 35, 102

382 Plato, *Laws*, 955E

383 Plutarch, *Solon*, 21

384 W. S. Ferguson, *Hellenistic Athens* (1911), 42; D. C. Kurtz and J. Boardman, *Greek Burial Customs* (1971), 121ff, 162ff

385 Scullard, *Roman Politics* (1951), 113f

386 Scullard, *op. cit.*, 222

387 Tacitus, *Annals* III, 42

388 Dio Cassius LVII, 15, 1

389 Pliny, *NH*, 35, 119

390 Pausanias V, 11, 3; Dio Chrysostom XII, 6; on Pheidias' own portrait, see Cicero, *Tusculanarum Quaestionum* I, 15, 34; Valerius Maximus VIII, 6

391 See *GTBE*, ch. IV, for fuller discussion

392 There are records of disputes ('strikes') between workers and city governments under the Empire, at Pergamon and Miletos in the second century AD, and at Sardis in the fifth, showing that the workers were calling for regulation of exactly the same points as are to be found in the Greek contracts—terms of payment, time limits, fines for default and penalties incurred because of the difference in price of contracts which had to be relet. See W. H. Buckler, 'Labour Disputes in the Province of Asia', *Studies Presented to W. M. Ramsay* (1923), 27ff

393 *IG* I², 105—shipbuilding in Macedon; *IG* I², 73 and 74—numbers in the shipyards

394 Livy XXVII, 45

395 The *lex Metilia*—Pliny, *NH*, 35, 197–8

396 Pseudo-Aristotle, *Economics*, 1346A. Athenaeus XII, 522D—dyers at Sybaris were exempted from a produce tax, so as to raise their morale

397 M. I. Rostovtzeff, *Social and Economic History of the Hellenistic World* (1941), 445

398 Jones, *LRE*, 431–2

399 Libanius, *Or.* XLVI, 22–3; Jones, *LRE*, 871–2

400 *Cod. Theod.* XIV, 7, 'de collegiatis'

401 See ch. II, p. 34, and note 47

402 *Clara Rhodos* VI–VII, 413, no. 38

403 *Lindos* I, no. 165

404 Ploutarchos—*Lindos* I, no. 131b; Theon—*Lindos* I, no. 172; Charinos—*Lindos* II, no. 327; *IG* XII, 1, 107; Epicharmos—*Lindos* I, nos. 232, 235–6, 246

405 *SIG*³, 707

406 *CIG*, 2024; cf. his epitaph, 2025

407 See ch. VI, p. 265

408 Pliny, *NH*, 35, 115

409 *Cod. Theod.* XIII, 4, 'de excusationibus artificum'

410 *Cod. Theod.* XIII, 4, 4

CHAPTER V

411 Vitruvius VII, pref., 12; the ships' arsenal—*IG* II², 1668; the trierarchy—*IG* II², 1622, 694

412 *RE:* Vitruvius, 419ff. Vitruvius said himself (VI, pref., 6) that 'the ancients

used to entrust work to architects of good family. . . . Such men would have no need of touting for patronage, but would be men of independent means and judgment'

413 Pliny, *NH*, 36, 83; Delphi—*FD* III, i, 299; Delos—*OGIS*, 66, 67. The people of Kaunos also honoured Sostratos in the Delian sanctuary, for his good services to their city—*OGIS*, 68

414 It is as likely as not that the wealthier craftsmen of the later sixth and early fifth centuries (i.e. those who made dedications on the Athenian acropolis, of whom more below) were more sympathetic to the aristocrats and the rich, the politically exclusive, since these were the fine craftsman's most generous patrons

415 See ch. II, note 99 for references

416 See ch. IV, p. 147 and note 392

417 E.g. Xenophon, *Memorabilia* III, 10, 1–15

418 Lysias XXIV, 19–20

419 See ch. IV, p. 130 and ch. III, p. 82 and note 184

420 Sophocles—*Vita* 1; Kephalos—Schol. Aristoph., *Ekklesiazousai*, 253 (the potter Kephalos—*ARV²*, and perhaps Raubitschek, *Dedications*, no. 209); Kleon—Aristophanes, *Knights*, 129ff; Kleophon—Andocides I, 46; Anytos —Plato, *Meno*, 90A—his father Anthemion was a self-made man; Hyper-bolos—*Knights*, 1315

421 Cf. the remarks above, ch. II, p. 30 and note 37, on the differences between Nikias and Kleon, and the source of their wealth

422 Cf. M. I. Finley, 'Athenian Demagogues', *Past and Present* 1962, 3–24

423 The Athenian army fortified Pylos, without benefit even of mason's tools (Thucydides IV, 3, 2–4, 3). Later in the Peloponnesian War, troops from Syracuse helped the men of Antandros complete their fortifications—'as a result they now enjoy the privilege of benefactors and the rights of citizens at Antandros' (Xenophon, *Hellenica* I, 1, 26)

424 Cf. Ramsay MacMullen, *Soldier and Civilian in the Later Roman Empire* (1963), 23ff

425 E. W. Marsden, *Greek and Roman Artillery* (1969), 185

426 The cult of Bendis in Athens has been discussed by W. S. Ferguson, 'Orgeonika', *Hesperia*, Supplement VIII (1949), 130–63. On Greek associations in general, see F. Poland, *Geschichte der Vereinswesens* (1912); on Hellenistic and Roman associations, see Waltzing I–IV—the inscriptions are presented in vol. III

427 Waltzing III, no. 179

428 See below, p. 171, for reference to the miners' dedications

429 Collingwood and Wright, *op. cit.* (note 131), no. 156

430 Waltzing I, 90ff

431 N. Lewis and M. Reinhold, *op. cit.* (note 380), 326ff, no. 84

432 Tacitus, *Annals* XIV, 17

433 Pliny, *Letters* X, 33 and 34

434 O. Gradenwitz, 'Das Statut für die Zunft der Elfenbein-arbeiter', *Zeitschr. d. Savigny-Stiftung* 1890, 72

435 *CIL* VI, 1060; Frank, *Economic Survey* V, 215

436 Dubois, no. 56

437 *ILS*, 7237; see above, pp. 18–19

438 See below, pp. 182–3 and note 522

439 *ILS*, 7687

440 R. S. Young, *op. cit.* (note 185), esp. 222–3

441 These calculations are based on a summary count of the dedications and epitaphs published in *IG* I² and II², and an estimated citizen population of no more than 120,000 at any one time

442 As the merest glance at *CIL* (an unwieldy publication) indicates

443 Marie Delcourt, *Héphaistos, ou la légende du magicien* (1957), discusses Hephaistos, Prometheus and Vulcan; she lays rather too much stress on the possibilities of magical powers in the operations of these deities. On Athena as patron of the crafts, see e.g. Sophocles, fr. 760N, 844; Pausanias I, 24, 3; and, with Hephaistos, Plato, *Laws*, 920E

444 Thucydides III, 88

445 M. Delcourt, *op. cit.*, 41

446 See W. Burkert, 'Jason, Hypsipyle, and New Fire at Lemnos', *CQ* 1970, 1–16, in which he suggests that the smiths of Lemnos played an important part in the fire festival. Otherwise, there is little or nothing to indicate that smiths had any more magical or ritual importance in the eyes of Greeks and Romans than other craftsmen

447 W. B. Dinsmoor, *Observations on the Hephaisteion*, *Hesperia* Supplement V (1941), 125ff

448 Dinsmoor, *op. cit.*, 129; cf. Homer Thompson, *Hesperia* 1936, 126

449 M. Delcourt, *op. cit.*

450 Ovid, *Fasti* V, 725

451 M. Delcourt, *op. cit.*, 212

452 But see below, pp. 175–6, for some hints that quarry masons took more heed of religious influences in their work than other craftsmen

453 *Corinth* XV, 1: *The Potters' Quarter* 22, 51f

454 *ID*, 2473

455 Strabo X, 1, 6

456 Vitruvius X, 2, 15; cf. the article by W. Alzinger, 'Ritzzeichnungen in den Marmorbrüchen von Ephesos', *Jahreshefte* (Wien) 1966–7, 62ff

457 Raubitschek, *Dedications*, no. 70

458 Raubitschek, *Dedications*, no. 48

459 Raubitschek, *Dedications*, no. 178

460 The incidence of dedications itself presents problems. No strict correlation can be made between dedicating and social standing, because the practice seems not to have been observed with any regularity. If craftsmen's dedications became fewer after the mid-fifth century (one or two as

compared with ten or a dozen previously), then so did the total number of dedications made

461 *IG* II², 4921a

462 Of twenty-two workshop scenes, four are on vases found in Athens, one on a vase in Rhodes, the provenance of six is unknown and the remaining ten went to Italy. Three in fact were found on the Athenian acropolis, but it is by no means certain that they were dedicated

463 Pollias, who dedicated a painted terracotta plaque *c.* 500, signed by Euthymides, is probably to be identified with the sculptor who was also Euthymides' father (M. Robertson, *Greek Painting* (1959), 95; cf. Raubitschek, *Dedications*, nos. 522–3). Another sculptor, Demetrios, set up a dedication *c.* 400 B C (Raubitschek, *Dedications*, no. 143)

464 *IG* I², 784–7, and *AJA* (1903), 263ff, on the cave-shrine at Vari

465 Discussed by Lauffer, *op. cit.* (note 66), II

466 *IG* II², 2940; 4598; 4633. Cf. Lauffer, *op. cit.*, 172ff

467 E.g. *IG* II², 4545–7; 4646–7; 4650–1

468 *IG* XII³, 1075. Cf. L. H. Jeffery, *Local Scripts of Archaic Greece* (1961), 320

469 *SEG* III, 464

470 *BSA* 1907, 134

471 Herodotus IV, 87–8

472 *Lindos* I, no. 165

473 *CIL* II, 2559

474 *CIL* X, 8146

475 *ILS*, 5405

476 *ILS*, 3534

477 Calabi-Limentani, no. 98; *ILS*, 5442

478 *OGIS*, 590; Calabi-Limentani, no. 143; Collingwood and Wright, *op. cit.* (note 131), no. 274

479 Calabi-Limentani, no. 67

480 Waltzing III, no. 95

481 Waltzing III, no. 198

482 Waltzing III, nos. 148, 225

483 Waltzing III, no. 617

484 *ILS*, 7392

485 Dubois, no. 63

486 Dubois, no. 131

487 Dubois, no. 58

488 Dubois, no. 125

489 Dubois, no. 135

490 Published by H. Sandars, *Archaeologica* 1905, *pl.* LXIX

491 The craftsmen's epitaphs are mostly of the fourth century B C

492 Some impression of the sentiments often expressed in such records can be gained from R. Lattimore, *Themes in Greek and Latin Epitaphs* (1942)

493 *IG* II², 10051. See Lauffer, *op. cit.* (note 66), II, 198ff

494 *IG* II², 11678–80; Lauffer, *loc. cit.*

495 *IG* II², 12618. The relief is now apparently lost

496 *IG* II², 11697

497 *IG* II², 11954; *JDAI* (1920), 69–72, and cf. A. Wilhelm, *Beiträge* (1909), 40ff

498 For Mannes' epitaph, see ch. I, p. 18 and note 14; Euthias'—*IG* II², 11387

499 Athenaeus XII, 543C

500 *IG* II², 11689—his trade name was *persikopoios*

501 *IG* II², 11175–6; 7967; *SEG*, XIX, 305; 13178

502 *IG* XII, 1, 381. It is all the more strange that Rostovtzeff should have remarked (*Social and Economic History of the Hellenistic World*, 688) that 'the Rhodians very seldom mentioned their profession, even in their funeral inscriptions, *differing in this from the inhabitants of other parts of Greece*, not to speak of Italy and the west' (my italics)

503 Various examples have been collected in an article by H. Gummerus, 'Darstellungen aus dem Handwerk auf römischen Grab- und Votiv-steinen', *JDAI* 1913, 63–126; cf. W. Deonna, 'Ex-votos Déliens: Instruments de métier sur un relief de Délos', *BCH* 1932, 421–90, who warns against identifying every gravestone which has mason's tools engraved on it with a professional craftsman. Tools of this kind seem to have gained a cult significance quite remote from the interests of skilled workers

504 *ILS*, 7733

505 Calabi-Limentani, no. 82

506 Calabi-Limentani, no. 53

507 Calabi-Limentani, no. 75; G. Calza, *La necropoli del porto di Roma* (1940), 279; W. Peek, *Griechische Grab-gedichte* I, no. 420

508 Calabi-Limentani, no. 77

509 *IG* II², 9611

510 Calabi-Limentani, no. 57

511 Calabi-Limentani, no. 94

512 See below, ch. VI, p. 208 and note 593

513 *CIG*, 2025

514 Calabi-Limentani, no. 5

515 Calabi-Limentani, no. 23

516 *ILS*, 7687

517 Calabi-Limentani, no. 127

518 Calabi-Limentani, no. 138

519 Contrast this poverty with the glory achieved in the monuments of other manual workers, such as that of the Roman baker Eurysakes

520 *ILS*, 7723

521 *SEG* IV, 105

522 *ILS*, 7715. Cf., for phrasing, *CIL* VI, 13481

CHAPTER VI

523 *Nikomachean Ethics* VI, 2, 5

524 Antiphon, *Concerning Truth*, 2. He is not necessarily condemning craftsmanship outright, but merely wishing to emphasize the difference between real and false, or natural and conventional forms

525 E.g. Plato, *Protagoras*, 326E–328C

526 Cf. M. I. Finley, 'Metals in the Ancient World', *Journal of the Royal Society of Arts* 1970, no. 5170, at pp. 598ff

527 For a recent study of these views and for what follows, see T. Cole, *Democritus and the Sources of Greek Anthropology* (Philological Monographs XXV, American Philological Association, 1967). As he points out, the wide currency of the anthropologists' opinions is reflected in their having become part of the rhetoricians' stock-in-trade

528 Lucretius, *On the Nature of Things* V, 940ff; Vitruvius II, 1

529 Lucretius V, 1457

530 Vitruvius II, 1, 6–7

531 In Diodorus' version (I, 13, 3) Hephaistos is spoken of as the discoverer of fire, but at this point he is seen simply as a representative of man, not yet a *divine* being

532 Tzetzes speaks of *promethesteroi* men, the 'more forethoughtful', drawing close to see the new phenomenon of fire; cf. Lucretius V, 1107

533 See ch. V, p. 167. on the possible significance of the cult of Hephaistos to the Athenians, and the importance of enlarging his sanctuary during the 450s

534 436ff. G. Thomson suggests in his edition of *Prometheus Bound* (1932), that the third play in the trilogy was *Prometheus the Firebearer*, under which epithet he was worshipped in Athens, together with Athena and Hephaistos in the Academy (schol. *Oedipus Colonus* 54–6). In this final stage of the trilogy, Athena perhaps reconciled the conflicting parties, and saw to the institution of Prometheus' cult in the city

535 As stated in the opening of the *Prometheus Bound*

536 See Cole, *op. cit.* (note 527), and A. Kleingünther, Πρωτος Εὑρετης, *Philologus*, Supplementband 26 (1933); the fullest list surviving is that of Pliny, *NH* 7, 191ff

537 *NH* 7, 198, 199; 197

538 *NH* 7, 195; or, alternatively, the Phoenicians made the discovery

539 A worthy counterpart to this oft-repeated tale is offered by Diodorus Siculus IV, 76–7, who recounts that Daidalos' nephew Talos 'invented' the saw as a result of playing about with the toothed jawbone of a serpent

540 Hellanikos, *FHG* 112, 113

541 Hesiod, fr. 76

542 References given by Kleingünther, *op. cit.* (note 536)
543 Thucydides I, 13, 3
544 Herodotus III, 60
545 Pliny, *NH* 7, 198
546 Kritias, Bergk³, fr. I, 12–14
547 As is the case with the sculptors Dipoinos and Skyllis, 'the first men to make a name as sculptors in marble' (Pliny, *NH*, 36, 9); or Boutades of Sicyon, the potter who 'first invented portraiture in clay from an outline drawing' (*NH*, 35, 151)
548 Vitruvius X, 2, 11–12
549 Vitruvius IV, 1, 10. Indeed he was spoken of rather disparagingly elsewhere as 'over-complicated' or 'too-clever-clever', even 'over-craftsmanly' (Pausanias I, 26–7)
550 Vitruvius IX, pref., 9–12. To be sure, the good inventor is able to seize unexpected opportunities, as well as to apply a theory which he has already thought out; and this is an element in the success story of the Rhodian engineer Diognetos, who is supposed to have disabled Demetrius Poliorcetes' *helepolis*, not by constructing an even bigger and better machine, but by flooding the place where the *helepolis* was to be brought up, so that it foundered in the mud (Vitruvius X, 16, 7–8)
551 Vitruvius X, 2, 15. Cf. ch. V, p. 169 and note 456
552 For references see Kleingünther, *op. cit.* (note 536). The Titan smiths offer some parallels to the magician-smiths of other cultures, such as R. J. Forbes enumerates in *op. cit.* (note 157), VIII, ch. iii, 'Evolution of the Smith, his Social and Sacred Status'. But the magical aspect of the smith's work seems to have dropped out completely in classical antiquity. Cf. Finley, *op. cit.* (note 526)
553 *CIG*, 2025; see ch. V, p. 181
554 Hesiod, fr. 178
555 Cf. M. Delcourt, *op. cit.* (note 443), who goes rather far along this line of speculation
556 *RE:* Hephaistos, VIII 332, 14–333, 19
557 *RE:* Daidalos, IV 2002, 10—productions as craftsman; 2002ff—productions as sculptor; 2005, 31ff—productions as architect; 2006, 8ff—productions as inventor. Michael Ayrton's novel *The Maze-Maker* (1967) presents a compelling account of the strange and powerful craftsman
558 Homer, *Odyssey* XI, 609
559 See also ch. III, pp. 122–3—the few pieces of evidence for the use of apotropaic charms, and the *Potters' Hymn*
560 Plutarch, *Numa* XV, 2–4, 13, 1–7
561 See above, p. 82 and note 187
562 Homer, *Iliad* XVIII, 468ff
563 Homer, *Odyssey* XXIII, 190
564 Cicero, *Brutus*, 18, 70

565 *Institutio oratoria* XII, 10, 1–10
566 *ibid.*
567 Diodorus Siculus XXVI, 1
568 Pliny, *NH*, 34, 43
569 Pliny, *NH*, 34, 140. Silanion's work is similarly described in Plutarch, *Quaestiones Convivales* V, 2, 1: 'We find pleasure in and marvel at the modelled statue of Jocasta, in whose face they say the sculptor mixed silver so that the bronze might take on the surface colour of a person whose life is being slowly snuffed out'
570 Zeuxis was said to have painted the picture of a boy with a bunch of grapes. When some birds flew down to eat the fruit Zeuxis remarked with annoyance that this showed he had not painted the boy in as realistic a manner, for otherwise the birds would have been frightened off
571 Pliny, *NH*, 34, 46
572 Famulus—Pliny, *NH*, 35, 120; Protogenes—35, 102; Pasiteles—36, 40
573 See ch. IV, p. 129 and note 337
574 Pliny, *NH*, 35, 103
575 Pausanias III, 17, 2
576 So Pausanias II, 11, 6 reports that Alexander, son of Machaon and grandson of the hero-healer (later, healing god) Asklepios, built the sanctuary of Asklepios at Titane and made the image of the god
577 Plutarch, *Kimon*, 4; Pliny, *NH*, 35, 58
578 See ch. IV, note 379, for reference to Pheidias' notoriety and associations with Athenian notables, and Plutarch, *Pericles*
579 Plutarch, *Alexander*, and L. Pearson, *The Lost Historians of Alexander* (1960), show how Alexander the Great was taken over. This problem is discussed at length—with perhaps excessively 'historical-developmental' conclusions —by E. Zilsel, *Die Entstehung des Genie-begriffs* (1926)
580 Apelles—Pliny, *NH*, 35, 84
581 Pliny, *NH*, 35, 85
582 Pliny, *NH*, 35, 101
583 Pliny, *NH*, 35, 104 and 105
584 Lysippos—Pliny, *NH*, 34, 61
585 Suetonius, *Augustus*, 50; Pliny, *NH*, 37, 38
586 Overbeck, *op. cit.* (note 149), 553–88
587 Pliny, *NH*, 35, 112
588 Plotinus, *Enneads* V, 8, 1. J. M. Rist, *Plotinus, the Road to Reality* (1967), 183–4, suggests that sculpture served as a parallel to the activity of the seeker after the Good, and that Plotinus is reacting against Plato's view that the artist merely copies the copy of the object by saying that Pheidias went back to the original form of Zeus for his statue. But the whole image still seems remote from the reality of the working sculptor. Cf. Seneca, *Letters to Lucilius* I, 9, 5: 'If Pheidias lost a statue, he would quickly make another one'—seeming to suggest that Seneca saw some deeply personal connection

between the craftsman and the work of art; Seneca makes the point to illustrate that to be making new friends was a better state than to keep the same old friends—'just as it is more enjoyable for a painter to be actually painting a picture than to have finished it'. Once more the only individual cited is Pheidias and here clearly the crafts are being used figuratively

589 Porphyry, *Life of Plotinus*, 1
590 Solon, frag. 13, 11, 49–52 (Edmonds, Loeb edition, *Elegy and Iambus* I)
591 However, see below, p. 208 and note 594, on craftsmen's records in which the term *sophia* occurs
592 See p. 205
593 Miss Joyce Reynolds has kindly allowed me to make use of this unpublished inscription
594 *IG* XII, 5, 147. *Sophia* here must surely serve as the equivalent of *technē*—'know-how'—not wisdom in any inspired sense; as far as I know it only occurs in one other craftsman's statement, that of Kapiton and Janouarios in the second century AD (see below, page 209) and in the personal name Cheirisophos, p. 211
595 Pausanias VI, 10, 4
596 Athenaeus XII, 543C–E
597 See ch. V, p. 178, and cf. Wilhelm, *op. cit.* (note 497), 40f
598 See ch. V, p. 177
599 See ch. V, p. 182
600 *JRS* 1967, 43, no. 8
601 Calabi-Limentani, no. 107
602 See ch. V, p. 181
603 See ch. V, p. 180 and note 508
604 See ch. V, pp. 182–3 and note 522
605 See ch. V, p. 181 and note 517
606 Beazley, *ARV²*, 1027
607 *Inschriften von Pergamon*, 136; *CIL* VI, 29796
608 See ch. III, pp. 84–7
609 Pausanias VI, 3, 4
610 See ch. III, p. 85 and Pliny, *NH*, 35, 182
611 See ch. III, p. 24 and Pausanias VIII, 53, 8
612 Pausanias I, 40, 4
613 Cf. Athenaeus XII, 541A, on competitive displays at festivals, and Pliny, *NH*, 35, 125
614 Pliny, *NH*, 34, 53; cf. 36, 17
615 *ID*, 4
616 See ch. III, note 248
617 Calabi-Limentani, nos. 87, 60
618 Calabi-Limentani, nos. 68, 91
619 Collingwood and Wright, *op. cit.* (note 131), nos. 149 (Priscus, son of Toutius, *lapidarius*, a tribesman of the Carnutes, i.e. the district around

Chartres) and 151 (Sulinus, *scultor*, i.e. sculptor). 149 = *ILS* 4661; 115 = *CIL* VII, 37

620 *CIL* X, 6126 and 6339

621 Loewy, 339

622 *CIL* XII, 186; *ILS*, 5637

623 Kleon—*IG* V, 1, 690; Zenon—*CIG*, 4342d; Aristainetos—see p. 212

624 *CIL* IV, 3884

625 *ID*, 2288

626 See Calabi-Limentani for the varied character of mosaic workers' signatures

627 *Archaeology* 1955, 256ff

628 Pliny, *NH*, 37, 8, mentions, in addition to Pyrgoteles and Dioscurides, Apollonides and Kronios

629 See C. Kraay, *Greek Coinage* (1966), on the coiners of Syracuse and other Sicilian and south Italian cities at this period

630 R. M. Cook, *Greek Painted Pottery* (1960), 256

631 *loc. cit.*

632 Beazley, *ABV*, 112

633 Nikosthenes, a potter working towards the end of the sixth century, signed over 120 of the surviving 150 vases attributed to him, an unusually high proportion. His partner Pamphaios signed 31 out of 50 surviving pieces; other potters and painters are known from half a dozen signatures at most

634 Beazley, *op. cit.* (note 240), commenting on *fig.* 7. See ch. V, p. 170 and note 462

635 The makers' marks on Arretine pottery cannot really be called signatures. Their purpose was surely to serve as a check on production; it is not that the mould maker wished to be identified with every pot turned out of his mould

636 *ILS*, 8562. Cf. the earlier inscribed fibula from Praeneste (sixth century BC?): *Manios med fhe fhaked Numasioi* ('Manius made me for Numerius'), *ILS*, 8561

SOURCES OF ILLUSTRATIONS

French School of Archaeology at Athens, 1, 71, 72; Alison Frantz, Athens, 2, 58; Ashmolean Museum, Oxford, 3, 31, 47; Trustees of the British Museum, 4, 6, 10, 14, 21, 22, 23, 25, 29, 42, 43, 46, 78; P. Dumont and J. Babinot, Rheims, 5; Mansell, 12, 19; Mansell-Alinari, 7, 54, 70, 86, 88; Maurice Chuzeville, 8; Fotofast, Bologna, 9; National Museum, Copenhagen, 11, 37, 77; Staatliche Museen zu Berlin (East), 13, 15, 16, 18; Antikensammlungen, Munich, 17; Museum of Fine Arts, Boston, 20, 30, 44; American School of Classical Studies at Athens, 24, 35; Toledo Museum of Art, 26; C. Macdonald, 27, 28; Deutsches Archäologisches Institut, Athens, 32, 75, 80, 84; Yorkshire Museum, York, 33; Cliché des Musées Nationaux, 34, 59; Deutsches Archäologisches Institut, Rome, 36, 41, 48, 56, 82, 83; Staatliche Museen, West Berlin, 38, 39, 40; Hermitage, Leningrad, 45; John Webb, Brompton Studios, 49, 50; Ray Gardner, 51, 52; Bibliothèque National, Paris, 53; the author, 55, 60, 63; Yale University Museum, 57; Max Hirmer, Munich, 61, 81; Foto Marburg, 62; Fototeca Unione, Rome, 64, 67, 68, 69, 74; Georgina Masson, 65; Gabinetto Fotographico Nazionale, 66; Sonia Halliday, 73; Metropolitan Museum of Art, New York, 76; Royal Ontario Museum, 79; Museé d'Aquitaine, Bordeaux, 85; Ch. J. Makaronas, 87; Figures 2 and 3 drawn by Miss G. D. Jones.

MUSEUM LOCATIONS

Delos Museum, 1; National Museum of Antiquities, Athens, 2; Ashmolean Museum, Oxford, 3, 31, 47; Rheims Museum, 5; British Museum, 6, 10, 14, 21, 22, 23, 25, 29, 42, 43, 46, 49, 50, 51, 52, 78; Ostia Museum, 7; Louvre, 8, 59; Ravenna Museum, 9; National Museum, Copenhagen, 11, 37, 77; Berlin (East) Museum, 13, 15, 16, 18; Antikensammlungen, Munich, 17; Acropolis Museum, Athens, 19; Boston Museum of Fine Arts, 20 (gift of Martin Brimmer), 30 (H. L. Pierce Fund), 44; Agora Museum, 24, 35; Toledo Museum of Art, 26 (gift of Edward Drummond Libbey, 1930); Olympia Museum, 32, 80; Yorkshire Museum, York, 33; Cluny Museum, Paris, 34; Vatican Museums, 36, 41, 54, 56, 81; Berlin (West) Museum, 38, 39, 40; Hermitage, Leningrad, 45; Private coll. Rome, 48; Bibliothèque Nationale, Paris, 53; Yale University Museum, 57; Epidauros Museum, 62; Metropolitan Museum of Art, New York, 76 (Rogers Fund, 1945); Royal Ontario Museum, 79; Palazzo dei Conservatori, Rome, 82; Museo Nazionale, Rome, 83; Chalkis Museum, 84; Musée d'Aquitaine, Bordeaux, 85; Museo Nazionale, Naples, 88.

INDEX

accounts for public works, 24–5; *see also* Delos, Delphi, Epidauros, Eleusis, Erechtheion, Parthenon
Aeschylus, 53, 186, 189–90
Agatharchos, 133
Aischines, 170
Akesas, 87
Alxenor, 208, 211
Amabilis, 71, 181
Ameinokles, 110, 191
Andocides, 94, 170
Antenor, 85, 112, 128, 176
Apelles, 69, 137, 199, 204
Apollo, 11; quarrymen's cult, 168–9
Apollodoros, architect, 67, 96
Apollodoros, sculptor, 129, 202
apotropaic signs, 122–3
apprentices, 87–91, 92
Archedemos, 170–1
Archermos, 85, 208
Archias, 110
Archimedes, 67, 96, 102, 104, 134, 135, 193
architects, 21, 66, 91, 93–5, 102; architectural development, 112–13, 119–21; carpenters, 86–7; dedications, 173; epitaphs, 176, 179; family interest in craft, 59–60; harmony, 131–2; military architects, 158; patrons, 124, 126–7; in public life, 153–4; salaries, 136–8, 141–142; sculptors, 86; signed works, 214; training and experience, 102–6
Argos, 63, 66, 85, 111, 191; *see also* masons, sculptors
Aristaichmos, 101, 163–4
Aristainetos, 21, 212, 214
Aristandros I and II, 84
Aristeides, 102
Aristokles, 85
Aristophanes, 53, 54; trade names in, 99; the new philosophy, 134–5; *banausia* complex, n. 334
Aristotle, 25, 30; *banausoi* and political rights, 34; barbarians, 53; the economy, 57; mechanization, 58; patron and craftsman, 126; slavery, 43; teaching crafts, 88; technological development, 185
Arkesilaos, 142
armourers, 91, 92, 129, 160
Arretine pottery, 24, 60, 61, 95, 107–8
ars, artifex, 14

Athena, 122, 181, 211; with Hephaistos, 166; in Athenian vase-paintings, 168, 170, 194; transmitter of skill, 194–5; statues of, *see* Pheidias
Athens, craftsmen concentrated at, 111; cult associations in, 159, 160; democracy and craftsmen, 154–7; industry, 30–1; intellectuals and craftsmen, 128–9, 156; land-owning and citizenship, 29–32; prices and wages, 138–9, 140–1; *see also* labour market, masons, metics, miners, potters, sculptors, shipwrights, slaves, smiths
Atotas, miner, 56, 177, 209
Atotas, sculptor, 91
Auctus, L. Cocceius, 91

Bakchios I, 178, 209; II, 67, 150, 170
banausia complex, 25–6, 179, n. 334; *see also banausoi*
banausoi, 12, 25, 29–30, 72, 207; and Athenian democracy, 154, 156–7; and gentlemen-craftsmen, 203; and intellectual pursuits, 128–35; philosophers' attitude to, 185–6; political limitations, 29, 34, 39–40, 41, n. 24; professions admitted in epitaphs, 176; and technological development, 119
Beitenos, P., 182
Benignus, Q. Candidus, 163, 182–3, 210
Blesamus, Novius, 180
Boethos, 150, 172
Brentes, 84
building contracts, 36, 147, 155

Cadgat, Iulius, 181
Caecilianus, 41
Camillus, P. Longidienus, 164, 179, 182
Capitolinus, C. Vettius, 181
carpenters, 18, 86–7, 96–7, 99–100, 102, 110, 162, 163, 182–3, 209
Cato, 30, 55, 146
Chares, 115
Charopinos, 84
Cheirisophos, 211
Cheirisophos, silversmith, 24, 211
cheirotechnēs, 14
Chersiphron, 86, 192
Chrysothemis, 88, 208
Cicero, 30, 54; and slave architect, 42, 126, 129; *banausia* complex, n. 334; craftsmanship, 199

citizenship, 23, 28–41, 43
city economy, 57–67, 97; *see also* labour market, specialization
clothes-cleaners, 160, 171
coiners, 216–17
collegium, 18–19, 27; compulsory membership, 149–50, 159–63; funerary function, 180–2; group dedication, 173–5; lack of concern in training craftsmen, 90
competitions, painters', 200–1, 211; potters', 211; sculptors', 211
Corinth, attitude to *banausoi*, 34; labour force, 66; 'first discoverers', 191–2; *see also* carpenters, lamp-makers, masons, potters, shipwrights
craft associations, *see collegium*
craftsmanship, 68–9, 96–7, 114, 184–90; standards of, 98–9, 107–14; price of, 135–6; names reflecting, 210–11
Cyrene, treasury, 131–2
Cyrus, 42, 126, 129

Daidalos, 82, 96, 112, 192, 196–7, 198, 203, 210
Daidalos of Sicyon, 210
Damophon, 172
dedications, 11–12, 13, 26, 91, 164–76
Delos, 11, 25; architects and carpenters, 86, 99–100, 141–2; contract regulations, 147; salaries, 59; smiths, 101; workers from elsewhere, 67, 79–80
Delphi, accounts, 25; architects, 86, 141–142; Alcmeonids and temple, 128; carpenters, 102; manumissions, 47; salaries, 59
Demetrios, 91
dēmiourgos, 14, 191
designers, 93–6; interaction with patrons, 124–8; *see also* architects
Diodorus Siculus, on craftsmanship, 15, 200
Diophanes, C. Valerius, 90, 182
divine inspiration, 207
divine intervention in crafts, 189–90, 194–195
division of labour, *see* specialization
Douris, 94, 100
dyers, 78

economic factors, *see* city economy, labour market, land-owning, prices, specialization, wages
Egypt, apprenticing, 89–90; tax on craftsmen, 149; *see also* mines, quarries
Eleusis, accounts, 45, 46 – slaves; 120–1 – transport; 140 – price of tools
engineering, 58, 115–16, 134; military, 117, 118, 173; Roman, 64, 102–5

Ephesos, marble discovered at, 169; privileges for manual workers, 34, 150; quarrymen's cult, 169; sculptors' competition, 211; temples, 82, 91, 169, 193–194
Epidauros, accounts, 25; architect and sculptor, 95; economy, 63; salaries, 59, 136, 138, 142; temple building, 63, 65–66, 98; workers from elsewhere, 85; workshop, 78
Epikrates, 13, 66, 150
Epimenes, 113
epitaphs, 18–19, 26, 47, 163, 164–5, 176–183
Erechtheion, accounts, 24, 59, 62, 79; division of labour, 100; salaries, 138–9; workshops, 91
Erigonos, 91
Euboulides I and II, 85, 211
Eucheir, 85, 211
Eucheiros, 211
Eupalinos, 22, 103, 115
Euphranor, 132, 135
Euphronios, 94, 100, 113
Eutelidas, 88, 208
Euthykartides, 11, 20, 112, 165, 168
Euthymides, 94, 100, 113
Eutyches, T. Ascharenos, 91
Eutychides, 90, 180
Exekias, 217

faber, 14
family tradition in crafts, 82–8, 102–3, 163, 198
Felix, T. Sen., 91
figurine makers, 107, 108, 111
foreigners, 28, 35; *see also* metics, racial prejudice
freedmen, Greek, 47–8; Roman, 32, 38–9, 41, 55–6, 91
fullers, 78

gem engravers, 113, 114, 205, 216
glue boiler, 99
Grophon, 172, 211

Hagelaidas, 91
harmony, 131–3
Harpokration, P. Aelius, 150, 181, 210
Helikon, 87
Hephaistos, 5, 58, 72, 165, 207; and the crafts, 190, 194–5, 196, 198; cult of at Athens, 82, 166–7, 189
Heron of Alexandria, 105
Hesiod, 20, 29, 97, 186
Hilarion, T. Fl., 18–19, 163
Hippodamos of Miletos, 135
Homer, 14, 58, 97; and craftsmanship, 196–7, 198–9; and *banausoi*, 207

Ianibelos, 177
Iktinos, 95, 103
individualism, 19–20, 202–3; public's appreciation of in craftsmen, 95–6, 201–6; *see also* signatures
intellectual interests, 128–35
invention, 97, 186–8, n. 309; 'first discoverers', 190–4; *see also* magic, technological development
ivory workers, *collegium* of, 161

jeweller, 90, 181
joint efforts, 95–6

Kallikrates, 103
Kallimachos, 192
Kallonides, 83
Kanachos, 85
Kapiton, 209
Kephisodotos, 85
Kittos I, 170; II, 34, 67, 150
Kleitophon, 129
Kleoitas, 102, 116, 211
Kleon of Athens, 30, 54, 78, 80, 156–7
Kleon, engineer, 77
Koroibos, 95, 103
Kritios, 85
Ktesibios, 104, 134

labour market, 15–16, 56, 57–67; effect on products, 119, 125; state control of, 58–9, 88, 99, 148
Lacer, C. Iulius, 102, 173
lamp makers, 107–8, 110
land-owning, 28, 29–31, 32, 37, 118
Leptines, 178
Lucian of Samosata, 12, 55
Lucretius, 186–8
Lykon, M. Plautius, 151
Lysippos, 85, 96, 111, 115, 137, 205, 208

magic, 121–3, 196–8
Mandrokles, 103, 172
Mannes, 18, 53, 56, 178, 218
masons, 23, 75–7; Argive, 85; Athenian, 82, 85, 111, 170; Corinthian, 109; Naxian, 11, 76, 115, 120–1, 126, 213; epitaphs, 176, 180; irrational attitude to material, 119–23; pride of workmanship, 209; signatures, 213, 215; *see also* quarry cults
Maximus, 182, 209
mechanics, 134
mechanization, 58, 116, 118–19
Melos, terracotta reliefs at, 109–10
Metagenes, 86, 192
metalworkers, *see* miners, smelters, smiths
metics, 23, 28, 35–6, 86
Mikon, 97
miners, 30; Athens – conditions, 74–5,

80, cult and associations, 160, 171, epitaphs, 176–7, family connections, 87, slaves, 47, 54, 63–4; Egypt, 80; pride of workmanship of, 209; Spain, relief from Linares, 176; techniques, 72–5; *see also* smelters
Mnesikles, 103
Moderatus, C. Vedennius, 158, 179
mosaicists, 91, 150, 215
Myron, 66, 85, 133, 206, 210

Naxos, discovery of marble in, 190; attitude to, 121, 213; *see also* masons, quarries, sculptors
Nealkes, 91
Nearchos, 165, 170
Nesiotes, 85
Nikias of Athens, 30, 43, 157
Nikodemos (Nikon), 132
Nikosthenes, 94, 170

Oltos, 94
Onatas, 207

Pagus, 90
painters, 69, 85–6, 97, 147, 150; competitions, 200–1, 211; connoisseurs and, 199–201, 204–5; dedications, 173; epitaphs, 181; pay, 137; pride of workmanship, 208–9; scene-painters, 133; Sicyon, 91; signatures, 215; stylistic development, 113; theory, 133–4; and vase-painters, 100
Paion, 209
Paionios, 112, 125–6, 211
Palmyra, 66
Pamphaios, 71, 94
Pamphilos, 137, 170, 199
Panainos, 86
Paphlagonia, slaves from, 45, 54, 177
Pappos, mathematician, 105
Parmenon, 213, 215
Paros, *see* masons, sculptors
Parrhasios, 85–6, 100, 129, 178, 199, 200–201, 207, 208–9, 211
Parthenon, accounts, 25, 62, 136; architects, 103; and sculptors, 95; marble, 75, 76; older Parthenon, 119; workshop, 78
Pasiteles, 201, 207
patron and client, Roman, 19, 37–8; craftsman-employee, 108–9, 124–52, 204, 210
Pausanias, 172
Pergamon, sculptors, 95–6, 213
Persia, Athenians and, 53; building record, 20; Greek craftsmen in, 66; slaves from, 45
personal records, *see* dedications, epitaphs, signatures

Pheidias, 12, 86, 87, 89, 91, 95, 203, 206–7; competition, 211; impiety, 147; pay, 136, 142; and Pericles, 129; statues, 101, 115, 121; versatility, 86, 96; workshop, 78, 122
Phereklos, 82
Philon of Eleusis, 95, 153
Phyles, 150
Pistias, 92, 129
Pixodarus, 169
plasterer, 98
Plato, 25, 46; and *banausoi*, 154, n. 334; and craftsmanship, 112, 130; family tradition, 84, 87; and technological development, 185, 186, 187; and training, 88, 89
Plautios, Novios, 218
Plautus, trade names in, 99
Pliny the elder, 26; on supernatural marble, 121; on inventions, 190–1; on craftsmanship, 200–1
Pliny the younger, on public works in Asia Minor, 67
Plotinus, and art, 206
Plutarch, on *banausoi*, 12, 207; on magic, 197–8
political privileges, 150–2, 158; under the later Empire, 151–2
Pollio, C. Postumius, 91
Polygnotos, 86, 100, 203, 210
Polykleitos, 12, 85, 87, 89, 96, 111, 200, 203, 207, 210; competition, 211; on harmony, 133; II, 85, 133
Polymedes, 111
Polynices, Camillus, 163, 181
potters, Athenian, 24, 34, 60, 61–2, 67, 94, 156, 191–2; Corinthian, 60, 107, 110, 191–2; Kabeiran, 110; south Italian, 109; competition, 211; cults – at Corinth, 168, of Hephaistos, 167, Vulcan, 167; dedications, 164, 165, 170; epitaphs, 177–8; family tradition, 84; signatures, 212, 217–18; technique, 71–2, 93; workshop connections, 94; workshop discipline, 91; *see also* Arretine pottery, magic, vase-painters
Praxiteles, 85, 90, 210
prices, 22–3, 24–5; of staples, 138, 143–4; of works of art, 134–7; *see also* wages
Prometheus, 165, 166, 186, 189–90, 194
Protogenes, 137, 144, 199, 201, 202, 204–205, 207
public life, 153–8; membership of *collegia*, 160–1; *see also* political privileges
public works, 79, 101–2, 114; *see also* accounts, architects, engineering, labour market
Pythagoras, 132–3
Pythios, 96, 105–6

quarries, Corinth, 109; Egypt, 77, 175; Gaul, 175; Naxos, 11; Numidia, 74; Pannonia, 76; Roman imperial, 75ff; *see also* masons
quarry cults, 168–9, 175–6
Quintilian, on craftsmanship, 199–200

racial prejudice, 52–6
religious beliefs, 164–76
rhetorical figures of speech, 121, 202, 206–7
Rhodes, Colossus of, 115; political privileges at, 150, 172; workers from elsewhere at, 67; *see also* sculptors
Rhoikos, 110, 191
Roman army, 64–5, 76, 102, 158
Rome, citizenship, 31, 32–3, 36–41; labour force, 64–5, 111; Diocletian's edict, 143–4; tax on craftsmen, 148–9; *see also collegium*, labour market, potters, Roman army, state controls, state factories, tanners, working-class districts

Samos, 110–11, 191–2
Satyros, 66, 84
sculptors, Argive, 85; Athenian, 62–3, 85; Chian, 85; Naxian, *see* masons; Parian, 84; at Rhodes, 85, 111, 150; Sicyonian, 85, 88; and architects, 95–6; competitions, 211; dedications, 170–2, 173; epitaphs, 176, 180; mobility, 66, 218; pay, 136–7, 142; personality, 203, 205, 208; signatures, 121, 212–13; stylistic development, 111–12, 114–15, 119–23, 124–8
Scythia, slaves at Athens, 44–5; Greeks working for, 66
Secundus, L. Arrius, 90
shipwrights, Athenian, 64, 77, 79, 87; Corinthian, 110, 191; canvas for ships, 70; colossal ships, 115; epitaph, 182; state control of labour, 148; technique, 114
shoemakers, 114; at Athens, 82; and Socrates, 129–30, 178; at Rome, 64
Sicyon, 85, 111; *see also* sculptors, painters
signatures, 26, 207–17; evidence of family training, 83; joint, 95–6; potters' and painters', 85, 94; sculptors', 121, 212–213; unsigned works, 213–14
Simon, 82, 130, 156
Skiapos, 177
Skopas, 66, 84, 95, 210
slaves, 19, 22, 23, 28, 32, 42–52, 58; at Athens, 30, 43, 44–5, 46, 47 (mines); at Rome, 33, 36, 42, 48, 60, 162; apprentices, 87–8, 89; competition with free labour, 59–60; convicts in quarries, 75ff; cost of, 140; on equal terms with

free workers, 90–1; manumissions, 47–48; numbers, 43, 49–50; mine slaves, 73–4; slave wars, 155; see also freedmen, racial prejudice
smelters, 114, 116, 177; see also miners
smiths, associations of, 163; at Athens, 101, 163, 171; dedications, 174; epitaphs, 176, 181–2; Hephaistos, 166, 167, 171; magic, 196–8; prices, 136–7; signatures, 216; specialization, 101; trade names, 101; working conditions, 72
Socrates, 92, 103, 129–30, 156, 157
sophia, 207, 209, 211
Sophilos, 217
Sosinos, 101, 176
Sossios, Loukios, 13, 150–1, 181, 208
Sostratos, 102, 154
Sparta, 31, 34, 43, 44
specialization, 61, 96–101
Spintharos, 66
state controls, 144–52
state factories, 65, 92–3
strikes, 147, 155, n. 392
Sybaris, 77
Syracuse, Dionysios of, 66; Hieron of, 67

tanners, 30, 78, 80, 156–7, 178
technē, 14, 197, 198–217; technitēs, 14
technological development, 22, 114–23, 185–96
temple building, see accounts, public works
terracotta, reliefs from Melos, 109–10; Corinthians in Italy, 210–11; see also figurine makers, lamp makers, potters
textile workers, 41, 70, 87, 187
Thalassius, 41
Thallus, P. Cornelius, 87
Theodoros, 96, 110, 191–2
Theodotos, 95, 136, 138
Theokosmos, 211
Theon, 150, 179
Thous, 177
Thraix, 178
Thrasymedes, 95, 136
trade titles, 97–9, 101

training, 69, 82–91, 119–23, 205
transport, land, 57, 117, 119

vase-painters, and picture-painters, 100, 210; signatures, 85, 94, 217–18; versatility of, 100
versatility, 86, 94, 96–101; see also architects, specialization
Veturius, Manurius, 198
Vipasca, mining at, 75, 80
Vitalis, Ti. Claudius, 86–7
Vitalis, Vireus, 182
Vitruvius, 26, 169; on an architect's education, 102–6; architects' families, 86; his own, 153; higher mathematics, 131; optics, 133–4; patronage, 124; technological advance, 186–8, 192–4; versatility, 96
Vulcan, 165, 166, 167

wages, 22–3, 24–5, 135–44; slave and free, 59; standard day-wages, 138–40; see also prices
woodcutter, 18, 53, 56, 178, 218
working-class districts, 80–2, 163
working conditions, 70–8; state legislation, 144–5, 147–8
workshop owners, 91, 119, 137, 156–7; see also Kleon, Nikias
workshop relations, 44–7, 51, 94, 155, 160, 162; discipline, 91–2
workshops, 58, 59–60, 78–80; processes, 97; scenes of activity in, 70, 79, 89, see also Athena; size, n. 177

Xanthippos, 71, 178
Xenophon, 25, 29, 31, 61; on banausoi, n. 334; on jacks-of-all-trades, 96; on Socrates, 129, 157; on training of craftsmen, 88, 89

Zenodoros, 67, 201, 206, n. 13
Zenon, architect, 86, 214
Zenon, sculptor, 180, 210
Zeuxis, 89, 137, 138, 144, 199, 200–1, 211
Zosimus, M. Canuleius, 181, 210